Spring in Winter

The Global Security Programme in the Faculty of Social and Political Sciences spearheads the University of Cambridge's response to the challenges of the new global security agenda of the 1990s.

The Programme offers teaching and training at undergraduate, graduate and postgraduate levels. It also operates as the University's node of domestic university, national and international co-ordination for both global security research and policy discussion.

The Programme commenced operation in October 1989. Five weeks later, the Berlin Wall was broken, ending a forty-year post-war world order and signalling with irresistible power the arrival at centre stage of the global security issues which are the Global Security Programme's concern and with which many of the essays in this book are preoccupied.

Traditional International Relations is concerned with inter-state issues, and there is emerging a growing concern with environmental security. Both these are necessarily within the remit of global security. Yet neither alone provides a sufficient scope for the major tasks of theoretical and empirical integration which circumstance now demands. It is the central mission of the Cambridge Global Security Programme to develop those issues which lie across, between and especially beyond these current concerns.

Further details of the Programme's activities and of opportunities for PhD research and other work in the Programme may be obtained from the Global Security Programme Office, Faculty of Social and Political Sciences, Free School Lane, Cambridge CB2 3RO

Spring in Winter

The 1989 revolutions

Preface by **Vaclav Havel**

Gwyn Prins
Editor

Manchester University Press
Manchester and New York

Distributed exclusively in the USA and Canada by St. Martin's Press

Copyright © Manchester University Press 1990

Whilst copyright in the volume as a whole is vested in Manchester
University Press, copyright in individual chapters belongs to their
respective authors, and no chapter may be reproduced wholly or in part
without express permission in writing of both author and publisher.

Published by Manchester University Press
Oxford Road, Manchester M13 9PL, UK
and Room 400, 175 Fifth Avenue,
New York, NY 10010, USA

*Distributed exclusively in the USA and Canada
by* St. Martin's Press, Inc.,
175 Fifth Avenue, New York, NY 10010, USA

British Library cataloguing in publication data
Spring in winter : the 1989 revolutions.
  1. Eastern Europe. Political events
  I. Prins, Gwyn
  947.0854

Library of Congress cataloging in publication data applied for

ISBN 0 7190 3444 2 *hardback*
ISBN 0 7190 3445 0 *paperback*

Typeset by Saxon Printing Ltd., Derby, England.
Printed in Great Britain by Biddles Ltd, Guildford and King's Lynn

947
SPR

Contents

Vaclav Havel

Preface

Perhaps I'm not the most appropriate person to judge and assess with an impersonal, scholarly overview and at a distance the unbelievable shift that came about in our part of the world during the past year. Many journalists and scholars will look for the correlation of that chain of spectacular transformations that changed, as if at one blow, the fates of tens of millions of individuals and the hitherto firm bipolar picture of the modern world. I believe that this book will be one of the first important impulses in that direction.

Today, many people are talking and writing about the role of the intellectuals, students, and the theatre, or the influence of the Soviets' perestroika and economic difficulties. They're right. I myself as a playwright would also add the influence of humour and honesty, and perhaps even something beyond us, something maybe even unearthly. I think that above all, however, we were witness to the awakening of people who in the past had already repeatedly resisted violence and were repeatedly defeated with a violence still greater and more sly. But suddenly that violence ceased to be effective. Non-violence became the power of the hitherto powerless.

We search for causes and at the same time we search for fundamental, categorical imperatives that prevented the return to totalitarianism. And we find them again in the most simple, always valid – because the most just – causes. The first Czechoslovak president, Tomas Garrigue Masaryk, said in this context, "Do not fear and do not steal." We probably cannot find better words. I hope that the readers of this book will, after having read it, believe that it is up to each of us.

Acknowledgements

The editor and authors of this book could not have accomplished their work without the advice, support and generosity of many people and organisations.

The original suggestion that, as its first major lecture series, the new Cambridge Global Security Programme should address the revolutions which had just burst upon us, came from my colleagues in the Faculty of Social and Political Sciences, John Barber and Paul Ginsborg. I am grateful to them and indebted to the Faculty for its general support of what seemed at the outset a breathless, not to say reckless, undertaking.

Once decided to proceed, my next act was to contact John Tusa, Director of the External Services of the BBC. His practical advice at this initial and stressful moment was invaluable, as was his support throughout the enterprise. I was pleased that a good number of the authors were able subsequently to find their way on to the airwaves of the BBC World Service. I am grateful also to Dr Chris Hann of the Faculty of Social Anthropology for expert advice both at the planning stage and later, and similarly to Christopher Lee, Whitaker Fellow at Emmanuel College.

However, good intentions and good advice could not suffice. The Global Security Programme had no funds available to realise them. Three bodies responded swiftly and generously to fund this undertaking. At very short notice, Trinity College, Cambridge provided an initial facilitating grant to get things started, and I wish to express gratitude to the College, and most especially to Professor Julian Hunt and to the Master, Sir Andrew Huxley. The British Council in the person of the Cultural Attaché in Moscow, Mr Terry Sandell, instantly agreed to underwrite Dr Piontkowsky's participation. The British Foreign and Commonwealth Office and the Central Office of Information then, at a stroke, took over the financing and the practical logistics of bringing the East Europeans to Cambridge. I am indebted to the Embassy staffs in Warsaw, Prague, East Berlin and Budapest, and most particularly to Messrs Bernard McGinley and Murray Angus at COI. Without their help this book would not now exist.

As we moved from lecture to essay format, the support of the Foreign and Commonwealth Office continued. In the process of editing, I visited most of the authors at home. The FCO made possible my visits to Prague and to Budapest, for which thanks are due to Mr David Thomas. I owe a particular debt to Mr Lawrence O'Keeffe, HM Ambassador in Prague. The Minister of State at the FCO, Mr William Waldegrave, took an interest in the Office's support to the enterprise, for which I am also grateful.

In the task of editing, I drew extensively upon the advice of colleagues, all given unstintingly and at short notice. Terry Sandell and Michael Bird in Moscow helped over the Russian chapter, and in Cambridge I am grateful to Professor Ernest Gellner for assistance and wise advice in several areas, drawn from his encyclopaedic knowledge of Eastern Europe. I am also grateful to Professor Eniko Bollobas, Dr Chris Hann, Dr Frances Pyne and Dr Jarek Skadarek for allowing me to pillage their expertise!

A particular debt is owed to my friend, the sculptress and professional photographer Gabriella Bollobas, who, on her own initiative, began photographing the authors before I realised that it should be done, and whose foresight thus gave us the portraits which grace this book.

The production of the book was made swift and efficient by Richard Purslow, our editor at MUP, and the team at the Press. But the preparation of the typescript owed much to several people without whose work the Press could not have moved so fast. Thanks are due to Lizzie Gosling of Forum Executive Centres for typing early drafts, to Vince Woodley of the Personal Systems Division of the University Computer Service for keeping our disks and machines talking to each other most of the time (and us to them), to the Toshiba Corporation for inventing my laptop, which trundled faithfully around Eastern Europe with me, and without which editing would have taken months rather than weeks, and to Scott Nathan, the 1990 Harvard Scholar at Emmanuel College, for help with proofreading and editing, especially of the Czecho-slovak chapter. The debt of all who use this book to Sarah Humphrey will be evident from the excellence of her Comparative Chronology.

More than any other single person, my assistant Dee Noyes was indispensable to this project. She has had a vital role at every stage - helping to arrange the lecturers and to run the lectures, typing and retyping large portions of the text, researching points of information, making editorial and sub-editorial suggestions and compiling the index. I could not have done it without her.

Thanks are due to the Vice-Chancellor of the University of Cambridge, Professor David Williams and to the Secretary-General of the Faculties, Mr James Wright, for their active and sympathetic support, both of the *Spring in Winter* project in particular, and of the Global Security Programme in general. It is an exciting moment to be initiating a new dimension in the life of the University - more momentous than anyone could have anticipated when the idea was originally mooted several years ago.

That the Global Security Programme was there at all to respond to the challenge is due entirely to the generosity of the John D. and Catherine T. MacArthur Foundation of Chicago, which by providing core funding for the initial phase of Global Security studies at Cambridge, has made it possible for the University to fulfil its commitment to remain at the forefront of responsible scholarship on the leading issues of the day.

© Gabriella Bollobas

Gwyn Prins

Introduction

I had never been to an evening at the theatre like it. It was a first night in Prague. *Largo Desolato* was performed in a narrow, dark theatre - the same theatre, indeed, where the playwright had worked as a stage-hand many years before - in the presence of the playwright and his friends. The previous year, many of the audience had been in prison, or were being pursued and harassed by secret police. At this performance in April 1990, the Theatre of the Absurd embraced both stage and auditorium; for as Jan Urban remarked to me, probably some of the bodyguards who stood in the aisles, watchfully protecting the President of Czechoslovakia, were the same men who a few months before, as good Communist bodyguards of President Husak, would at the very least have approved of the hounding of the notorious dissident playwright, Vaclav Havel.

Here, in a small Prague theatre, was jammed a good portion of the new Czechoslovak government, roaring with laughter at the moral dilemmas, political and sexual impotence of the anti-hero of the piece, a timorous dissident writer, buffeted variously by his women, by friends and by solicitous and Kafkaesque secret policemen, as he wrestled with the question of whether to denounce a piece of his own writing. Next to the Playwright/ President in his dinner jacket, who was rocking with mirth, the Prime Minister; over there, the Foreign Minister's Adviser; nearby the new Mayor of Prague and next to me, one of the guiding forces of Civic Forum, the spontaneous alliance which overthrew the Old Guard. The plot and the people in Havel's play expressed the claustrophobia of the dissidents' predicament, intimately familiar to the members of the audience, but now presented to them from a world unexpectedly, suddenly fictional and far removed.

In the interval, in a cramped theatre bar thick with the smoke of the furiously puffing makers of revolution, casually dressed and bearded people talk energetically. The conversation is of what positions to take at the Bratislava Summit of East European Presidents the next day. One group calls over the hubbub to another. They agree to meet again on the presidential helicopter in the morning and everybody troops back into the auditorium for the second half, always under the inscrutable gaze of the besuited (some leather-jacketed), tie-wearing bodyguards. What on earth do they think?

After the final curtain, the playwright is reluctantly persuaded on to the stage, where he first shakes hands vigorously with the cast, bobbing along the row at the back of the stage, before making a dash for the wings, only to be dragged back again downstage to receive flowers and more applause. Bashful, the man who had engaged the famous talking crowds of Wenceslas Square in slow, contrapuntal conversations, which endowed the crowd with a unitary life and which had helped to decide the course of the November revolution, ducked out of sight.

What is an historical turning-point? How do we know one when we meet one? In the modern western world of instant and saturated reportage, can we know, or are we imprisoned in the media's flimsy and self-fulfilling exaggerations? This book is about the time when spring blossomed in winter in Europe and it is mainly written by people who were intimately involved in those revolutionary events, in two cases (and in the Preface) by people who led them. It is not a collection of further and large speculations by observers from the outside. These essays project their authors' intense and ineradicable clarity of recollection from inside the Whale, linked here in several of them to their first extended reflections upon the causes and courses of the year.

To the outside world, the sequence of revolution in 1989 looked like a powder-trail fired spontaneously by the sparks from the pickaxes biting into the top of the Berlin Wall. From the inside, it didn't look like that because in each country there was a long and particular preparation. The image of clocks is less explosive but more apt. The various East European clocks ran at different speeds, and the internal mechanisms of each brought them to chime in 1989. This is not to deny a demonstration effect, and certainly not to deny the vital harmonising role of Mr Gorbachev and of Soviet military *non*-intervention; only to propose the virtue of proper context to secure understanding. Among its functions, this book may assist westerners to discern a reliable picture of Europe's *annus mirabilis* by offering views which sometimes contrast sharply with the received wisdom (which John Kenneth Galbraith names Simplistic Ideology in his chapter) that swiftly established itself as the Western media and much of the western establishment rushed to premature judgement.

The genesis of this book was in late December 1989. The University of Cambridge's Global Security Programme had commenced operations on 1 October. On 9 November, as all the world knows, the Berlin Wall was breached. By early December, it seemed to me and to one or two colleagues in the Faculty of Social and Political Sciences (notably John Barber and Paul Ginsborg, now of the University of Florence) that there was a pressing need for someone to provide an English-language platform for a reflective and authoritative examination of the causes and the conduct of the amazing events of preceding weeks, especially since many of the issues which the new enterprise of Global Security studies addresses were prominent within them. Given its new Programme, the University of Cambridge was clearly an appropriate place in which to do this. Accordingly, I resolved to arrange a series entitled "Understanding the Revolutions in Eastern Europe" at very short notice as the 1990 Global Security Lectures. My debts to those who, in addition to the lecturers, made this possible and successful are listed in the *Acknowledgements*.

As the lecture series proceeded, with such varied and, unbe-known to each lecturer, complementary insights, I began to wonder whether there might be a role for a collection of essays by a collection of lecturers well qualified to write from within and at the forefront of the 1989 revolutions. Others encouraged me in this feeling which was further reinforced as I read some of the early outpourings of what we may expect to be a torrent of both participant observation and observation from afar. Before things went too much further, a different sort of book - this sort of book - seemed called for, so that the testimony which it represents, as well as its analyses, could enter the fray. *Spring in Winter* is in different parts both a contribution to explanation and a piece of primary historical evidence. As I have edited it, both functions have always been in my mind. Seeing the importance of the latter role as the book took shape caused me to commission Sarah Humphrey's *Comparative Chronology of Revolution*, to make the book more useful for those using it as a primary source.

What was as plain as the need was the inappropriateness of merely reproducing the East European lectures from the Cambridge series. Yet the lecturers were mostly under heavy burdens of office and of impending elections. I put to them the case for this book, the value of speed in producing it and the implication in terms of additional work. All accepted, and we are all in their debt for having in some cases extensively expanded their accounts in the passage from the spoken word to the written essay despite the pressures of their daily obligations.

As editor I have implied no argument in my arrangement of the structure of the book. The chapters are simply placed in chronological order of the onset of political change, with the American and British perspectives placed fore and aft and the great questions about the Russian revolution still in process at the time of writing following the lesser questions about the unfinished nature of the Romanian December (which has burst into flames again as this book goes to press).

The different chapters each highlight themes particular to each national experience, some signalled in the chapter titles. Elemer Hankiss argues for the applicability of the "Tocquevillian sce-nario" to explain Hungary's transformation: de Tocqueville's famous and controversial view that the principal achievement of the French Revolution was to delay a bourgeois–capitalist revolution that was already under way. This, he thinks, is the best analogy for the Communist detour since 1948. Hankiss explains how the Communists systematically "demobilised" Hungarian society by destroying all means of public association except through the Party, and how, once this process had begun, Hungarians continued to demobilise themselves by the abuse of alcohol, by gross overwork and by a rising suicide rate. He places the "fake liberalisation" of the 1970s in context, and identifies the sources of residual strength which have endured despite this long erosion and from which a new Hungarian society can be built. Like Hankiss for Hungary, Janusz Ziolkowski dwells upon the social and cultural resources present in Polish society which may be mobilised to sustain the reconstruction of civil society and which were important in nourishing the roots and branches of Solidarność in the years between the declaration of martial law and the June 1989 election victory. In Hungary and Poland, a residual entrepreneurial tradition and an intact peasantry respectively ballast the new foundations. Ziolkowski stresses the fundamental and formative role of the Roman Catholic Church as embodiment and protector of an alternative social vision, a role which the Hungarian churches did not play.

The next pair of chapters, on East Germany and on Czechoslovakia, are rather different in approach. Both Jens Reich and Jan Urban write autobiographically as a way of leading the reader into an understanding of the 1989 revolutions. Their essays are remarkable documents of the revolutions as well as analyses of them. The course of events following Spring in Winter has been vastly divergent in the two countries. As this Introduction is written, Civic Forum has triumphed at the polls in Czechoslovakia's first free elections and in the DDR, the extinguishing of national identity is proceeding apace and Neues Forum holds a tenuous position in the first and last freely elected Volkskammer.

It is logical that Reich writes reflectively, dividing his chapter to answer the three central questions: how one became a dissident under the omnipresent gaze and cruel control of the Stasi state; what the Wall meant and what it did, and what it means to lose a country. He writes poignantly of "Wall-sickness", a mixture of melancholy, introspection, a sense of loss and of boredom, which afflicted an entire generation. He describes vividly the upwelling of courage and imagination which broke the Wall and which, he fears, may not be properly rewarded in a harsher, brasher united Germany.

Jan Urban's joyful and gripping history of the Velvet Revolution (as President Havel described it), seen from one of the key posts within The Magic Lantern - the Prague theatre which became the headquarters of Civic Forum and from which the new Czechoslovak Spring was led - is a gem set within two other, quite different accounts. One is a description of life in 'Absurdistan'. It tells of living split lives, of the "One Chance Philosophy" - where you could not afford to slip up once, for that mistake would be your last. It tells of the depth of humiliation into which Czechs were plunged after the suppression of the Prague Spring of 1968, when winter came in summer with the Soviet tanks in August. It witnesses to the raw courage of the dissidents of Charter 77 in the face of a régime that rode to power on those tanks and whose lack of legitimacy translated itself into an obsessive and continual (and it must be admitted largely successful) humiliation of its own people. The other account is of what power resides in humiliation when people find the will to transcend it. This is shown in the central role of the People of the Arts - actors, painters, playwrights - in the Czechoslovak revolution and it is shown in Urban's frank and detailed discussion of the ethnic, economic and especially ecological problems which now face the Civic Forum led government. To this I shall return below.

Jonathan Eyal's anatomisation of Romania's recent history and of the bizarre career of the Ceausescus shows forcefully how the West made the cardinal and self-serving mistake of failure to enquire into the reasons for Ceausescu's divorce from Moscow. The fact of divorce was deemed sufficient on the principle that "my enemy's enemy is my friend". The reason, Eyal explains and illustrates, was that Ceausescu remained a Stalinist when Khrushchev did not. Running through this chapter is the consistent contempt of the Ceausescus for the Romanian people: a belief in their limitless ability to absorb insult and injury which proved to be for the two dictators, he and she, in the end fatally misplaced. They were members of a tiny ruling caste and the nature of their régime was such that it could only end in blood. The nature of their removal (by hasty execution, before their colleagues, who then ran the National Salvation Front, could be compromised by them), Eyal suggests, made it likely that as the May 1990 elections and June violence confirmed, the reconstruction of civil society expressed as the return of fully-fledged combative democracy in Romania, would not be as swift or as successful as it has been in neighbouring Hungary.

The Romanian future may be profoundly in question and that is extremely important to Romanians and to their neighbours. But the Russian question is titanic both in scale and in implication. Russia is the inscrutable Sphinx, wrote the great St Petersburg poet Alexandr Blok in "The Scythians", from which Andrei Piontkowsky's chapter takes its title. He looks at the 1989 Revolutions from the East. He examines both cause and effect. He shows how events and the development of views about Europe in the USSR since Gorbachev's accession to power were axiomatic to Spring in Winter. The Soviet role was everywhere that of the famous clue in Conan Doyle's story "Silver Blaze": the curious incident of the dog in the night-time. ' "The dog did nothing in the night-time." "That is the curious incident," remarked Sherlock Holmes.'

Jens Reich writes of the importance of Gorbachev's unofficial and inflammatory comments during his visit to East Berlin for the fortieth anniversary of the DDR. Several authors refer to the speculations upon the role of Soviet restraint in preventing bloodshed in Leipzig on 9 October. The confidence which spread across Eastern Europe as the revolutionary process unfolded that Soviet tanks would not again roll westwards to crush the people and to restore the Old Guard, underpinned everything. Piontkowsky, writing from the radical democrat wing of Russian politics, explains why he thinks that this came about. He attributes much of the credit for the liberation of Eastern Europe to the *mujahadin* of Afghanistan.

He also believes that the success and decisiveness of the European revolutions gives valuable support to his wing in the battle for the soul of Russia, although he feels no confidence in their definitive success in the short term. However, since completing his chapter, Boris Yeltsin's successes in the Parliament of the Russian Federation have brought forward the moment of choice for Mr Gorbachev, which Piontkowsky here predicts, and also the challenge to the Russian democrats to find a *modus vivendi* and a means of alliance with the Russian Nationalists; for it is Piontkowsky's view that the tension, even hostility, between democracy and nationalism in Russia is an insuperable obstacle to the ultimate civilising of Russian politics to which he looks.

But before that moment comes, Piontkowsky sees another essential task and in the bulk of his chapter, he endeavours to help remove a more immediate impediment. What is it, he asks, that has caused so many millions of Russians to die violent deaths at the hands of their own people during the seventy-three-year history of the Soviet state? For him, it was not Stalin and his henchmen who were to blame. They were only pupils. Piontkowsky rejects indignantly the view of liberal Communists (like Gorbachev) that the humane and lofty vision of the Old Bolsheviks was hijacked and contorted by Stalin. He accuses directly the "inhuman relativity of Leninist morality". His chapter is, in his own description, a contribution to a necessary act of repentance which must precede success in the current Russian Revolution.

In two ways Sir James Eberle's chapter complements that by John Kenneth Galbraith. It also looks for lessons for the West, notable among which, Eberle suggests, was the role played by modern mass communication; and like Galbraith, it eschews simplistic triumphalism. In so doing, Eberle touches one of the four themes which may be traced across *Spring in Winter*. Several of the authors acknowledge the role of the example of the West, although there is considerable divergence among interpretations of that fact. All the authors see roles for market forces in reviving their countries. None of the authors holds with the view expressed by those subscribing to the Simplistic Ideology castigated by Galbraith, that a wholesale adoption of free-market capitalism, red in tooth and claw and unmoderated by what Galbraith calls the mellowing effects of government intervention, is the correct prescription for the newly free nations. Jan Urban states simply that while he wishes to borrow much from the West, he does not want to import "carelessness with people". Jens Reich fears that in this he has no choice as, with a sense of "oppressive unease", he says farewell to the DDR, an unloved and deformed creature of the Cold War.

A second theme which threads the book is the entwined tension between nationalism and democracy. For Andrei Piontkowsky, these two forces are two strong horses who must pull together, or the cart will remain stuck. As each of the relevant chapters explains, they did yoke up for different reasons in Hungary, Poland, East Germany, Czechoslovakia and Romania; but in the USSR, they pull against each other. Indeed, Piontkowsky sees the danger of a dark and bizarre alliance forming between the extreme Russian nationalists and the old Communist *nomenclatura* as they discover a community of interest in denying the European and bolstering the Asiatic identity of the Russian Sphinx.

A third theme is concerned with communication. Many chapters discuss communication between and within the different revolutions and several, notably the first and the last, look directly at the way in which the outside world perceived them. There is disagreement about the demonstration effect of electronic images of the West. Reich, for example, suspects that they were less important in triggering the East German revolution than many, especially in the media, themselves suspected at the time. This is because by and large the outsiders did not and could not know how the mechanisms of the different East European clocks, which moved their hands towards synchrony, worked; so they substituted a mechanism of explanation which they did understand. Certainly the role of television in the Romanian events in December is well attested and seems clear. It is less the case for November.

So what was it that co-ordinated the striking of the clocks whose cacophony dismissed the *ancien régime*? This book contains evidence of the efforts of Polish, Czech and Soviet dissidents to harmonise their efforts; but forest picnics at the border would never be enough to rouse the masses. They needed to be touched directly. The catalyst would best be a spectacle which was enacted before their eyes.

Chapter by chapter, theatre by theatre, the same heralds stagger onto the stage to announce the coming drama. They arrive by train, on foot and in lines of stinking Trabants and Wartburgs. First it is Hungary; then it is Czechoslovakia. Always clawing westwards. The refugee army from the DDR swarms across the map of modern revolutionary Europe like an army of tired crusaders from another age. Wherever they go, they galvanise, and as they go they increase the moral and material pressure upon the public fabric of the state and the private morale of the leadership of the DDR.

No symbol of political turbulence is more potent, packs more semeiotic punch, than a March. The East German refugees seem to have served for the 1989 revolution the same mobilising function for many otherwise apolitical or inwardly demobilised people as did the Long March from Jiansxi to Yan'an for the Chinese Revolution earlier in the century. The spectacle of a March forms a most efficiently compressed and memorable image. Crowds, by coming into being, make power.

Aspects of Spring in Winter reverberate with old and honourable themes of popular protest, adding and renewing items in the European lexicon of public symbolism. Such were the uses of candles. Candle-bearing crowds walk through several chapters of this book. Nor has their light been extinguished. The informal institutionalisation of these many, tiny flames of the revolution has become an apt monument to the spirit and the message of 1989. These were popular movements in a swathe of Europe where civil society is recalled to life.

In Wenceslas Square, in front of the equestrian statue of St Vaclav which has presided over and carried the flags and posters of both the Prague Spring and of Spring in Winter (and now constantly a poster of the new Vaclav), a dark circle lies permanently on the pavement. As one approaches, the circle begins to twinkle. In the middle, garlanded with flags and flowers, are the portraits of Jan Palach, of Tomas and Jan Masaryk. The wall of wax from the encircling candles was over a foot high by

Easter 1990, constantly replenished. It is a truly popular equivalent to the state-prescribed and gas-fed "eternal" flames in whose continuing *raison d'être* one can never have complete confidence. The Palach/Masaryk flames have only burned if people constantly willed them to do so.

A fourth theme which appears throughout *Spring in Winter* is green; or rather it is greenness emerging through the grime. Forty years of smokestack industry run with worn and wasteful Soviet plant has left a legacy of deeply poisoned land, water and air. The casual contempt for people was matched by a lordly disregard for Nature. In its exuberance about human power and in its linearity, Marxism–Leninism shared intimate qualities with free-market capitalism. Both projected a very nineteenth-century way of looking at the world. Jan Urban sees how following the revolution, unexpectedly, Czechoslovakia has an opportunity to pioneer a new, ecologically sensitive and sustainable politics fit for the twenty-first century. Jens Reich asks for a mode of political analysis which works constantly from the perspective of fifty years on. Concern about environmental degradation in a situation of powerlessness to act is mentioned as an early and powerful stimulus to mobilisation.

The first and most explicit signal of the inextricability of sustainable stewardship of the natural world and human freedom of knowledge and expression was the Bulgarian movement EcoGlasnost. (The absence of a particular Bulgarian chapter in this book is an omission which I acknowledge and regret.) For all the Danube riverine countries, the Hungarian/Czechoslovak Dam project at the Danube Bend provided a focus of anger and a school of dissident politics. The Dam appears in column after column of the *Comparative Chronology*. Groups like EcoGlasnost in Bulgaria and the Duna Circle in Hungary spearheaded protest against the Old Guard in three ways. First, they did it by being first; second, the insult to Nature expressed eloquently the moral vacuum at the heart of the *anciens régimes* and third, perhaps because the question was not "traditionally" political and yet was intensely political, it proved able to mobilise many people. The "green" objections to the Danube Dam were the first to win a notable success against one of the incumbent Old Guards. In this, as in other ways, the political process of Eastern Europe's Spring in Winter may prefigure a greening of pan-European politics.

What is meant by this "greening" is one of the issues at the heart of the new discipline of Global Security studies. Questions of environmental security sometimes cross borders and are physically large-scale, such as in the debate over the Dam (in which the interim Czechoslovak government, between the Revolution and the June 1990 election, maintained much of the overthrown government's commitment to the project, creating friction with the new democratic Hungarian government that was committed to abandonment of the scheme). Considerations of environmental security may mould the shape of strategies for national economic recovery. Josef Vavrousek, a member of the Civic Forum Co-ordinating Committee, an ecological protester of long standing and the new Minister of the Environment in the Czechoslovak government, is quoted as believing that about two thirds of Czechoslovakia's existing factories must be closed down, and that seventy per cent of Czechoslovakia's forests are dying. In Slovakia, the first student protest of November 1989 was against an unsafe nuclear power station. In East Germany, as more and more information has become public about the dangerous condition of the Griefswald nuclear power complex, the point has been made tellingly that this technology only persists where there is a heavy pall of Official Secrecy (a point underscored by the release of information about Chernobyl, mentioned in Piontkowsky's chapter). Protest against the gigantic steelworks and other gifts of "eco squared (economic and ecological) imperialism" from Stalin and his successors, which has created a Rust Belt all over Eastern Europe from Nova Huta in Poland to Kosice in Slovakia to Ceaucescu's maniac heavy industries in Romania, converges with the rural crises which arise from abuse of the land by industrialised agro-business and the expropriation of peasantries (except in Poland), the other main sources of regional ecological injury. Together, they frame the hard choices which the new governments will have to make.

Global security is also about the much more intimate scale of the balance between risk and trust which ties each individual to each other and to structures of superordinate power. The transformation of these relationships has been part of the "green" theme of Spring in Winter, but also, as many of the chapters attest, a central aspect of the remobilisation of collective conviction and of collective action. Under the old régime, people turned inwards, focusing emotional energy and investment in private relationships, often destructively. Positive networks woven from private trust underpinned strategies both for survival in poverty, beset with shortage and, for the courageous minorities, for protest against totalitarianism. Trust systems of this sort hedged against material and political risks. The corollary was a significant general erosion, and for dissidents a total failure, of faith in the good intentions of the Old Guard. The discovery which seems to have been made first in the school of "green" protest in 1988/89 was of the immense potential to capitalise upon the sort of popular unity, exemplified by Solidarność in one country earlier in the decade, but now across the whole region, when the reconstruction of civil society permits a renovation of the social contract between, on the one hand, individuals assailed by a host of environmental and economic threats and on the other, institutions rendered legitimate (and thus competent to take unpopular actions) by an infusion of democracy. Without implying a judgement of relative merit, one observes that the "green" agenda has had a power much in excess of one composed solely or largely of concern for the rights of dissent. It is because of the prevalence and importance of these new issues, and the evident insufficiency of traditional international relations theory to embrace them, that this book and this episode fit squarely within the terms of Global Security studies.

Spring in Winter is a book of the revolution. Although raising the questions, usually in terms of the new opportunities to re-phrase them, the following chapters are not principally concerned with speculation about what comes next. There will be plenty of occasion for that elsewhere. As it goes to press, no one can yet say for certain whether the astonishing events of 1989 throw Europe back into the morass of ethnic and imperial conflicts of the world before 1914, pitch Europe forward decisively into the new politics of global security, mark a conclusive triumph of bourgeois and capitalist values (mellowed by a welfare state or not), or are themselves only a temporary point of light before a return of blackness.

What *is* certain about this exhilarating moment I understood best from studying the face of one of the audience at Havel's first night in Prague. Sitting not far from me, and in my line of sight, was a striking woman. I do not know who she was. She was in her fifties, had a strongly sculpted face with high cheekbones, animated eyes and mouth. The play amused her hugely. She laughed with abandon, and frequently. There was in the carriage of her head and in the deliberateness of her hand gestures both poise and great vitality. To a stranger, they signalled an inner tension between practised self-control and powerfully held views. But what drew my attention to her, and held it, were the lines on her face. They were in contradiction. Her face was plainly in the process of metamorphosis. The dominant lining of her face was sad. Around her eyes and her mouth and across her brow, they spoke of the trials and conflicts of the dissidents' life being acted out on the stage that night and described by many of the authors in this book. But cutting across them, as I watched her watch the play, were laughter lines. They spoke of the transformation of the previous six months, and clearly so; for in repose, I observed how the lining of the old face was receding. The new one, not yet dominant, was creating a new and happier geography. In the meantime, the criss-crossed lines of old and new gave the appearance of an aged skin that was quite belied by the sparkle of her eye and of her laughter.

There is a fragility in these times of metamorphosis and expectation. The purpose of this book is to search for its beginning while the memory is still fresh, to think about our ways of knowing, both as observers and as participants; to look to the future, especially to Russia, and throughout to preserve a sense and to offer a privileged witness of Europe's *annus mirabilis*.

Gwyn Prins
Emmanuel College
Cambridge
15 June 1990

© Gabriella Bollobas

1 John Kenneth Galbraith

Revolt in our time: the triumph of simplistic ideology

John Kenneth Galbraith was American Ambassador to India from 1961-3, and for many years, Paul M Warburg Professor of Economics at Harvard University. He was born in 1908 in Ontario, Canada. After graduating in agriculture at Toronto and taking a PhD at the University of California, he became Social Science Research Council Fellow at Cambridge, England, and went on to teach at the universities of California, Princeton and Harvard (1945-75). In 1970-1 he spent two years at Cambridge University as Fellow at Trinity College and Visiting Lecturer at the Faculty of Economics and Politics.

During the war, at the American Office of Price Administration, he headed the wartime price-control activities, and later was a director of the US Strategic Bombing Survey and of the Office of Security Policy, receiving the Medal of Freedom and the President's Certificate of Merit for his work. He has been closely identified with the Democratic Party.

Professor Galbraith has contributed to leading journals and reviews. His books include A Theory of Price Control, American Capitalism, The Affluent Society *(which held its place on the best seller lists for some thirty weeks)*, The Great Crash of 1929, The Liberal Hour, The Non-potable Scotch *and* The New Industrial State. *He is also author of a book of satirical sketches*, The McLandress Dimension, *a best selling novel*, The Triumph; *a study of Indian painting*, Indian Painting: Scene, Themes and Legends *(with M S Randhawa)*, Ambassador's Journal, Economics, Peace and Laughter, A Chinese Passage, *a record of his visit to China*, Economics and the

Public Purpose, Money: Whence it Came, Where it Went, The Age of Uncertainty, Almost Everyone's Guide to Economics, The Nature of Mass Poverty, The Anatomy of Power, A History of Economics: The Past as the Present *and a volume of memoirs*, A Life in Our Times. *He delivered the Reith Lectures in 1966.*

The author, who is an enthusiastic skier, is married with three sons. Much of his writing is done in Switzerland and on an old farm in Vermont.

1

The events of the last months of 1989 in Eastern Europe, building on earlier changes in Poland and the Soviet Union, have, not surprisingly, nurtured a major economic discussion. Some of this has been eminently sensible; some, rather more, has been aberrant to the point of mild insanity. The aberration extends to both sides of what was once the Iron Curtain or, in more recent symbolism, the Berlin Wall. We need a name for it; it can, I believe, best be denoted Simplistic Ideology.

It has been my fortunate experience over the last years to see something of the countries of Eastern Europe, including the economists and public figures therein. I have had discussions in all the European Communist states except Bulgaria and Albania (though rather distantly in Romania) and more than a few in the Soviet Union. In the autumn of 1989, just prior to the great explosions, I lectured in Leipzig and Budapest and talked at some length with scholars, journalists and politicians there. I cite this not to suggest superior insight – although some believe that over my lifetime I have not been wholly reluctant in this regard – but to qualify in a small way my interpretation of developments in this part of the world. I find myself, as will be evident, in serious disagreement with widely accepted views of what has occurred and is now occurring.

The Simplistic Ideology that extensively interprets these events pictures a starkly bipolar world. On the one side Communism, on the other side capitalism. Each exists in its unadulterated form. Now, reversing all Marxian prediction, capitalism is triumphant. Communism having failed both economically and politically in Eastern Europe, the countries once so afflicted will now make their way to the capitalist *nirvana*. As will, if more gradually, the USSR. The prospect is a blessed improvement in economic life; this will combine with the freedoms that we in the West enjoy. Interim pain and shock are possible and perhaps to be welcomed; "Shock Therapy for Poland", a recent *New York Times* headline proclaimed. There is no question, however, as to the ultimate reward.

The prime essential is that the transition to capitalism be complete. And this view is being advanced in both East and West. Lecturing on these matters in Budapest, I was questioned severely by a Hungarian journalist who was distressed that I had not mentioned Freidrich Hayek as a guide to needed reform. Did he not offer the most workable economic and political model? My interrogator was visibly depressed when I replied that it was a design we in the West would not care to risk.

The risk would be very great – greater than even our most ardent free enterprise ideologists would accept if actually in office. In the last century when Marx wrote, and continuing on into this century and the years of the Great Depression, the survival of capitalism in its original and ideologically exact form was very much in doubt. There was the highly unequal distribution of power and income as between employer and employed. And over the society in general a few rich and many poor. Workers were discarded without income when unneeded. There was cruel exploitation of the notably vulnerable women and children. The perils of old age and illness without income were extreme in the new industrial towns. Many were spared them by early and exhausted demise. There was the deeply conditioned discontent of farmers. Most threatening of all, as Marx foresaw, were the recurring economic crises or depressions that swept millions into unemployment and deprivation.

From all this came anger and alienation and for many the strong feeling, perhaps the near-certainty, that the system could not survive.

The system did survive because the welfare state mitigated the hardships and the cruelties of pristine capitalism. Also trade unions were legitimized and exercised countervailing power. And the Keynesian Revolution gave to the state the responsibility, however imperfectly discharged, of smoothing out the business cycle and limiting the associated hardship and despair. The prevention of mass unemployment and the assurance of economic growth became the prime tests of government competence. So, to repeat, the system survived. It should be noted, no doubt, that the fortunate thus saved accorded the most ardent resistance to action on behalf of their own salvation.

Meanwhile changes in the structure of capitalism rendered obsolescent even the term capitalism itself. There came, in the words of the late James Burnham, the Managerial Revolution; it denoted the passage of power in the modern great industrial and commercial corporation from the provider or possessor of capital – from the capitalist – to the professional management, the managerial bureaucracy.

Given the specialised knowledge and experience required in the operation of the modern large enterprise and the diversity and complexity of its tasks, the capitalist or, more often, his questionably competent or committed descendants were pushed aside. In no country did the managerial bureaucracy encounter the same motivated resistance, even hostility, to the claims of its labour force or those of a civilised society as had the primeval capitalist. Here, as from the welfare state and from Keynes, came a solvent for the old anger and antagonism (and for many primeval capitalists the righteous pleasure) in primitive class conflict.

Let us be clear. What the countries of Eastern Europe see as the alternative to socialism or, in the common reference, Communism is not capitalism. Were it capitalism in its classical form, they would not for a moment want the change. The alternative they see is the modern state with a large, indispensable, mellowing and stabilising role for government.

Mr Reagan and now Mr Bush in the United States and Mrs Thatcher in Britain have enjoyed power in these last years only because earlier and effective *public* action has made a majority of

their citizens economically comfortable and secure. In consequence, as with comfortable and secure people over the centuries,
these citizens are self-protective in mood – conservative. Had Mr
Reagan or Mrs Thatcher sought to restore the austerities,
insecurities and cruelties of pure capitalism, an intention that Mr
Reagan in his innocent way regularly avowed, neither of them
would have survived in office. Their debt for their survival, sadly
unacknowledged, is to what an earlier generation did to modify
capitalism and to what they themselves were kept from doing – or
undoing – in office.

I turn now to socialism.

The capitalism to which the Eastern European countries seek
to escape bears little relationship to the Marxian model. Neither
do the economic and political structures under which they have
lived and visibly suffered in these last decades. Socialism, as it
matured, had a task that Marx and Lenin did not foresee: the
production of consumers' goods in all their modern diversity of
styles, designs and supporting services. This was the model set by
the non-socialist world. With this a centralised planning and
command system could not contend. Nor in general could it
contend with the special problems of agriculture. The latter is an
industry that functions well only when blessed by the self-
motivated energies of the individual owner and proprietor or some
close approximation thereto. It requires in less agreeable terms
the exploitation by the individual proprietor of himself and his
family. Except as people might be rescued from what Marx was
pleased to call the idiocy of rural life, agriculture played little part
in his thought and not a great deal in Lenin's.

A further and greater misfortune of advanced socialist development was in close parallel with the advanced capitalist experience.
That is the increasing and eventually the overriding role of
organisation, of bureaucracy. As the modern great industrial firms
– General Motors, General Electric and Exxon in the United
States; Shell and BP in Britain – develop a large bureaucratic
apparatus, so also and much more does mature socialist production. Much more, because in this system the producing enterprise
is united in greater or lesser measure with a supervising and
controlling ministry. The result is a truly massive organisational

structure; by some counts the bureaucracy of the USSR numbers some thirty million inhabitants.

The basic characteristics of great organisation, massive bureaucracy, are common to all systems, all cultures, There is, first, the ineluctable effect of age. Individuals, we accept, decline in effort and initiative with the passage of years. But so also does the bureaucratic establishment or enterprise. Accordingly, with the passage of time socialist ministries and enterprises matured and passed on to an intellectually sterile senility. As also, let it be noted, did US Steel, the once-great British automobile companies and now, many avow, General Motors. There is a further tendency of great organisation to proliferate personnel; nothing so measures bureaucratic significance and prestige as the number of one's subordinates. Nothing so eases bureaucratic life as having willing subordinates who spare one thought and action. Here too is prestige. The most common of all questions in a bureaucracy are: How many people does he have under him? For how large a department is she responsible? The result is the cost and immobility of great and persistently growing mass.

But most important of all, bureaucracy defines its own truth. We see this currently and with exceptional clarity in the United States. Our vast military establishment, as also the State Department and the intelligence agencies, are now struggling to preserve the sense of need and urgency which, for so long, served stable thought and expanding budgets so well. Some have spoken out in open regret over recent changes which might mean diminished budgets and painful thought. The Deputy Secretary of State Mr Lawrence Eagleburger, perhaps our leading current exponent of institutional truth, recently regretted the passage of the Cold War – "a time," he said, "of remarkable stability in international relations."

But again the western commitment to bureaucratic or institutional truth has been less than that of the Eastern European countries. In the West inconvenient thought and its consequences, however deplored, could not, to the regret of many, be suppressed. The justification in the United States for our present scale of military expenditure is now being sharply questioned. There has even been official talk of reduced budgets, the reductions so far suggested being, alas, in planned increases. Officials and some scholars, whose minds, books and lecture notes are also committed firmly to the threat of Soviet expansion, have recently been reduced to expressing their concern over Soviet ambitions in Nicaragua, El Salvador and Ethiopia. Not even General Noriega in Panama could persuasively be called a Kremlin agent.

Again, however, the hold of bureaucratic truth was far more unrelenting in the socialist world. There it enforced comprehensively the belief of those within the bureaucratic structure; there it extended its reach comprehensively to those outside. As I've noted on another occasion, the aged men who headed the East German government could not have lived in total innocence of what was happening in that country. The better level of consumer life in West Germany was disastrously visible on television. The secret police almost certainly reported rumblings of discontent from below. (Intelligence agencies, we know, regularly report what their masters wish to hear, but they could not have been that incompetent.) The reality however, could not be accepted. Bureaucracy enforces its truth not least on those at the top. Theirs was to see with surprise the eventual explosion.

So, to summarise: capitalism in its original or pristine form could not have survived. But under pressure it did adapt. Socialism in its original form and for its first tasks did succeed. But it failed to adapt, and it nurtured an oppressive and repressive political structure. Having shed this last, how does it now adapt?

Two things will be clear. First, those who speak, as so many do so glibly, even mindlessly, of a return to the Smithian free market are wrong to the point of a mental vacuity of clinical proportions. It is something we in the West do not have, would not tolerate, could not survive. Ours is a mellow, government-protected life; for Eastern Europeans pure and rigorous capitalism would be no more welcome than it would be for us.

Equally to be avoided are those who see, out of short-run shock and hardship, the promise of prompt economic betterment. In this view the hardship itself is therapeutic. Out of any suffering must come good. Elements of theology intrude here: self mortification, as in notable religious rites, is the path to righteousness.

The citizens so afflicted will not be as easily convinced as are those who, from a distance or from positions of some personal comfort, see virtue in hardship. And the political consequences are· far from attractive. This is a moment of great and welcome liberty in Eastern Europe. It would be tragic indeed were liberty to be there identified with unacceptable economic deprivation. I would especially urge against any prescription of hardship from western capitals, including Washington. There is little to be said for therapy that, again, we would not wish to suffer at home.

Were I counselling the Eastern European countries, I would, indeed, urge the release of less urgent consumers' goods and services to the market along with the productive resources therewith required. And I would also urge loans from the state banks to facilitate this process and any necessary steps to accommodate banks to this purpose. There should be no hesitation, as now in the Soviet Union, about having a private employer/employee relationship. This is a relationship, however identified with capitalism, that millions have survived and enjoyed.

I would be more cautious and gradual in releasing basic foods, rents and health services to the market. Here hardship and suffering would be acute. And, it should be recognised, it would involve action that the capitalist countries, as they still are called, would find unacceptable. All of the major industrial counties now heavily subsidise their agricultural production. In all, in consequence, farm prices are higher and/or consumer prices lower than they would be without such government intervention. All industrial countries also take special steps to provide lower-cost housing; capitalism does not anywhere supply good inexpensive shelter. Health care is only satisfactory where, effectively, it is socialised.

I do not urge that prices to farmers be kept low; that is a serious past error. I would urge recognition of the fact that all current capitalist practice combines higher prices to the farmer and lower prices to the consumer than the classical free market provides. If in a transition period some rationing continues, I would think that the least adverse of alternatives.

As to the characteristic large producing firm, one would urge that, indeed, it be released from ministerial supervision. And in response to market demand it should be responsible for its own operations with its management and workers enjoying the rewards of good performance. This means that it should be free to set its own prices and bargain with similar freedom for production requirements from firms similarly released to the market. Loans should again be available to finance innovation and expansion. And, a difficult matter, the penalty for miscalculation and failure should fall on the defaulting management.

It does not seem to me greatly important as to where the ultimate ownership resides. In the capitalist world this is normally with stockholders unknown to the management. It would make no decisive difference were it the state, as in notable cases it is. What is important is that the producing firm, not less that the individual, be the expression of its own personality with the reward of its own success and the penalty of its own failure.

There has been much talk of moving to convertible currencies. This reflects an equally Simplistic Ideology. What is – or would have been – far more important is the immobilising of accumulated currency surpluses within the country.

The persistent and damaging tendency of socialism in the past has been to supply more money than goods. These funds make market liberalisation identical with inflation, as currently in Poland. Anyone holding spendable money above a certain amount should have been required through a currency conversion to hold it off the market in long-term interest-bearing bonds. This would seem still to be a plausible design in some of the other socialist countries, including the USSR.

I advance these suggestions with caution: on the great problems of conversion and change the socialist countries are, as I've noted, now in receipt of more western advice that they can possibly use or should ever contemplate. I read of a recent American mission to the Soviet Union that urged the adoption there of the gold standard in support of a fully convertible rouble. This would, admittedly, be welcomed by the few who would immediately be in full possession of all the gold. It is a fair reflection of much of the advice now traversing the onetime Iron Curtain.

On one step there should be no hesitation. That is for the western countries and Japan to come promptly and generously to the assistance of the countries now in the process of liberalisation. This is the moment of need; freedom as I've emphasised, must not be seen to have a heavy economic price. Debt service should be suspended, as my colleague Jeffrey Sachs, with whom I perhaps differ on the effect of shock therapy, has wisely urged. Nor is this a time for lectures from the IMF on austerity. The affirmative help in grants and loans should not be confined to capital goods; it must extend generously to food and consumers' goods, the areas of most serious past socialist failure and thus of present need. Let there be no hesitation in providing support to the requirements and even the modest enjoyments of life. These, not plant and machinery, are of the most immediate importance. Needless perhaps to say, these countries should be accorded relief from past capital charges; this, assuredly, is not the time for assigning resources to the financial errors of the past.

The resources are available in the West, for one consequence of these months of revolution, which is visible in the West with a clarity that cannot be resisted by even the most ardent exponents of bureaucratic truth, is a diminished military threat with its resulting claim on public resources. It is the most obvious and elementary of steps that some of the resources so freed must be used to ease the transition – the transition to a world of greater economic success, political freedom and military security.

I do not minimise the reluctance to be encountered here. Bureaucratic truths supported by the economic self-interest of a vast weapons industry are still strong. So doubtless in other countries and so certainly in the United States. When I urged these matters in Washington before our Senate Committee on Foreign Relations in company with administration officials recently returned from Poland, I heard much of the advice that might be given that country. The particular reference was to "institution-building"; that has the advantage of being wonderfully inexpensive. It has the highly probable disadvantage once again of being advice that we would not accept for ourselves. The triumph here of Simplistic Ideology once more.

As to more substantive help of the kind just mentioned, there was a short reference to "budget constraints". Budget constraints are not thought to be similarly decisive where something as remote from reality as anti-missile defence – Star Wars – is concerned. Or the Stealth bomber, the sacrifice of only a few of which would pay the cost of greatly expanded economic aid. Here is the bureaucratic truth, as distinct from reality, in its starkest and, alas, also its darkest form.

Eastern Europe and the Soviet Union are now experiencing one of the greatest moments in their history. That moment is also ours. I return to Simplistic Ideology. Nothing would be more disastrous in the West than a return to the economic order envisaged in early capitalist doctrine and still celebrated by its more devout theologians. The system has survived only because of its capacity, in a liberal political context, to adapt.

Socialism encountered revolt because it failed to adapt. Adaptation and not a dramatic descent to primitive capitalism is now the need. It is an untrod road; it cannot be negotiated by adherence to rigid rules. It requires, alas, the painful processes of thought. That has in all economic ages been resisted, as it is being resisted now. There is, sadly, no alternative.

© Gabriella Bollobas

2 Elemer Hankiss

What the Hungarians saw first

Born in 1928. A philosopher by training, he took a PhD in philosophy at the University of Budapest. Has taught at many universities around the world and is Professor of Political Sciences at the University of Budapest and Research Director of the Institute of Sociology of the Academy of Sciences. Author of several books and many essays in the field of political sociology and the sociology of values. Newly appointed Head of Hungarian Television.

2

It is not easy to understand East European societies nowadays. Maybe it has never been easy to understand this crazy part of Europe. Eastern Europe has been called by some, I think appropriately, "Absurdistan", and it is true that these countries have a long history of absurdities, which makes them difficult for foreigners to understand.

A short Hungarian anecdote illustrates how absurd those countries are and how difficult it may be to understand what has happened there. There is a story about the Hungarian Ambassador in Washington going to the State Department in 1941 to submit Hungary's Declaration of War on the United States.

The high official in the State Department doesn't know too much about this far away country, very understandably, and asks some cautious questions. First he asks, "Where is Hungary? It's a republic isn't it?" "No sir, it is a kingdom." "I see, so you have a king?" "No sir, we don't have a king, we have a governor. He is an admiral." "So you have a fleet?" "No sir, we don't have a fleet. We don't have a single ship. Hungary is a land-bound country. We have no sea coast." "Oh, well, I see. So now you want to declare war on us?" "Yes sir, we do." "And why? You surely have some claims on us?" "No sir, we don't." "You may have then some claims on our allies the French, or the Poles?" "No sir, we have nothing against the French; and the Poles have been our best friends for centuries." "I see. Then on whom do you have any claims?" "Well, the Romanians." "So you have declared war on the Romanians have you not?" "No sir. They are our allies." The situation is no less absurd and no less complex nowadays in Eastern Europe than it was in '41. Therefore I am not surprised that Jan Urban and I independently use the same point of reference in this book. It bears repetition!

Due to this absurd complexity experts could draw up a great number of hypotheses about what has happened during the last few years and what may happen in Eastern Europe in the near future. Let me offer here only three scenarios which I believe to be among the most illuminating.

The first is best called the "Colonisation Scenario". According to it, we have to go back forty years if we want to understand what has happened in the last two. In 1947/48 East European countries were colonised by the Russian empire, were kept as colonies for forty years and now in the last two years there have been anti-colonial revolts and national liberation movements. This is the essence of what is happening: the revolt against a colonial empire. Certainly there is something in this interpretation.

According to a second, which we may label the "Social Democratisation Scenario", after the Second World War, East European countries were still backward countries with hybrid feudal–capitalist systems – authoritarian systems of the type which in *The Social Origins of Dictatorship and Democracy* Barrington Moore ascribed to Germany and Japan. Thus there was a need for a kind of social revolution. This revolution happened in 1947/48 in most East European countries. But this revolution de-railed, however, after it ran into the Communists coming down the track the other way. Now disoriented and deranged, the Communists kept these countries in a kind of amnesia and suspended animation for forty years. But in the 1970s, in certain places a kind of social democratisation began. Already during the late sixties, in Hungary the Kadar regime introduced a more tolerant policy to the opposition and to society in general. It allowed a kind of "second economy" to evolve; it allowed a process of cultural pluralisation to emerge, though of course it did not allow political pluralisation. There was also a strictly limited liberalisation of the whole system. This has been viewed by some experts as a kind of slow progress towards a social democratic polity.

Personally, I don't think that the Communist "revolution" in 1948 was necessary. I don't believe the argument that without this revolution Hungary, Poland and Czechoslovakia would have fallen into a process of "Latin Americanization" meaning that it would have developed towards a conservative, right wing, populist, and nationalist régime. The disaster into which right wing politics had earlier led the country under Admiral Horthy, the disintegration of the *ancien régime* and of the traditional ruling class, Land Reform and nationalisation, the presence of the Allies, the general (West and Central) European trend of democratisation were all factors which could, and in my mind would, have protected the country against this danger.

The Hungarian Communist Party crumbled on 7 September 1989 and one of the parties which emerged from the debris calls itself a "Socialist Party". It considered itself to be a type of Social Democratic Party. A Western European social democracy would certainly be an effective model for many Hungarians nowadays. So again, I would say there is something of value in this scenario. It points out how in these Communist parties there was a change from Bolshevism to a more social democratic type of development. This is what Hungarians saw first, but it was also to be seen on a less extensive scale in some other countries, notably in Poland.

A third hypothesis to explain what has happened in Eastern Europe, may be labelled the "Tocquevillian Scenario". According to Alexis de Tocqueville, the French Revolution was not necessary, because the main forces of the real, transforming revolution, the bourgeois revolution, had been there already starting to be active before the 1789 revolution. The French Revolution was therefore a disruption. It interrupted a normal evolutionary process, which without the detour via the Terror and the Guillotine and the Napoleonic Wars, would have led much earlier than happened in reality to a kind of bourgeois capitalist democratic society. So the achievement of the French Revolution was to lose two or three decades for France on the pathway of normal (ie bourgeois) development.

Applying this model to Eastern Europe, we can say that all these countries have made a big Tocquevillian detour in the last forty years. After the Second World War they began to develop market economies. They began to develop their own multi-party parliamentary systems. In 1945 or 1946 in almost all these countries there were free elections and parliaments began to function: Czechoslovakia was a democratic republic, in spite of the presence of a strong Communist Party and the pro-Soviet policies of Benes, until the *coup d'état* in the Spring of 1948. In Hungary, the Independent Smallholders' Party won a strong majority (57 per cent) in the elections of 1945, while the Communists got less than 17 per cent. In 1948 this healthy revolution embracing a relatively well functioning multi-party system was destroyed. In other East European countries, for in instance in East Germany and Poland, evolutionary trends were disrupted earlier, in 1933 or 1939, and after the war they fell victim to Soviet colonisation and communist domination too early, without a genuine attempt at re-marketisation and re-democratisation. Now, after forty years, people across this part of Europe have to begin where they left off in '48. I think this scenario best interprets what has happened; but the other two scenarios also have something to say for them.

If we now try to see how these three scenarios work when applied to various East European countries, we get different results. Poland first. Poland has its own idiosyncratic development, which is similar to, but not the same as Hungarian development and very unlike the development which is taking place in East Germany or in Czechoslovakia.

Poland was the country which first got into a deep economic crisis in the 1970s and during that decade it led a series of economic bankruptcies in Eastern Europe. Second, in Poland the process of proletarianisation went furthest and its social fabric was most deeply penetrated by Bolshevik power. In Poland independent economic autonomies – middle class autonomies – were destroyed more than in any other country in Eastern Europe. Third, the Polish economy was, and is, more dependent on the Soviet Union than the economies of any of the other East European countries. Fourth and finally, a very important factor is the power of the Church. Poland was the only country where there was a countervailing power, a strong and almost autonomous countervailing power, which could counterbalance in any meaningful sense the power of the Communists. The Polish Church played a very important part in the last few years in organising the transition to a new type of society.

In this respect, one should stress the contrast with Hungary. The Hungarian Churches didn't play any kind of role in the Hungarian revolution; nothing like in Poland or in East Germany. The Hungarian Churches were compromised and became very conformist throughout the forty years of Communism. We didn't have a Polish Catholic Church; we didn't have an East German Lutheran Church. We simply had Churches and Church hierarchies which were deeply conformist – they even helped the State to oppress independent Churches. After the 1989 revolutions, they are at a loss, confused, and don't know what to do. They have even let down their own party, the Christian Democratic Peoples' Party, which tried unsuccessfully to get some help from them. The Hungarian Churches are much criticised, and are still very passive in this field. Perhaps this is for the best; I wouldn't like them to be too active in politics!

Due to these four factors in Poland we have a mixture consisting of the germs of a Social Democratic politics, of a sort of Christian Democratic model and now, thirdly, it is also mixed with a Thatcherite radically libertarian economic programme. They have their millions of workers now well organised. They are ready to adopt and fight for a kind of Social Democratic model. At the same time they have a Christian Democratic Trade Union movement, not a classical Social Democratic type movement. And they have their new economists who try to implement a Thatcherite programme. These are the three Poles of Poland: Social Democracy, Christian Democracy and Free Market economics. They form a triangular field of force which now determines what is happening in Poland.

The Czechoslovaks were latecomers in the East European revolutions. Their Spring in Winter came on 17th November 1989 after a deep freeze of twenty years which had killed any mass political pluralism root and branch in that country. Only the small and immensely hardy plants of the Charter 77 Dissidents managed to survive in this latter-day Ice Kingdom of Narnia, realm of Husak, whom the Czech novelist Milan Kundera has immortalised for posterity as the "President of Forgetting."[1] The Czechs and Slovaks have their differences, but the Czech Civic Forum and the Slovak Public Against Violence worked closely together during the 1989 Revolution. Compared to other places, they have the advantage of relative unity.

They were able to adopt ready-made models very quickly and very skilfully and to plant them in virgin soil. Their exceptional suffering had given them an exceptional advantage when the thaw came; for they were able to initiate the transformation of their societies while in a pre-democratic, pre-pluralistic mode. It is more difficult to transform a country quickly when it has a multi-party democratic parliament than when it has a single charismatic leader or a small group of leaders such as the Czechoslovak ex-dissident "revolutionary aristocracy" provides. In contrast, the problem of Hungary and also of Poland is that they have to transform their countries while a multi-party system is already in existence and in both cases has been operating in some fashion for some time.

Czechoslovakia is the best candidate for a predominantly social democratic socio-political form as it makes itself into a new country and new system. They have strong traditions in this field, as strong as or even stronger than the East Germans. They don't have, however, the kind of entrepreneurial class which, for instance, Hungary has. So they may be tempted to rely more on a sort of "managerial socialism" or a "managerial capitalism": in short on Keynesian economics. They may be forced to keep a relatively large number of existing state companies for a longer period than Hungary. So it is possible that they will have a market economy dominated by relatively big state companies and controlled by a strong social democratic society and parliament.

---

[1] Milan Kundera, *The Book of Laughter and Forgetting*, Alfred Knopf, New York, 1980.

The trajectory of Hungarian life since the Communists took over in 1948 has been rather peculiar. First, the Communists set out systematically to "demobilise" civil society. The seventeenth Trades' Union Conference of October 1948 incorporated the Unions as agents of state power in the economy. Simultaneously, independent actors in the economy – peasants, small entrepreneurs – were expropriated and hounded. Parliament was subverted and given the typical East European function of "vote delivery", while new patronage systems, controlled by the new oligarchy, were installed. As a late Christmas present, on 26th December 1948, Cardinal Mindszenty was arrested, signalling an undermining of the Church which successfully cowed it for a generation; indeed the Hungarian Church was denied any equivalent to the role of the Church in Poland, for example.

In short the Communists aimed to atomise society: to drive people in upon themselves, to force them to live very private lives and to render them unable to defend themselves against the new oligarchy in the public domain. A telling indicator of this is the precipitate decline in the number of clubs and societies (that is, interest-group clubs not connected with sport). In the early 1940s, there were 13-14,000 in Hungary. After the Communist takeover there remained less than 1,000. The means of public association other than through the Party were stripped away.

Once begun, this process could be relied upon to proceed under its own momentum. People "demobilised" themselves, by illness, suicide and alcoholism. It is well known that both the latter rise at times of crisis. In Hungary, the suicide rate was in the low 20s per 100,000 in 1948. It was 45 per 100,000 by 1984. Alcohol consumption followed a similar path, from 4.9 litres per capita per annum in 1950 to 11.7 in 1984.

But the peculiarity of the Hungarian situation became most strikingly apparent in the 1960s. Hitherto, this dismal story of social atomization and political crippling matches that of other East European countries. But in the 1960s, the Hungarian oligarchy did something different. (All this story so far and the story of the fake liberalisation of the 1960s is told in full in my book *East European Alternatives*).

In the 1960s the oligarchy began to want to have two contradictory things. On the one hand they wished to maintain the atomised, disheartened state of civil society. This required maximum decentralisation of popular institutions, maximum centralisation of State power and information. On the other, they wanted to stimulate innovation, which required some "re-heartening" to encourage people to be creative. But the stuffing had been so knocked out of Hungarian society in the 1950s that it remained diffuse and inarticulate. The effect of the Hungarian liberalisation was in some ways a precursor of what has happened since 1985 in the USSR. When the pressure was released, the victim was unable to stand up. This led directly to the growing crisis of the formal economy which by the mid 1970s was bad and by the mid 1980s severe. Only two things kept the situation from unravelling earlier: self-exploitation and the continuation of the informal sector or "second economy".

According to a social survey made in 1989, Hungarian adult males work fourteen hours a day, six days a week. Fourteen hours a day is unacceptable. We have a very high rate of early death and heart attacks. People are ruining themselves physically in order to survive economically. This general damage to health, compounding the suicide rate and alchoholism, was the price paid to prevent Hungary starving in the sixties and seventies. The Communist economy, which was more inefficient than in either Czechoslovakia or East Germany, would have starved our country. But thanks to the second economy and to this gruelling fourteen hour day, the country was relatively more prosperous than those countries. Yet at a price, and that price has been paid in human lives and in the lives of broken families.

With respect to political pluralism, Hungary has had a one-party system for forty years. But change began in 1985, when we had a general election which was still controlled by the Communists. Despite this, suddenly and unexpectedly, there was a huge popular groundswell to try to have independent candidates run for parliamentary seats. The Communist oligarchy tried to frustrate this demand, but in spite of their attempts, 10% of parliamentary seats were gained by independent candidates. This was something quite new in Eastern Europe at that time, where practically all the parliaments were controlled 100% by mixtures of the Communists (in preponderance), some collaborating, dependant and conformist small parties, and by the so called Popular Fronts.

The pattern of parliamentary life changed further, but only with any speed in 1988. This may be demonstrated. The number of laws passed by parliament was, from the late nineteenth century up to 1948, an annual average of thirty-seven per year. After the Communists took power the yearly average of laws passed in parliament sank to five per year. This means that in practice the parliament actually did not work. As I have observed, its role was as a vote machine, cranking out spurious legitimation of Party actions. It was the executive power which did everything; the parliament had no role. During the period 1987-90 there has been a sudden regeneration. Twenty-six laws were passed in 1988 and there were many more in 1989. In the first session of 1990, in one single session twenty-six laws were passed. This is even too much I think! But now, we really are in a hurry. Hungary is seeking to transform everything and to have democracy as soon as possible.

As far as the state of the parties is concerned, we had a one-party system until late 1988. The first Hungarian alternative party of opposition was founded only in September 1988. This was the so called Hungarian Democratic Forum. It was not yet a party at this time, but it worked like a party. And then in the next year there were about twenty parties founded. In the last couple of months of that year and the first of 1989, an additional *thirty* appeared. Now Hungary has *fifty-two* parties running for seats in the parliament, which is maybe a few too many according to British standards! Yet I think that it is healthy after having had only one party for forty years. Consider that after the end of Franco the Spaniards, in the mid 1970s, began with exactly the same figure: they had more than fifty parties running for the first elections in Spain. Now they have five or six serious parties. Hungary may hope to follow a similar profile and to have a similar number after the elections.

Such a regenerative process is not without its unpleasant sides. One, a familiar spectre from the European past, returned to Hungarian politics in 1989. Anti-semitism reappeared in December 1989 and early January 1990 in Hungary. This question divided the two major parties, the Democratic Forum and the Free Democrats. Between the two World Wars, there was anti-semitism in most East European countries, mainly in Poland and Romania but also in Hungary and Czechoslovakia. After the Holocaust and the Second World War, everybody hoped and believed that this question would never re-emerge in any of those countries. In any case, after the genocide, very few Jews came back to Poland, and only a few more to Hungary. Those remaining were urban. Indeed, of the twenty districts of Budapest, full deportation to the death camps only occurred in one. But still we are not talking of a large Jewish population.

In its modern recurrence, the pith of the hatred was not any longer composed of economic and social grievance as it was before the War. So the question is, why did it emerge so suddenly in 1989? To understand, we must know its context. Anti-semitism has a slender social basis in contemporary Hungary, indeed virtually none in the countryside and only little in society as a whole. It is almost uniquely an issue which exercises intellectuals and people living in Budapest. For many reasons, the Jewish community, which reorganised itself after the Second World War, earned its living mainly in the media, in the field of culture, and to a certain but not great extent in finance and industry. In these fields, the non-Jewish community felt that Kadarism and especially Aczel, Kadar's Secretary of Cultural Affairs in the Central Committee, was biased in favour of the Jewish com-munity. Ethnic Hungarians are full of grievances and sincerely feel that they were discriminated against for thirty years and that the Jewish community had privileges in those years. In late 1989, certain political figures began to voice these grievances. The reaction came very soon and was, understandably, strong and emotional. In the ensuing debate both sides sustained injuries and the whole issue spun more and more out of control. It became a party issue and unfortunately there were parties prepared to use this issue for campaign purposes. I think that it was a kind of chain reaction. It began on the nationalist side of the non-Jewish community and then it became a kind of aberration and the whole thing became more and more ungovernable. What is good is that the leaders of the two big parties have realised the dangers lying in the fact that if anti-semitism becomes the major issue, along this dividing line none of the serious problems of the country can be solved. If the new government is defined by divisions on the issue of anti-semitism, this will herald the political bankruptcy of the country, for the new government and for democracy. Both camps realised by the time of the April 1990 elections that this was not the real issue. Underlying are very important economic, political, social and culture problems with which we have to deal. Co-operation is building up at the time of writing between the two parties to turn away from the leering shadow of the past towards the concrete challenges of the present.

I now turn to the material substance of politics. Economic recovery or re-generation is influenced in a basic way by the fact that everything was nationalised. In Hungary still 90% of all assets are owned by the state, (in reality the state bureaucracy). Almost all companies are owned by the state. Ownership is highly relevant because in Eastern European countries, the lack of real owners has caused many problems. There was no control and no motivation to try to make the most of the assets one had.

State companies ran totally inefficiently because nobody cared. Managers were appointed by a state bureaucrat, and the state bureaucrat was not interested in finding the right person to run the company in the best way, because he was not interested in the profit made by the company. The bureaucrat was interested in appointing someone by the appointment of whom he dispensed patronage to a select small circle, from which he could get back reciprocal favours in due course. This is the secondary circuit of interest in these countries. Appointed and morally endebted, the manager then had to make decisions which his friends in the mafia liked, because he in turn could then use the power of the small mafia for his own personal benefit. Patronage moves in a virtuous spiral for its beneficiaries and a vicious spiral for society as a whole.

Until we have owners who try to find the best managers, there is no way in which these state companies can be forced to become more efficient. So ownership is quite important; but of course personal initiative and mechanisms or institutions which would mobilise similar resources are also very important. What of organised labour? We had official Trade Unions in Hungary which were controlled by the Communists. Now this, which in 1948 had been one of the first, is in 1990 the last bastion of Communism in Hungary. The oligarchy of Trade Union leaders remains there and it is the strongest organisation – a nationwide network with many activists and many assets. The old Trade Unions were very strong and very dangerous. If the new parliament fails to control and solve the problems they pose, this Kadarist Trade Union oligarchy will be the first to organise, for its own purposes against parliament and against democracy, the workers, the poor and all those who feel themselves in a difficult situation.

There is a movement of independent Trade Unions, which began growing in recent years and which tries to challenge the oligarchy. But it is still really too weak to challenge the powers of the official Trade Unions. They suffered from political neglect. The new parties were not interested in Trade Union problems in Hungary in 1989. They were too much concerned with larger, more lurid political issues: maybe that was their duty. However, they neglected the whole industrial relations dimension. In 1990 they are trying to make a *rapprochement* with the independent Trade Unions. An attempt is being made to move this independent movement against the old inefficient Trade Unions. This would be a very important step in the evolution of Hungary.

But outside the classical, formal labour sector, regeneration has already begun. In 1948 there were about a hundred and seventy thousand independent craftsmen in Hungary. The number dropped to fifty thousand in 1953. Now again it grows, reaching again a hundred and sixty thousand in 1989. Thus we are back at the level where we were interrupted in 1948, a further buttress for the "Tocquevillian scenario". We have the same figures for shopkeepers and entrepreneurs and those employed by them. The number was sixty seven thousand in 1982 and now it is almost six hundred thousand: it is a tenfold increase in five years and rising.

According to a poll made in December 1989, 28% of Hungarians want to become entrepreneurs. This is ridiculous. They can't! But the fact that the motive force, the motivation, is there I think is very encouraging. The country has never been as entrepreneurial as it is now. To be fashionable, you have to be an entrepreneur. This is true not only for private individuals, but also for institutions. We now have entrepreneurial parties, entrepreneurial Trade Unions, entrepreneurial Churches. Everybody is now trying to become entrepreneurial.

There is activity also in the informal sector. One of the most important trends in Hungary in the last twenty five or thirty years has been the rise of a *petite bourgeoisie*, the rise of a middle class. But this is a bourgeoisie evincing a very low level of individual entrepreneurial activity, although great zeal. By the early 1970s, two million Hungarian families were involved in this "second economy". Each claimed that they had a back garden where they grew something, and they made money. They made such money on a very small scale entrepreneurial basis. But it means, when agglomerated, that two million families have been learning for three decades the basic skills of how to work decently, skills which they forgot in the state companies: how to meet deadlines, how to produce acceptable quality goods, and even how to have a very simple accounting system. These are skills, which are now very important national assets. We have two million potential entrepreneurs in Hungary. This is formerly covert, but now overt petite bourgeoisification, embourgeoisement on a small scale. Yet this is not the sum total of human resources available to assist in the regeneration of Hungary.

Another important process may be called the rise of a kind of nineteenth century "*grande bourgeoisie*". This *grande bourgeoisie* is a coalition and to some degree an amalgamation of three or four important social groups. Firstly there is the most dynamic generational group within the old Party and state bureaucracy – its children.

We speak in Hungary in 1990 of a phenomenon called "the conversion of power". Since the writing appeared on the wall in 1987, the Party and state bureaucracy have been trying to convert their bureaucratic power into a new type of power which will be an asset that can be preserved within a new system, namely in a market economy or even in a democracy.

There are various ways of converting to new power if you are a Kadarist oligarch. The first is by diversification. The characteristic oligarchic family in the mid 1980s was the father or the grandfather, a party *apparatchik*, a high-level party or state official; his son a manager of a British/Hungarian joint venture; his son-in-law with a boutique in Vaci Street; his daughter an editor for Hungarian television; his nephew studying at Cambridge or Oxford; his mother-in-law having a small hotel or boarding house on Lake Balaton etc. We sociologists have tried to explore these networks, but it is understandably difficult. These family businesses are absolutely top secret. However, we did discover more than two hundred and fifty businesses belonging to this kind of diversified oligarchic family and there must be several hundred more.

In 1989 there appeared another way in which as a party oligarch, you could convert your power on an institutional level. The party tried to transform its huge properties and real estate (Party headquarters, Training Centres, holiday centres) into semi-private companies or into joint stock companies. Once converted, this property was then withdrawn from state control. These new assets would be the basis of real power in a market economy, and the point is that such reserve wealth could be created by the oligarch's own fiat. In the last moments some of these redefinitions could be stopped, but not all. Some sales were still proceeding in 1990, but less and less because control had grown very strict after the loop-hole was noticed.

A third way for the régime to convert power was, ironically, to transform the Hungarian economy into a market economy. This may be in the general good of the country, but has been carried out in such a way that this new *grande bourgeoisie* profit most from the new laws. Here, I must add that beside those party bureaucrat families who are converting their power, there is also a managerial class whom we call the "Red Barons", and also the new entrepreneurs who are coming from elsewhere to the market. These three groups are slowly amalgamating into a new *grande bourgeoisie*, and the new laws, partly backed by parliament, favour this new *grande bourgeoisie*.

Let me illustrate. In 1989 two new laws were passed. One was called the Company Law, the other, the Transformation Law, which allowed the transformation of state companies into any other form of ownership – into joint stock companies or limited liability companies, or co-operatives, for example. In practice the managers of the state companies had the right to sell the old company to anybody: to foreign investors, to themselves, even to their friends in other companies. This they could do by a strange method which we called "cross-ownership". It works in this way. Company A sells its shares to four other companies B, C, D and E. Then A itself buys shares in B, C, D and E. So by interlocking in this fashion, the five managers own themselves and practically nobody can oust them, because there is no state control or external market control: the shareholders are themselves. This is most ingenious. It is reminiscent of that speciality of British capitalism – the interlocking directorship network.

There are various other ways to effect a secret privatisation of state property, transforming it into managerial property. It has been a very hot issue in Hungary. In 1990, a new law was made, trying to break this process; but it is still going on.

A new ideology has emerged since 1987. Originally, the whole market idea was thrown out easily by the Communists themselves and new ideas replaced it. More recently, the egalitarian ideology of Marxism has been replaced surreptitiously by a kind of meritocratic ideology, which has never been a Marxist value. Even more characteristic, after 1948, Marxism bore within it tangible, physical egalitarianism, which meant equality of living conditions, even if that meant equality of misery and squalor for all. The arch enemy of Marxism was the equality of chances. Marx, Engels and company all attacked as devilish bourgeois tricks or lies the bourgeois ideology of equality of chances. But suddenly, since 1987, the Hungarian Communist Party has adopted as the basis of its value system none other than that devilish lie, the equality of chances. A radical turnround!

The last item in the fundamental canon of Marxist values was work: physical, sweaty, heroic, Stakhanovite work; in short, blue-collar work. The blue-collar worker was the paragon of the Socialist system. With bulging muscles and lantern jaw he and she both stare from many Socialist Realist friezes. In Budapest, a classic example of the genre is to be found high on the Citadel. It graces the plinth of the Statue of Liberation, commemorating the Soviet defeat of the Germans in the 1945 Battle for Budapest.

Since 1987 physical work has disappeared from the ideology and value system of Hungarian Communism. It has been replaced by achievement, mainly by entrepreneurial achievement. If you are an entrepreneur you are the "right guy": you have all the prestige. If not you are practically nothing. This ideological reorientation has helped the new *grande bourgeoisie* to emerge.

Ideological flux combines with the enthusiasm for the free market to create what may be a tricky problem. Important media tycoons have come to Hungary since the autumn of 1989, and they are very welcome. Mr Maxwell is welcome, Mr Murdoch is welcome, Mr Springer from West Germany is very welcome, because we need the expertise, we need the money, we need new media technology. But it would not be in the best interests of Hungary if all the important papers, the daily papers, magazines or TV stations were to be bought by these gentlemen, although at this writing, in two cases they have been active in our temporarily, unnaturally free market.

This is a live danger because during the interregnum between the collapse of Communism and the crystallisation of democratic government we have literally an absolutely free press. There are no norms, there are no traditions which control a normal free press. Hungary in 1990 has an *anarchy* of the Press, not a freedom of the Press. This is not bad after forty years of nothing, but it has its own dangers. It may be some irritation for them because Mr Maxwell cannot buy all the British press and Mr Springer cannot buy all the West German press, but Mr Maxwell can easily, from one pocket, buy the whole Hungarian press and all the TV and all the radio stations in a week. That's the problem. We need some kind of regulation.

Once when I was in the United States the question of control of the media was discussed. Colleagues were trying to convince us that we would have to adopt an absolutely free market approach and that it would be very good if Mr Murdoch or Mr Maxwell bought all the media, because that is the free market, that is competition, and if they don't work well, then new people will come and establish new stations and why not? Hungary has the right to only three television channels by international agreement and it would not be good if they bought all three. Then I asked about the American Broadcasting Corporation and they told me that in the United States foreign citizens cannot buy a single share either in the TV or in the radio companies. But, don't learn from our mistakes, they said!

Hungary, in comparison to Poland, Czechoslovakia or East Germany, has difficulties because we have created our pluralistic system before we have made the big decisions about the transformation of our economy. The deliberation will be very difficult to make through ordinary parliamentary procedures. But we have the advantage over our friends of having these large entrepreneurial bases, the large *petite bourgeoisie* and having this aggressive new composite *grande bourgeoisie*. I think that on balance, Hungary is in the stronger position. Next comes Poland. They too have this new type of big entrepreneur to some extent, but the Hungarian position is more peaceful for many reasons.

I have tried elsewhere to answer the question: "Why did not they shoot?"[2] Instead of listing here all the factors that have been mentioned in this context, let me focus on one single factor which played an especially important part in the Hungarian (and to a lesser extent in the Polish) process of transition: loss of interest in preserving the Party. In the late 1980s a substantial part of the Hungarian party and state bureaucracy discovered a way of converting their bureaucratic power into lucrative economic positions and assets (and indirectly also into a new type of political power) in the new system based on market economics and political democracy. In the first years of Communism, the Bolshevik leaders coming back from Moscow needed to exercise dictatorial power in order to protect themselves as the ruling elite. By 1965 they were firmly established. They controlled all the economic, political, social, and cultural institutions, resources, and interactions. They had co-opted large numbers of activists and experts, and had begun to build up a large quasi-constituency of people

---

[2] "Pourquoi ils n'ont pas tiré?", *Documents Observateur*, No. 8, Paris, *Le nouvel Observateur*, Janvier-Février 1990.

who began to realize that they might profit modestly from the existing system. In this situation, the over-centralised and despotic rule exercised by the party leadership became anachronistic. It was time to decentralise power and to reward the faithful. With this, the development of oligarchic and neo-feudal structures began in Hungary. When in the late 1980s they discovered the possibility of transferring their power into a new and more efficient socio-economic system and of becoming part of an emerging new and legitimate ruling class or *grande bourgeoisie*, they lost their interest in keeping the Communist Party as their instrument of power and protection. And, as a consequence, on the night of 7 October 1989 they watched indifferently, or assisted actively in, the self-liquidation of the Party.

Like all the other countries which have experienced revolution, Hungary faces the question of what the party cadres will do now and what will be done to them. For the reason just mentioned, Hungary is curiously positioned in this regard, for the old oligarchy of the *ancien régime* has found bridges over and barges in which to retreat from the rising waters, and to save itself and part of its power and prestige in forms still usable within the new system.

First we must have regard to the upper leadership, because with the dissolution of the Communist Party, the national leadership and the county leaderships dissolved and disappeared overnight. It is very strange that the Party headquarters in the county capitals became empty overnight and nobody knew who would be there and for what purpose these big buildings would be used. Then slowly the Socialists, who were the haters of the Communists, began to occupy some of the offices; then they let some of the offices to other parties, or to other institutions.

As for the people of the old oligarchy, some of them remain in politics. Those of low and medium rank organise the Socialist party and they ran the campaign for the Socialist party. The more orthodox of them have retained their Communist Party, and after falling down the biggest snake in Hungarian political snakes and ladders, in 1990 they began to organise their national campaign from the beginning again. Most of those high-ranking cadres who were working for the national leadership were irretrievably committed to the old order and have lost their jobs. They were given thirty days notice and then they were sacked in late October 1989.

Now they are looking for new jobs and many of them are "parachuting" into various companies. As some of these are still state companies it's not too difficult for them to find a niche. They also tried to parachute themselves into some other existing organisations, (the Trade Unions or the still existing Popular Front) into some new institutions; or they went into private business. There are hundreds of them who tried to build up a small, or not so small private business. There were some attempts to transform Communist property into individual private property as described above and the new leaders of these new companies come inevitably largely from the old oligarchy and from the bureaucrats. This is the meaning of "dispersion" in the economy.

The real problem will come when the local oligarchies lose their jobs. Ten thousand people, many more than the national leadership, are already looking for new jobs. They are now buying up land, they are founding their new market-type farms together with the so called "Green Barons" (the managers of the agricultural co-operatives). So they are establishing small companies and consolidating their farms which will be absorbed within the market economy.

Whatever its merits or demerits, this process in Hungary is proceeding without violence. There was a law passed by parliament in February 1990 which said that Party national and county leaders had to give account of their wealth, and particularly the increase of their wealth, between 1980 and 1989. Within a month they had to submit accounts. This is not like shooting Ceausescu or imprisoning Honecker; but it nonetheless dangerous.

There is a debate about how to cope with this problem. It is hard to have a revolution without villains, and in a way, the society needs some kind of visible justice. Some kind of justice should be done. But how to do it, and not destroy too much? How to have justice and not destroy too many experts whose skills we sorely need? It is a familiar problem across Eastern Europe following the 1989 revolutions: not to fall into the trap described by the famous Latin phrase *fiat iustitia et periat mundus* – do justice and let the world perish. We don't want to destroy our society just for the sake of having justice, but we want justice all the same.

At the other end of the spectrum is Romania. The old régime still has important positions but does not have these bridges across which it will be able to withdraw its power and prestige. Maybe that is why they have shot the old leaders in Romania and they haven't shot them in Hungary. In East Germany there are no bridges between state economy and market economy, but one presumes that West Germany will help those people to find their position and place in the new system.

The countries which were changed by the Spring in Winter Revolutions of 1989 were different from Hungary – or rather Hungary differed from them in another way wherein, because we saw it first, we are less fortunate. They preserved the innocence of revolution for the period during and after late 1989. In Hungary, we unfortunately have lost our innocence. We are beyond the innocence of revolution and this poses one of our problems which we have to solve. We have also lost something even more important. We have lost our common enemy.

We have lost the devil against which we have been battling and fighting for forty years. It is reassuring and useful to have a common enemy. It is simpler. You can feel yourself innocent, heroic and beautiful. We have now lost this enemy because this enemy has played a dirty trick on us. This enemy destroyed itself last September. We were left without an enemy, so we turned against one another. Hungarians were so accustomed to having enemies that we found these enemies within ourselves; one party against the other, or failing that, the Jews. We entered a period of fears and dishonest and pitiful party struggles in late 1989. Perhaps we had to go through this period? Certainly the result of the April 1990 election giving a mandate only for a coalition seemed to be an accurate result in that it accurately mirrored this social landscape.

Hungary had a difficult couple of years from 1987-89 in several respects. Five problems are outstanding. First, a tribal war broke out. Various cultural entities: ethnic, religious, cultural – people with various sorts of backgrounds – began to fight each other.

A second problem evident by late 1989 and confirmed in the elections was that we would have a weak government. None of the parties was individually strong enough to gain preponderant power. Worryingly, none of the possible coalitions are strong enough to implement the enormous structural changes required in economy and in society. Imagine that in Britain absolutely everything belonged to the State, not only the roads and the trains, but all the companies as well; also Cambridge University. Now you say we have to go back to private property. How do you go back? What to do? How to redistribute the whole national wealth? Who will buy? This of course Mrs Thatcher said she would do, and she had spanking great parliamentary majorities with which she could force any measure through Westminster. While she has successfully sold off some public utilities, what is most striking is how even she has eventually run up against public resistance and been forced to slow down and in several areas to stop this programme. In the case of the Channel Tunnel link, force of circumstance has driven her Government to reverse its preference; or, as with her National Health Service break-up, the Conservatives appear to press forward at grave electoral cost.

In Hungary, there are various programmes, at least four or five, on how to privatise and thus to redistribute the whole national wealth in a couple of months or years. We may confidently predict that a weak government will not be able to sort out these problems. It will then be easy for extra-parliamentary forces to topple the government, to organise nationwide strikes and hunger marches, to prepare a right wing or a left wing authoritarian restoration. This would not be impossible if the 1990 parliament or new government cannot handle efficiently these very difficult problems.

The next problem, we should call the problem of the twenty thousand *grande bourgeoisie* versus the two million *petite bourgeoisie*. There are various party programmes. Most of them favour the twenty thousand rich families and big business, which could, I think, run the country and economic recovery quite easily and quickly. But the social cost would be exorbitant, leading to very high figures of unemployment and a very high level of pauperization.

On the other hand, we have those two million very small-scale businesses and potential entrepreneurs whom I earlier described. I think that the best would be to build our recovery on two pillars, on both the twenty thousand and the two million. This would mean perhaps a slower economic recovery, but with much less chaos and a much sounder social basis. The two main parties, the Democratic Forum and the Free Democrats, have both come close to this "double pillar" programme and so there are hopes that they will try to present such a programme.

The penultimate problem which we have to face is the vacuum between high-level politics, or party politics, and everyday family life. I described how social life, civil society and social networks were deliberately sabotaged and destroyed by the Communists. It is very difficult spontaneously to regenerate all those clubs, associations, organisations and networks which are the essential part of a western-type democracy. You cannot have democracy with a good parliament and nothing beneath. This rich network of civil society is not there. We have large numbers of associations, but it is not enough yet. How to regenerate quickly the cells and network of the fabric of social life? That again is one of the issues which has to be solved by Hungarians with the help of the new parliament.

Lastly, Hungarians have to recover their dignity and self-assurance, of which they were deprived. Throughout forty years, the Communists tried to convince people that they were good for nothing, that they were fascist, that they were nationalist, that they were entirely worthless. The people didn't fully believe this, but if they are told such things often enough slowly they become indoctrinated, feeling inferior to other countries.

In particular, the West was the "Golden West" in their eyes. On the one hand the West was something admirable, of high quality, attractive, and represented the whole future, while on the other, at the same time this vision placed a big burden on people's shoulders and minds.

In Hungary, Czechoslovakia or Poland, if you speak to a child in the street about something which is produced in Hungary, it is synonymous with being shoddy. Good is Western, whether it is a car, a toothbrush or a nail. If it is Japanese or German or British it is by definition of high quality. If it is Hungarian, Polish or East German, also by definition, it is bad. People have lost the feeling that they can produce anything good and decent.

I saw the East Germans coming through the Wall in the first week after the 9th November 1989, and I saw how depressed and how humiliated they were by the failure of their own country, as compared to the achievements of West Germany. So we have to recover dignity and self-assurance, which will be a difficult process since it must be done simultaneously with weathering of economic crises.

But at the same time as confronting these problems, it must always be remembered that Hungarians have achieved something very important since 1987. They blazed a trail. In 1990 Hungarians see aspects of the European transformation which other East Europeans may see a little later. Again the Hungarians are seeing things first – the depressing as well as the exhilarating! So I think there is hope for us to be able to solve the problems.

Meanwhile, we have a daily prayer. Let Gorbachev survive until the last Russian troops leave Hungary. After that I think that we will not really be affected by anything that may happen in the future in the Soviet Union.

3 Janusz Ziolkowski

The roots, branches and blossoms of Solidarność[1]

Professor Janusz Ziolkowski is by profession an academic. He is Professor of Sociology at Poznan University. He did early postgraduate work at the London School of Economics. In the 1960s and 70s, he worked for UNESCO. Was elected in 1981 Vice-Chancellor of the Poznan University and removed from office after the introduction of martial law. As the winds of change swept Poland, he played a role in March 1989 as a participant in the Round Table Group on Science, Education and Technical Progress. As a Solidarity supporter, he was elected to the newly constituted Polish Senate in June 1989, where he is now Chairman of the Senate Foreign Relations Committee.

---

[1] In preparing this text I have drawn upon the articles (appearing at the end of 1989) of: G. F. Kennan, A. M. Rosenthal, R. J. Samuelson – *International Herald Tribune;* M. Mandelbaum – *Time*; P. Johnson – *The Spectator*.

3

The term revolution aptly depicts the character of the changes which occurred in the last part of 1989 in East Central Europe. One should stop referring to what has been going on in the "other Europe" as reform. It was revolution. By revolution I mean the overthrow of the existing political, economic and social order. The fact that the revolution has so far been peaceful does not make it any less genuine. Reform is, comparatively speaking, a gentler process that seeks to assimilate new realities within an existing political and economic system. This does not describe what has occurred in the countries of East Central Europe.

It is not simply that these societies are moving away from Communism, from One-Party control towards democracy, or that they are shifting from state run economies towards market systems, or that they are rapidly ending four decades of physical and cultural isolation from the West. They are doing all of these revolutionary things simultaneously. It is difficult to grasp the scale of what is being attempted. These societies are discarding familiar political and economic institutions with no assurance that they can develop adequate substitutes. There are no simple rules for proceeding.

There has not been any model of how to be a democracy *within* (I stress within) a totalitarian system. There are no exact forecasts; the complexity of the problems involved and the dizzying speed of change ought to temper our excitement. Forces have been unleashed that are leading us in unknown directions. The course of past revolutions belies the power of prophecy. Events may take surprising twists; that is what revolutions are about. Who could – or would – have predicted in 1988, still less in 1978, a non-communist Prime Minister in Poland, the demolition of the Berlin Wall or the beginnings of the multi-party system in the Soviet Union?

The changes sweeping across Central and Eastern Europe are momentous and mark the end of a status quo which has existed in the region for four decades. Whatever else may be said about these changes, it is safe to say that Europe will never again look as it did during the years since the end of the Second World War. What has happened in that part of the continent is vital for the whole of Europe and indeed for the world at large.

There have been such moments in the past. In 1848, King Wilhelm of Württemburg excused his inaction faced with the revolutions of that year. He addressed his remarks to the Russian Minister at Stuttgart (who was interestingly called Gorchakov – almost, but not quite, prescient!). To him he made the famous remark, "I cannot mount on horseback against ideas!" And so it was in much of Eastern Europe during 1989. The recent revolution has been as much about ideas and morality as it has been about the inability of concentrated armed force to rescue the bereft Communist regimes that were swept away.

The comparison with 1848 may be pressed further. Jan Urban's description of 1989 as Spring in Winter, from which this book takes its name, directly echoes that other revolutionary year in European history. The events of 1848 were called the Springtime of the Nations. Between 1989 and 1848 there are both affinities and differences, and certain pregnant and still unanswered questions. Of these, the one which looms over all the rest is the recollection that 1848 failed. Will 1989 also come to be seen as a passing moment, rather than as the beginning of a new direction in European history?

The basic similarity lies in the European yearning for freedom. Europe is a continent of liberty. The Springtime of the Nations of 1848 was a chain reaction of democratic revolution which erupted against the autocratic rule of hereditary monarchs. In 1989, the wind of change was sweeping through nations escaping captivity, their condition being the result of Stalin's breaking of the terms of Yalta and the ensuing division of Europe. In 1848, as in 1989, men with little or no political experience were suddenly thrust into a position of leadership. Then, as now, the European uprising fanned the flames of nationalism and raised what came to be known as the German question – the possibility that all Germans would unite in one State.

To us, the Polish people, in 1990 "The German Question" may be politically and physically close, but it is, I believe, not our problem alone. If it is ours alone, then it is a problem. If seen as a European question, perhaps even a world question, then it need not be a problem. It is reassuring to know that most German politicians in West and East Germany, as well as Jacques Delors and the Mitterand Government, take this view also. I think that to raise the question of German transformation is, automatically, to raise the larger question of the political shape of Europe.

Since we are the neighbours of Germany as a people and as a nation and since the German nation is already culturally oriented towards reunification – in fact, will have monetary union in July 1990 and will be united as a political body not long after that – I would say that by and large, faced with German unification in 1990, Poles agree to the Germans being united. (Various opinion polls give figures of about one half in favour.) We Poles cannot deny them that right. We know that the division of Germany was the consequence of the Second World War, a war unleashed by the Germans, and therefore that division was imposed under the conditions of surrender. Equally, fifty years have elapsed since that time. Another generation has grown up and they have a right to be united.

With regard to the unification of Germany as a state, that is another matter, in the sense that it is not only a problem of self definition. It is also a political question for the neighbours, for Poland, Czechoslovakia and France, in particular. There is a special problem for Poland. We were shipped from the East to the West. At the end of the War, the Soviet Union took territory on the Eastern side, and gave us territory at the Western side which Germany had claimed under the Third Reich, including territory which the Reich had possessed before the War. This is a fact of history. It is also a political reality that we do not now lay claim to the Eastern provinces of Poland which are within the USSR. It would be foolish, irresponsible to do so; but equally we would like to have our South-Western frontier respected. The Oder-Neisse line has in the past been an iron pen which has inscribed bloody passages in our history, and must never be so again. That is why Poland insisted so strongly upon receiving, from both parts of Germany, unequivocal reassurance of the surrender of ambitions to (in the slogan of the ultra-nationalist Germans) seek reunification of the Fatherland, "All Three Parts of It".

We should not forget the past. We should remember it; but we should concentrate on the future. I must stress that this is not equally easy for everyone to do. I will give you only one example, a personal one. My eldest son is now aged forty. When he was in England about twenty years ago as a student, he met a German boy and they became good friends. For my generation, it is more difficult to think of a Polish/German relationship in a detached way than for the younger generation. For them, it is normal. That term "normality" in this context registers one of the great advances in European civilisation during the last generation. It now seems uncontroversial that Germany is part and parcel of Europe, a Europe admittedly within a framework which is still being defined. So the more Germany is integrated into Europe the more those dark and inevitably personal as well as public problems of the past are becoming irrelevant.

We also seek to ensure that our new relationship with the new Germany will be equable in other ways, for there is one serious danger, namely that Poland could become a German economic colony. The gap in economic development is tremendous and the largest tranche of our investment comes from Western Germany. We walk a tightrope, because we are looking for German help and investment at the same time as we seek to prevent it becoming a threat. We cannot manage this trick unless there is a counter-balance of involvement in some other forms with other countries, be it by bilateral dealings or be it through the channels of the EC or EFTA, or the Council of Europe. I shall return to this issue at the end of this chapter.

The German settlement is also a question for the four alliance powers, including the two former superpowers (although I don't think the second one, the USSR, should be called a superpower any more). In 1990, they will contribute through the so-called "4 + 2" talks, hopefully prior to the resumption of the CSCE (Conference on Security and Co-operation in Europe). So the matter is complicated, but my guess is that even these fearsome diplomatic complications cannot long delay the political reunification of Germany.

If the prominence of the "German Question" is one similarity with 1848, there are important and hopeful differences between the two springtimes. In 1848, multinational empires dominated Europe. The revolutionaries wanted to dismember them but could not agree on where the new boundaries should be drawn. At issue today is not the location of Europe's borders (at least not in northern Europe), but simply whether Communist or democratic governments should exercise power within them. The revolutions of 1848 failed. The leaders of the uprisings fell out amongst themselves and the forces of conservatism managed to regain control; in 1989 the latter-day revolutionaries seemed to succeed.

In the mid-nineteenth century great powers opposed the rise of democracy. By contrast, today's revolutionaries have the tacit blessing and sometimes the explicit encouragement of the great powers, including – and especially – the encouragement of the Good Tsar Mikhail in Russia. What Gorbachev is doing is vitally important. In his chapter in this book, Andrei Piontkowsky explains the nature of the risks that Gorbachev and the Soviet people run as they attempt their own regeneration.

Perhaps even more important for Europe is what Gorbachev has *refrained* from doing. The Spring in Winter Revolutions of 1989 could not have occurred without the reassurance, which grew as the pointer of history moved from the Berlin Wall to Prague, that Soviet tanks would *not* crash into the crowds, tearing apart the frail fabric of newly-spun democratic change, carrying the grim, grey men of the *ancien régime* back to power astride their gun barrels. Honecker failed to win the vote in the Politburo of the DDR to sanction the use of violence against the crowds. Indeed, it is said that the Soviet liaison officers were instructed to prevent the Volksarmee from shooting on their own people if it had come to that.

Whether or not this is true, the vital point is that last November there were *not* scenes reminiscent of Tienanmen Square in the streets of Eastern Europe, and that the Soviet policy was fundamental to that happy fact. One sign of the dramatic revision in the role of the USSR was that when the Romanian Army commanders, having sided with the people against Ceausescu, feared that the Securitate special forces might overwhelm them at the Bucharest Radio Station, they issued an appeal for Soviet military aid. Just imagine! Soviet forces were requested to come and *protect democracy against Stalinism.* As extraordinary, Secretary of State Baker signalled that there would be *no American objection* if the Soviets were to respond positively. The world turned upside down, indeed!

No less significant was the restraint shown by most of the European revolutionaries themselves. The enduring image of 1848 is that of the barricades often stained with blood. When in late 1989 citizens took to the streets, the demonstrations in Eastern and Central Europe, with the one grievous exception of Romania, were peaceful. Later in this book, Dr Eyal explains why the Romanian experience could not be otherwise, given the nature of the Ceausescu régime and what it had done to society. Today's revolutionaries show exemplary forbearance and political realism, which, combined with patience and ingenuity, should help them in their formidable task of building democratic institutions and in making the painful transition from planned to market economies.

Then there is the fact of Western Europe itself, democratic and prosperous. Unlike in 1848, there was in 1989 a model to which people could look. They did not have to fight purely on the basis of hope and imagination. Spring in Winter was a West European revolution too. It was to the West that the people of the surging nations looked, and from Western ideas that they drew their strength. However, one should caution against the attempts by several groups, both Left and Right, in Western Europe to claim exclusive copyright upon the ideas which East Europeans found attractive. We did not look at the West uncritically.

Indeed, the discipline and sophistication of Eastern Europeans today, as well as their access to information, may also mean that the popular image of revolution is itself undergoing a revolution. On the streets of Eastern Europe in 1989 and 1990, a different revolutionary tradition has replaced that of 1848. It shows a respect for non-violence and the rule of law and even a degree of forgiveness for those who have abused power. It is the tradition of Gandhi, Martin Luther King, Lech Walesa and Vaclav Havel. If that spirit is sustained, today's events, unlike those of 1848, could lead to the establishment of stable, durable and peaceful democracy.

But before one becomes complacent, we should note that the remarkable lack of violence during the 1989 Revolutions in all countries except Romania has not ensured a lack of politically motivated violence as we have entered the delicate period of post-revolutionary adjustment. There has been some street violence, due to the fact that in the months after the fall of Communism, the police have lost their power to engender fear. Also, the months after Solidarność's election victory have seen the emergence of some small, ultra-radical political groupings which reject the route of parliamentary democracy in favour of direct rule or of anarchy. Such groupings are especially to be found in Poland and East Germany.

Therefore, while society faces new challenges to public order, the police have become weak and fearful of popular revenge for their complicity as agents of the former régime. The army cannot be used in their stead, for obvious reasons. So, ironically, the streets have become more dangerous, after the peaceful period when the threat of State violence was so high and the uncertainty about intervention was still strong.

Should violence attend the next phase of revolution, there is little that we can do to protect ourselves. Early in 1990, there was a demonstration of a small group in the Polish Parliament. The Senate offices are on the ground floor and the demonstrators were able to penetrate the grounds of the Parliament, reach a window and break the glass. There was a lot of turmoil and there were no police to protect the Parliament. Parliament is absolutely unprotected. Anyone can enter the grounds and make any sort of demonstration or intervention. They could disturb the Assembly and no one would be able to intervene.

To read the press, or to hear some western leaders talk, you would think that history began with Gorbachev. His role is undeniable - *Glasnost, Perestroika*, the acceptance of the principle that each member of the Warsaw Pact is free to arrange its own internal affairs. All this created an ambience in which the revolutionary changes were possible. It was a necessary condition but it was not a sufficient condition. Freedom is not given on a plate – it must be fought for. In other words, the revolution was not brought about by Gorbachev alone. It detracts nothing from his role to say that he knows this and that all the people of Central and Eastern Europe know this.

So who created the revolution? Paradoxically, the revolution of 1989 was created by Lenin and Stalin. Almost from the moment when the Soviet empire, after Yalta, swallowed up the nations of Eastern Europe, the fight against Communism began. Most of the nations in revolt have always been part of Western civilisation in culture and history. One of the sad ironies of the almost half century of struggle was that the very fact of their imprisonment made so many Westerners forget this truth and psychologically identify them with their captors.

It is difficult for us, as well, to discover the right way out of this maze. Poles recall vividly that in 1956 there was an Soviet intervention in Budapest and that in 1968, tanks rolled into Prague (events which all the world remembers); but we Poles also remember that we escaped by the skin of our teeth from another intervention, against us. Except for the constant threat of the Red Army's intervention, the Communists would have fallen from power in Eastern Europe in the fifties. This gives the context to our present security dilemma, following the 1989 revolutions.

For the time being, Poland is a member of the Warsaw Pact. For how long is very hard to say; but in the meantime for as long as the Warsaw Pact exists, it will have to be transformed from a military pact, where the real command in each member country is in the hands of a Russian General or a Russian Marshal, into a political pact. Why should we, remembering the past role of the Red Army in our area, advocate such a thing? Simply because for the time being we don't want to frighten the Russians. Frankly, if we were to leave the Warsaw Pact abruptly and appeared to be following the road of the DDR, it would be dangerous, because it would be highly provocative evidence of Soviet military withdrawal. Therefore we prefer for the moment to change the nature of the Pact. Equally, we do not demand the immediate withdrawal of all Soviet troops. In the new political environment of Europe, I do not attach too much importance to the fact that we are members of the Warsaw Pact. It may be that the time for exclusive alliances is finally passing, as F. D. Roosevelt hoped in his final speech to Congress, reporting upon the Yalta conference. He proved to be sadly wrong – out by a generation in his timing. Maybe that time will come now?

Some governments of the West were fearful of instability. In the interests of preserving tranquil spheres of influences (another relic of the inter-war years which in 1945 Roosevelt hoped to see pass) they mumbled "slow, slow" to the prisoners in revolt. *Realpolitik* dictated that it not be remembered that this stability came not from freedom but from despotism; and that stability under repression finally creates citizens' revolution against it. That is why it is so vital to understand the roots and branches of what is really happening in East Central Europe. Even as history unfolds, it can be distorted in a chronic manner. It is both a distortion of truth and a cruel lack of grace to all who made the Spring in Winter revolution to say, after almost half a century of repression and of dissident struggle: "why so fast?"

One of the reasons that the truth of long repression is obscured is that so many of the Westerners who interpret what has taken place in 1989 have never truly understood. They thought that the phrase "captive nations" was just propaganda. Many preached that there was no ethical difference between Western capitalism and Communism, just different kinds of exploitation. Behind the Iron Curtain there was no such confusion, no "moral equivalency". East European fighters against Communism understand that if Moscow ever withdrew the threat of the Red Army to put down the struggle of the captive nations, the satellite régimes would eventually collapse. Even they did not foresee how quickly Gorbachev would do that, how soon he would have to jettison

Eastern Europe to save Soviet strength in order to apply it to the devastating problems at home, and how quickly we would slip out of his political control. Yet all these developments were a logical consequence of the retrenchment and disengagement which Gorbachev adopted as his military and diplomatic reversal of the Stalin and Brezhnev doctrines for Eastern Europe.

The revolutions of East Central Europe seem to be irreversible. Even if Gorbachev were replaced by some conservative alliance, it would still be extremely difficult to imagine the Soviet Union undoing by force of arms what they have now permitted to happen in Eastern Europe. After all, if they invaded one Eastern European country they would really have to invade them all; and then what would they restore? The shattered Humpty Dumpties that are today's East European Communist Parties? Nor is it easy to imagine the triumphant forces of reaction inside individual East European countries. So a reversal inside the Soviet Union would make life much less comfortable in the new Europe and directly affect development in a Germany still occupied by Soviet troops, but it would not, in itself, be able to turn the map of Europe back to what it was before the *annus mirabilis* 1989.

Until recently it was thought that democratic revolution, still a tender plant, was bound to stop spreading at the Polish/Soviet frontier. Gorbachev stated repeatedly that he did not intend to preside over the death of Communism in his own country. Wasn't he rather eager to preserve the system that brought Communists to power? And yet the Soviets cannot have their cake and eat it. Gorbachev cannot have both *perestroika*, a real economic change growing out of creative energy, and the existing Soviet system which kills initiative, and needs the power of the Soviet army to keep it alive, even at home.

Liberty is contagious, it does not know frontiers. Aren't we witnessing now a change in the thinking of reformers in the USSR? An attempt, in most dramatic conditions, to take the steps essential to full freedom – the creation of a multi-party system, an unshackled economy, an agreement to the independence of the various nationalities so eager to live their own lives? After the *annus mirabilis* in 1989 in Eastern Europe another *annus mirabilis*, this time in 1990, in the Soviet Union, may well follow.

All that I have written so far applies to Poland as well. But there are some specific features which characterise the Polish revolution. Mention should be made first of all of the long tradition of the democratic opposition and its grass-roots character. It would be presumptuous on the part of Poland to claim to be in the forefront of the long march of East Central European nations towards freedom and democracy: recall the Berlin upheaval of 1953, the Budapest uprising of 1956, the Prague Spring of 1968. But in the case of Poland, there has been constant advance towards a democratic pluralistic society; it has been a sort of cumulative process. Social pressure has been exerted all along using every opportunity which offered itself.

The milestones were the uprising in 1956, in Poznan, my own city; the Polish October Revolution of the same year; the student unrest in 1968; the wave of strikes of 1970 and again of 1976; the foundation of the Committee for the Defence of Workers in 1976, and of course August 1980, the beginning of the rise of Solidarność, the first independent Trade Union, with eventually ten million members.

Each of these events was eventually checked and met with coercive counter-measures; but each of them carved a further niche for freedom, had a far-reaching and lasting effect. The watershed was the year 1956 which launched an attempt to liberalise Communist rule. Poland has always enjoyed a relative freedom with regard to information, education, artistic creativity, contact with the West, travel abroad. It has a large, fiercely independent and articulate intelligentsia, and it has an overwhelmingly private agricultural sector (75% of the acreage).

It was in this context that, in retrospect, we may see that the Communist Party lost its last real opportunity for internal liberalisation. Gomulka stirred this initiative in 1947-8 and again in 1956 and it came from within the Party, initiated by the Party members. Gomulka was an extremely popular figure at that time; but he failed to follow through the chances for reform after 1956, and thus ruined the subsequent chances of the Communist Party to lead reform. There is no more Communism in this country. In my opinion, it was killed in 1956. Solidarność was born into a Post-Communist Society.

A central agent in creating this condition was the Church. Poland had its Catholic Church. The situation of Catholicism in Poland is a result of an interplay of challenge and response (to use Toynbee's terms): the challenge posed by the Communist state and the response give by the Church. The Church from the very beginning found itself in a position of open conflict or competition with the Communist system, mingled with the periods of reserved tolerance on the part of the latter. "Laicization of society," wrote the Polish bishops in 1980, "continues to be the State's official programme. It is meant to be a stage whose ultimate aim is atheisization of the nation."

Yet all the efforts of the State, equipped with a whole armoury of "rich means", have proved futile. The Catholic religion and the Church itself endowed only with "poor means", and despite the restrictions imposed on its activities, sometimes going through great sufferings and sacrifices (perhaps because of that) has emerged from this historical trial stronger than ever before. The vast majority of the population is Catholic, (about 85% are practising Catholics). For many Poles, at many points in Polish history, it was the Roman Catholic Church that was the guardian of Polish historic tradition. How relatively unimportant and irrelevant, as compared to the one thousand year old history of Poland, were the attempts of the Communist State to present the past as if it were pre-history, a mere run up to the splendours of the present.

The story of Poland strongly suggests that national solidarity – a duty imposed and a right to be claimed – patriotism and religion, in combination, are more important influences than class conflict. To an historically minded Pole, the Communist episode was only a minor ripple in the stream of history, merely bubbles that arose somewhere and disappeared before the next bend of the river. The river is formed from the indissoluble fusion which exists between Roman Catholicism and Polish culture. This term should be used comprehensibly and in two senses, to include both high culture and common culture, the "long tradition" that the people share. Polish culture fuses history and Catholicism, national and religious consciousness, to a degree rarely found elsewhere.

In addition, there exists also a body of ideals arising from secular sources, closely associated with *non-Communist* ideologies of the Left. These too have had a role in making our new society. Former members of KOR (the Committee for the Defence of Workers), like Jacek Kuron and Adam Michnik enter Jan Urban's story later in this book, as Polish participants in the now famous international woodland picnics of dissidents on the Polish/Czech border. Since that time, within Poland, they have become prominent members of the Solidarność government and the national political establishment (Kuron as Minister of Labour, Michnik as Editor-in-Chief of the pro-Solidarność daily newspaper, *Gazeta Wyborcza* [The Election Daily].)

Another trend arising from similar ideological sources must be noted to complete the spectrum. This is *Solidarność 80*, led by Marian Jurezyk. This organisation acts as a competitor to Walesa's Solidarność. It stresses principally the interests of working people and is opposed to "privatisation" of industry. So there are significant secular sources of the new public morality as well. In short, it has a wide and solid basis in many parts of society.

The history of Poland has shown also that moral law is the foundation of the social order. It was the Church that became the defender of freedom which is the inalienable right of every man, so that the violation of freedom by the State is at the same time a violation of the moral and social order. The cultural experience of Poland has been penetrated very deeply by the awareness of this Christian dimension of Man, Man who, to use the words of Karol Wojtyla "acts together with others", who is linked with other men through numerous bonds, contacts, situations and social structures. It is the awareness of the fact that persons are only fully themselves in a community. Community is also a state of mind and heightened awareness in individuals. In Poland's recent history, it received the name Solidarność.

This concept hides within an important ethical proposition, namely that Man is an actor or agent responsible for building his own attitudes and his own commitment in the community. Solidarność was rediscovery of the importance of participation. This made it inevitably subversive of the *ancien régime*. Once Lech

Walesa had vaulted over the fence at the Lenin shipyard, confrontation at the deepest level was engaged.

In a perverse (rather Hegelian) sense, Solidarność owed the clarity of its vision to the nature of its opponent. At the very beginning, Walesa himself put it succinctly:

If you choose the example of what we have in our pockets and in our shops, then I answer that Communism has done very little for us. If you choose the example of what is in our souls instead, I answer that Communism has done very much for us. Our souls contain the exact contrary of what they wanted.

The specificity of Polish cultural experience lies in an avoidance of many of the dangers residing in both individualism and collectivism. Individualism rejects socialist responsibility, and concentrates on self-fulfilment or self-preservation. Collectivism sets out to check and curb the individual, to subject him to its norms by coercion if need be. Both damage the human person. Both lack an authentic idea of John Paul II's "acting together with others". They lack the idea of community, a form of social organisation in which participation is taken seriously. They also lack any sense of common good: individualism is not concerned with it, and collectivism has decided in advance what it is.

I do not believe that it is impossible to be a participant in a general democracy. One may, at the same time, be a participant in a community and be a Solidarność participant acting in harmony with others. To make this clear, I think that a distinction should be made between the *individual* and the *person*. The Christian view is a personalistic philosophy. It speaks about a human person and being a person is closely connected with sharing, with being a part of a family and of a moral community. Of course we are at the same time individual human beings; but as is well known, in John Donne's famous phrase, "no man is an island." We are, by definition, as a species, social. That is what is meant by Solidarność; that is why it has such a significance for us and it is also how it is so intimately connected with the historical experience to which we have been exposed.

For the time being, we are not individualistic, and I would say, as Walesa observed at the outset of Solidarność, that it has proved to be most valuable that we have had an adversary, of the nature and with the philosophic outlook of the Communist Party.

Unlike in Romania, for example, Polish Communism has remained in a state of constant flux. Gierek's "quasi-liberalisation" of the 1970s loaded Poland with foreign debt. Sharply contending tendencies became apparent within the Party. In 1980-81, there occurred great erosion of Marxist-Leninism in the Party as grass-roots activists responded to changes in popular mood. This was expressed formally in Kania's "social democratic" phase of 1981, which persisted until the Declaration of Martial Law on 13th December of that year. It was in counteraction to this slippery opponent that we found unity, our solidarity, in the fight which occupied us throughout the 1980s with mounting intensity until the sweeping success of Solidarność at the polls in June 1989.

Success has a price, and poses many challenges, not the least of which is to the strength of our unity. In the period between the 1989 elections and the 1990 Solidarność Congress, the issue of unity versus diversity within our Solidarność parliamentary group has become more acute. The question is a familiar one in democracies, and familiar from recent Polish history also. Should we attempt to preserve a common front, or split into different groupings?

Poland has little historical experience of mass, competitive government. The norm in the twentieth century has a dominant "party of government": nationalist, after the Pilsudski Coup of 1926, Communist after 1948 and now, Solidarność. Yet within this have been episodes of many fragmentary parties – 92 after the enactment of the 1921 Constitution; and major fissures between urban and rural interests, expressed variously in terms of aristocratic or peasant power, at different periods. In 1990, we witness again a flowering of tiny parties – over one hundred! They express interests which are varied, but a sense of grouping within the range may be obtained from an analysis of the OKP (Citizens' Party Group) as it was in early 1990.

The "Left" counted about 40 seats. Lech Walesa's Trade Unionists counted another 60 and the Church candidates an equal number. The Centre-Right Peasants' Party held about 50;

the Liberal Conservatives (believers in radical Free Market philosophy), another 50 and the more extreme Right, 10 to 15.[2] This indicates that there has emerged a wide range of opinion, to which must be added extra-Parliamentary groupings, such as the Greens. So why not have political parties right away?

There are two reasons for not doing so. The first and most important in my view is that our job of securing the transition in Poland is not yet accomplished; and for this we need unity. We need a party of government. Furthermore, there has been such a dislike of the Communist Party as a political institution that the notion of the possibility of legitimate political power expressed through formal parties has been discredited after its overthrow. Poles, like other East Europeans, want other forms of association, loose confederations such as Solidarność. It is not necessarily a precondition of democracy to have formal political parties; yet we are prompted all the time in the Council of Europe to form political parties as a sort of test of our credentials as a democratic state.

I have deliberately raised the problems as well as the benefits which have come with the full flowering of Solidarność in 1989 and 1990. But a fundamental premise of this essay has been that this flowering could not have occurred without a long and particular preparation. Therefore we must look at the branches, and at the roots which feed and support them, if we are fully to appreciate the miracle of the blossoms that we saw after June 1989.

Timothy Garton Ash, in my opinion one of the best analysts of the situation in Eastern Europe, wrote:

If I were to be forced to name a single date for the "beginning of the end" of this inner history of Eastern Europe, it would be June 1979. The judgement may be thought excessively Polonocentric, but I do believe that the Pope's first pilgrimage to Poland was that turning point. Here, for the first time, we saw that large-scale, sustained, yet supremely peaceful and self-disciplined manifestation of social unity, the gentle crowd against the Party state, which was both the hallmark and the essential

[2] This analysis was quoted by J Reynolds in a paper on the current political party landscape in Poland at a conference on perspectives for Poland in 1990s in the Department of Social Anthropology, University of Cambridge, April 1990.

domestic catalyst of changes in 1989 in every country except Romania (and even in Romania the crowds did not start the violence). The Pope's visit was followed just over a year later, by the birth of Solidarity and without the Pope's visit it is doubtful that there would have been a Solidarity. The example of Solidarity was seminal. It pioneered a new kind of politics in Eastern Europe (and new not only there): a politics of social self-organisation aimed at negotiating the transition from communism. The actors, forms and issues of 1980/81 in Poland were fundamentally different from anything seen in Eastern Europe between 1949 and 1979: in many respects they pre-staged these seen throughout Europe in 1989.[3]

What was most characteristic and most remarkable about the Solidarność revolution was the complete lack of violence. It was exactly that historical contradiction in terms: "peaceful revolution". Recall that *ten million* people were actively involved. Discontent erupted on an unprecedented scale. After eighteen months of defying the Communist system and with no Bastilles stormed, no guillotines erected, not a single pane of glass broken, we triumphed.

The rationale of non-violence was to be found later on in the history of all democratic oppositions of East Central Europe throughout the 1980s, leading to Spring in Winter in 1989. Partly it was pragmatic: the other side had all the weapons. But it was also ethical. It was a statement about how things should be. It was not only a peaceful revolution but also a compromise revolution. The compromise was reached in August 1980 and a political contract was concluded. This contract was not honoured by the Communist Party.

In March 1981, a group of Solidarność deputies attempted to participate in a meeting of Bydgoszcz City Council. They were forcibly evicted and severely beaten in the process. This provocation led directly to Walesa's announcement of a General Strike to take place two or three days later. This strike did not take place because Walesa's advisers persuaded him not to implement the threat. There was a real fear of Soviet intervention and

[3] Timothy Garton Ash, "Eastern Europe: The Year of Truth", *New York Review of Books*, 15 February 1990.

secondly, with the Extraordinary Party Congress due to be held in July, there was still hope that the Party itself might reform and adapt itself to the new realities.

The Government and Party had engineered the provocation of Bydgoszcz. The episode was essentially the first attempt to gauge the strength and determination of Solidarność. What it showed was that direct physical force could be used against the Union without risking general and outright rebellion. This discovery had a high price for the régime. It breached not only the contract of 1980, but, in the eyes of Solidarność, the very legitimacy of the State's power.

Accordingly, in December 1981, Solidarność announced a Referendum to be held in February 1982. People were to be asked one question: "Is the Communist Party suitable to represent the political interests of Polish society?" In was in direct response to this dagger, pointed at the very heart of the Communist system, that Martial Law was declared. We were in *stan wojenny*. The declaration of 13th December 1981 was tantamount to being a declaration of war on society by the régime. (*Stan Wojenny* translates literally as "state of war".) The Solidarność movement was crushed in the short term, but a new pattern of political behaviour prevailed. It resulted after seven years of the unsuccessful deployment of counter-revolutionary force in the Round Table talks in early 1989.

Solidarność emerged from this long period numerically weaker but morally stronger. The basic idea remained intact. Intact, even heightened, was another specificity of Poland, namely the *entente cordiale* between the workers and the intelligentsia. The prestige of the charismatic leader, Lech Walesa, reached new heights during this period. This received world-wide recognition in the autumn of 1983 when Lech Walesa was awarded the Nobel Peace Prize.

Fearing that if he left the country, the authorities would prevent his return (just as they had sought to prevent his re-entry into the Lenin Shipyard in Gdansk at the inception of Solidarność), Walesa sent Danuta, his wife, and with her their eldest son, to receive the Prize on his behalf. This award dealt a body-blow to the régime's smear campaign against Walesa, which was then being actively conducted. He was represented as an uneducated simpleton, manipulated by evil advisers; in short, a dummy without a mind of his own. After the Nobel Prize, this calumny stopped, by and large. Walesa has remained a highly popular leader, although in the new shifts of power within the Solidarność government he is certainly not without his critics.

Solidarność was fortunate in having another charismatic supporter of world stature. The assassination attempt upon the Pope's life in May 1981 sent shock waves throughout Poland. The TV carried non-stop coverage of events and there was a spontaneous and massive public expression of grief, then relief when it became clear that the attack had failed. The episode gave a moral boost both to the Church and to Solidarność. After surviving the attack, John Paul II came to Poland twice, in 1983 and 1987, during the crucial seven years period between the Declaration of Martial Law and the 1989 June election victory. On each occasion his presence gave great uplift to the movement and reinforced our central moral propositions. The idea of Man as unique, by circumstance solitary and most fulfilled as participant in the community, Man who accepts his share in the construction of a humane society, was elevated to a height not known before. The point was given international prominence at that time in the much acclaimed film *Man of Iron*, by the prominent film director, Solidarność sympathiser and adviser, Andrzej Wajda.

A further and in many ways decisive watershed in the alienation of the Communist régime from society was the murder in November 1984 of Father Jerzy Popieluszko. He was well known as a supporter of Solidarność who in his sermons always emphasised the basic injustice of Communism and the moral right of all people to defend their interests against totalitarian states. This the régime could not stomach. Father Popieluszko was abducted, tortured and then killed by three members of the Secret Police. His grave became a shrine and a rallying point where people could display symbols of Solidarność. It was probably the only place in Warsaw where Solidarność badges were allowed to remain on display. After this terrible act, the State's remaining shreds of credibility in the eyes of the people were gone.

The seven years waiting was also a time for spadework with regard to the formulation of political and economic programmes. A tremendous clandestine publishing movement played a vital role in all this, as well as the support given by the Catholic Church. All the meetings of the various discussion groups were held in a more or less clandestine manner (with the knowledge of the Security, of course) in churches.

Another basic idea which emerged during those long seven years was that of "civil society". Of course, it was always present in opposition thinking. People had had enough of being mere components in a deliberately atomised society. They wanted to be citizens, individual men and women with dignity and responsibility, with rights but also with duties, freely associating in civil society. This dream came to full fruition about 1987/88. Thus a citizens' committee was formed around Walesa in 1987. It undertook the basic political responsibility with regard to the Round Table talks in spring 1989. It gave rise to thousands of local citizens' committees which took care so splendidly of the electoral campaign. Finally, when we, Solidarność's parliamentarians, came to give our group a name, in recognition of this mood, we called it the Citizens' Parliamentary Club. The Civic Forum of Czechoslovakia or the *Burgerinitiatiren* in Eastern Germany are in the same line of thought and action.

The rest of the story is well known and may be reported only briefly. The Round Table talks began on 6th February 1989 with the ruling Communist Party and Solidarność as the principal parties among the many at the table. The aim of the talks was to reach agreement on a programme of economic stabilisation and political reform, including the re-legitimisation of Solidarność. The resulting political contract led eventually to the parliamentary election in June 1989.

The Round Table talks were fraught with uncertainty at times. Various participating groups, for example the Official Trade Unions led by Alfred Miodowicz, tried very hard to de-rail the negotiations in order to preserve their own status quo. A major strike over pay occurred at the big Belchatow lignite mine, south of Warsaw. It was the first of many. Labour unrest resulted in the talks being postponed several times and only being resumed after frantic efforts on the part of Solidarność and the Government, jointly. On 10th February, Lech Walesa called for a six week moratorium on strikes, suggesting that there was a plot to stir up labour unrest in order to undermine the Round Table talks. This view was echoed on 21st by Jerzy Urban, speaking of the then Government's concern about the role of members of the official Trade Unions in the escalating number of pay disputes. (Fifty such stoppages had occurred already in February 1989 alone.) Solidarność and the Government each had their own powerful but, upon this one issue, convergent reasons for wishing to keep the talks going.

The June 1989 elections were partially democratic for the lower house (*Sejm*) and fully democratic for the Senate. Here the principle was very simple: the winner takes all; and we took 99% of the seats. What in fact was not foreseen was that Solidarność would emerge as such a convincing victor, with about 80% of the total vote. In the *Sejm* the Communist leadership managed to lose even the uncontested seats which it had been "guaranteed" as a concession at the Round Table. Perhaps most remarkable was that the Communist Party accepted the defeat. By the same token, it was accepted by the Russians. And that was most important. It seems that at that moment, for practical reasons, Gorbachev wrote off Eastern Europe. A completely new pluralistic political constellation emerged from the June election. The Communists still had the army, the police and the *nomenclatura*. But all this was crumbling.

There are still dangers. There is a gap between the political advance and the disastrous economic condition of the country. It must be bridged otherwise, democratic achievements will be in jeopardy. We do not know to what extent the people's patience and endurance can be tested. For the time being, the Poles have been remarkably patient, contrary to their nature. There is confidence in the new Government, there is hope. A public opinion poll held in January 1990 revealed that the popularity of Prime Minister Mazowiecki was 88%.

Poland after its early start in the 1989 Revolution is confronted with the daunting tasks of establishing the rights and institutions which characterise modern democracy and building a market economy. Added to this, there is the need to overcome enormous economic problems centring around production, distribution, over-employment, shortages, inefficient and polluting industries and antiquated farming practices. We not only have to restructure rights and institutions, but in cases where they were nonexistent, we have to create them.

Poland has already set to work. The parliament and the new Government are working very hard indeed. Since coming to power, we have drafted and enacted numerous laws which provide a legal framework for an independent judiciary, for freedom of the press and freedom to organise, for freedom to found political parties and for the reformed conduct of local government, which, with the forthcoming municipal political elections, will soon become effective. We are preparing a new constitution of the Polish Republic which will become a democratic state subject to the rule of law. Since the beginning of 1990, we have embarked upon a very difficult economic programme, one which aims not only to check inflation, but also to establish the foundations for a modern market economy after the pattern of the institutions in the highly developed European countries.

We intend to continue on this path, successively introducing new elements, among which importance will be attributed to reforming the system of ownership and introducing certain forms of state intervention and social protection within the market economy. We wish our future economic system to combine effective mechanisms for stimulating the creation of wealth, but with adequate protection for the social groups which require assistance within a free and competitive market economy. We seek help in a variety of ways. We have not only problems of capital, experience, training, exchanging people or exchanging experiences. Poland would like to be a full and integrated part of the European economy from which we have been forcibly separated for quite a long time.

We have always been part and parcel of Europe culturally; but economically where are we? What sort of country have we inherited? It is a shambles. So economically we would like to be part of Europe again and this is perhaps the main problem. This is why we gladly welcome any kind of help with training; not only capital investment, but all kinds of involvement of the Western democratic societies in our economic and social life. Cultural exchanges, for instance. The amount of money involved is not great; what counts is the purpose to which it is put. Small investment can produce disproportionately high results in certain fields, for instance in education. There are so many possibilities here.

We would also like to have help in a highly diversified form, not only in order to broaden our contact but also to avoid becoming too dependent on one country. Here is the danger to which I referred early in this chapter, namely that German investment and German aid would come to Poland more easily than from other sources. We would like to have aid in a much more diversified form. That is why we were glad to receive financial help from Japan (more than one million dollars) and from South Korea, in order to have a much more diversified economic scene.

The political division of Europe may softly and suddenly vanish. One feels that the political transition may be easier than anyone anticipates, for it turns out that people have a remarkably good idea of how to run a democracy, even without first-hand knowledge and experience. Somehow the knowledge is just there, as if innate. What will then remain is a deeper and arguably far more intractable economic division of Europe. Not East and West, but East as South and West as North. If this is going to continue, there will be no social peace in Europe. To erase the economic division of our continent is our common European challenge. Yes, prosperity and economic regeneration are important. But Europe is not just a continent of producers, merchants and consumers. It is a cultural entity. Europe is a system of values, the main value perhaps being liberty. Liberty is irrepressible. In struggling for liberty the peoples of East Central Europe are giving back to Western Europe a new sense of purpose. We are reminding Europe of its destiny.

4 Jens Reich

Reflections on becoming an East German dissident, on losing the Wall and a country

Jens Reich was born in 1939 in the University town of Göttingen in West Germany. He was brought up in Halberstadt in the GDR and then attended the Humboldt University in Berlin where he studied medicine. He was working in Berlin when the Wall was built in 1961. For many years he worked as a hospital doctor and general practitioner in the provincial town of Halberstadt before becoming a research microbiologist, with special interests in computer and statistical applications. While he had been permitted to travel in the 1970s, in the 1980s he was denied foreign travel. With a group of friends he founded Neues Forum on September 9th 1989 and he is presently a Member of Parliament in the Volkskammer for the Neues Forum-backed list "Alliance 90". He is Speaker of the Coalition and Member of the Committee on Science and Medical Affairs.

4

On becoming an East German dissident

How did we become dissidents, I and the group of friends who created Neues Forum at accidentally the crucial moment in September 1989? I have been asked this question many times, wonderingly, by western journalists who know only how grim and seemingly solid was the former East German Communist state and how it seemed to be the most efficiently repressive of the *anciens régimes*. Nor are they wrong. It was a grim regime, as I shall explain; and it was obsessed with maintaining uniformity of opinion. So how did one become a dissident in such a situation?

I think that westerners presume it must have arisen from some sort of agonized decision. I cannot speak for others. My answer is simply that I have been always a dissident throughout my life. For much of it, I was a quiet dissenter, but never was I convinced that the imposed system was something with which one could or should live peaceably, or to which one should give tacit consent. At best it might be tolerable if it could be liberalized and reformed; but the nature of the East German regime precluded that possibility.

Why was I like that? I grew up that way. I learned these values from my family culture and in my childhood experiences. One of my earliest memories comes from the war years. We children lay in our bed while our mother crouched under the blanket and pillows of her bed trying to listen to the news broadcast of the BBC from London, with its unmistakable (although if overheard, very dangerous) station signal of the first beats from Beethoven's Fifth Symphony – "V for Victory" in Morse Code. I will never forget the feeling of anxiety and excitement mingled. I knew that what mother was doing was wrong in the eyes of the authorities but right, very right, in her eyes. She wanted, desperately, to know the truth. She especially wanted to know the truth about the Eastern Front, where my father was serving as a medical officer in constant danger of his life. The Nazis were obviously lying about the state of affairs, and mother wanted to know what was really happening.

She was not German, but Austrian (in fact, a citizen of Czechoslovakia after the First World War). She had been against her fellow-countryman Hitler from the first moment of his rise to power, although inactively, powerlessly so. Listening to London was an act of dissidence that could result in denunciation to the Gestapo with the certain prospect of arrest. So we children learned from her a hard yet simple lesson in how the individual should regard tyrannical powers; how the individual could and should withhold legitimacy from tyrants. We did not need to read Hobbes and Rousseau to learn about the Social Contract, even if we could have done so!

Towards the end of the war we had to flee from Northern Bohemia. Other of my memories come from the bombing of towns like Plauen and Dresden and Halberstadt, one after the other. I was then six years old. There were many corpses in the streets. I remember standing in the staircase of a house which had been hit by a bomb. My mother was crying: "Jump! Jump over, I'll catch you in my arms!" Behind me the house was burning, but in front of me was a deep bomb crater, going right down to the basement, and I was afraid of tumbling into it. I was petrified and did not dare to jump. Finally a man picked me up and jumped with me in his arms.

Another scene etched into my young memory was of being attacked in a field by a Stuka pilot who amused himself by strafing the refugees with his machine guns, as we ran from Halberstadt. Shooting, flying over us, turning, coming back, attacking again, while terrified, we crouched in the roadside ditch, the bullets striking the ground around us, and then pelted along the road like mad while he was wheeling around to make another pass. Such experiences combined with the moral lessons from my mother to forge a sense of the need to know within oneself where one stands; to know that there is right and wrong and to accept the individual's responsibility to make, hold and when opportunity presents, to act upon one's judgements.

Well, these were the early days. Later on life became quieter. After the war, my family returned to and settled in Halberstadt which is near the border with West Germany. My parents still live there. My father is a doctor of internal medicine. From that time onwards throughout the DDR experience, we were what was in those days called "contra" : people against the whole system. My father was a bit pink; he had some socialist ideals. My mother saw to it that we were instructed as Roman Catholics, which was not without disadvantage at the time. Our family attitude may be best described as one of "internal resistance." We thought that the system could not last for long, but that we had to endure it as a result of the war, of Hitler's despotism and of the despicable conduct of the Third Reich regime against the other European nations. As I grew, literature added to the influence of my stock of family experiences. I read *Darkness at Noon* when I was still a boy and was moved by Arthur Koestler's novel about the imprisonment, interrogation and death of an Old Bolshevik under Stalin, a novel about the perversion of idealism; also I had read historical accounts about Hitler: why he was never overthrown.

We were always afraid of being denounced. In the next chapter, Jan Urban writes of what he calls the "One Chance Philosophy" – where you could not afford to betray yourself once, for that would be the last time. We had to live the same sort of split lives as children. Mother was anxious, telling us, "Don't say anything political", when we went to school. My decision to become a doctor and scientist was directly a response to living in this poisonous environment. It was a sort of camouflage. Given a free choice, I would have preferred to have pursued liberal arts or literature, but they were pervaded by the ideology of Marxism-Leninism, which you were forced to confess, and which it was impossible for me to do. My father said, "Go into science or medicine. This is where you can survive as a person."

In the late sixties, we were very, very depressed. I remember watching the 1968 student revolution from afar. We saw a film afterwards about the Californian student movement at Berkeley which I remember very vividly. I watched with envy. I thought that here, locked up in East Germany, we were condemned to live in the dullest period in the whole of history. People lived lives of quiet desperation. Men waited to become sixty five, women until sixty. This was the age when they were officially allowed to go abroad.

There were always other ways to leave, but all carried great risks or costs. One way was via Budapest or another international airport of Eastern Europe. You could sneak on to a plane to Frankfurt instead of back to East Berlin. Or you could try one of the dreadful escapes inside prepared trucks. You had to sit for many hours in fear and darkness. Embarking on a truck escape was always a major risk. The Border Guards had detection equipment at the frontier able to sense the presence of people concealed inside trucks. Families, and especially children, were made to take sleeping pills. Everyone had to sit motionless and silent until the border control was over. A friend of ours, a woman with three children escaping to West Germany, told later a terrible story of how one of the men in the truck with her went berserk from anxiety when it stopped for what he considered to be too long. He began to shout, and the others had to beat him senseless in order to silence him. Afterwards, when they arrived in the West, the unfortunate man had to be taken to hospital for treatment.

There were also other, even more risky and ingenious ways of trying to cross. But climbing The Wall, ramming barriers, swimming, flying in balloons or light aircraft all carried a certainty of being shot at if discovered, and therefore a high risk of being killed or wounded. If you were caught and arrested, you went to prison for two years at least. *Republikflucht* (flight from the Republic) they used to call this special crime in the penal code of a country which had this special way of keeping its citizens in. Nonetheless, desperate people tried all of these means.

After 1971, it was also possible to apply for legal emigration. But it meant years of waiting and in the meantime, subjection to extreme discrimination. Your children could not attend secondary school; you lost your job at once. But in principle this was a way out, and it was undertaken, in spite of all the humiliation, by many of our friends, very many. In these cases, we knew that it was probably farewell for ever, because we were not allowed to travel to them and they could never return. From my own family, nobody went until 1987 when one of my daughters left. She married someone who had emigrated earlier on political grounds. My children had argued: we are not going to spend our lives the way that you have. This hurt us emotionally, but my wife and I did not reproach them in the way that my parents had done when we were young. (They had argued that we were had a duty not to leave family and country). However, if one stayed, in order to make any headway in your profession, one had to make a lot of compromises. For instance, one had to be cleared by the Security Police.

Travelling abroad is necessary for a scientist. You really can't keep up in professional competition without this contact. Being cleared for professional travelling was called *Reisekaderstatus*. In recent years, I was denied this status for political reasons. One of those reasons was that I declined to break my contacts with a friend in West Berlin who visited me from time to time. He was an old friend of our family, a paediatrician. Our parents had been friends before us. He was politically completely harmless. But they set me the breaking of this friendship as a loyalty test. They hinted, "Well, it has to be done! We have information through our channels that this man is not clean and we expect for the greater good of science and of our country that you cease these contacts."

I declined, and was in consequence no longer eligible for promotion in my profession. Let me give an example of what this meant. After I had blotted my copybook with the authorities, I worked on a modern computer but I was prohibited from having knowledge of its operating system. This was kept secret (I guess partly also because the machine was obtained by circumventing embargo regulations). Since I was deemed to be unreliable, I could not know the secret, which is rather basic information for anyone engaged in programming. I was thus prevented from doing more sophisticated applications. I had to ask colleagues to do these for me, which, in a perverse way also "demonstrated" my unreliability. Nor could I respond to invitations from abroad. I had several very flattering ones, including one from Cambridge. I was not even allowed to answer in writing; I had to do this through friends.

Goethe said: *Leben is ein Gleichnis* (life is a metaphor). Our East German metaphor is that we have been living in a snail's shell, hidden and stubbornly defending what was considered worth living for. The snail sits in its cramped but cosy shell, making itself as comfortable as possible under the circumstances, occasionally putting out its antennae to find out what life outside is like. It isn't all bad inside the snail's shell. In our shell we had always time for other things and other people. In our circle of friends we became a little like the Slavs, I think, who during their long winters have time to play chess, to chat and to discuss their religion and philosophy. I hope these hospitable attitudes will not wane in the unified Germany, but on this I'm not too optimistic. That was life in Goethe's snail-shell.

Then came the time of Neues Forum. The origins of our enterprise lay in the emotional frenzy which seized the country in the summer of 1989, as a result of the mass exodus of refugees to the West, first via Hungary, then via refuge at the FRG Embassy in Prague. Week by week, more and more people, among them many young and bright people, voted with their feet. We felt that something had to be done. My own children indicated it to me and our friends shared the same feeling. Before us we had the example of the success of Solidarność in Poland, and of the Russian dissidents, like the great Andrei Sakharov, now restored to public life.

For years there had been dissidents in East Germany, just like those in Poland and Russia, but more hidden. Then in the early eighties we came to the surface. The new opposition was individualistic and bohemian, and composed of a kaleidoscope of "counter-culture" social groups: hippies, Maoists, anarchists, human rights groups, greens, gays, lesbians, the protesting "church from below" – a very colourful mixture, with lots of rock music; in fact, to professional people and academics, frankly somewhat alien! My wife Eva and I felt like fish out of water in this crowd, although they were all very friendly among themselves and towards us.

Of crucial importance to the emergence of the opposition was the role of the Church and in particular of the Protestant Churches. They gave shelter to all these groups (peace groups and ecological groups) which often were not particularly religious in the formal sense, although they had beliefs about preserving Creation which bordered on the religious. But only some pastors made this decision; others were against. There was always a struggle within the Church, and I would say that the majority of the Protestant Church was against these troublemakers. Even so, sometimes the dissidents attacked the church and its administration, which gave them shelter, as being bureaucratic. There were a lot of fights between the groups. It turned out later on that some of them were even steered and provoked by Stasi informers and *agents provocateurs*.

The political problem was one common to all of Europe. The appearance of mysticism or extreme rejection of the status quo of such fractions of Alternative or Youth culture really could not become a mainstream political force. It was too isolated from the culture of the bulk of the population. What they did was extremely brave, and some of them were harassed or expelled; but their approach and message could not reverberate on a greater scale. We had to reach out to a more "respectable" middle-aged generation, to give them the courage to come out of their snail-shells and the reassurance that they wouldn't look silly (which under any political system is the one thing that people cannot abide). We had to appeal to the ordinary man and woman in the street, taxi-drivers, doctors, nurses, bricklayers.

Finally, on 9th September 1989, a fine Indian summer's day, thirty of us, at that time not all fully acquainted with each other, congregated in the cottage of the widow of Robert Havemann (the famous dissident scientist who died in 1982), near Berlin. It was a more or less fortuitous collection: the principle upon which we invited the people who came was simple. We wished to ensure that we were properly representative; to ensure that Neues Forum incorporated not only clergymen, not only Berliners, not only intellectuals, not only young dropouts from the social ghetto. This criterion brought us together. There were of course pastors, there were of course Berliners, but there were also people from the provinces, so the result, although not fully balanced, was a cross-section of normal people with normal professions and different political leanings. For example, among those present that day, to indicate the range, there was Sebastian Pflugbeil who later became a minister in Modrow's cabinet, a specialist in Energy politics. Women also were represented in the group; not in great numbers, but they were influential. Bäebel Böhley, for example, the Jeanne d'Arc of the whole movement, and Katya Havemann, the widow of the dissident scientist in whose house we met.

We hammered out a Manifesto, whose aims are still pertinent, and we published it. It said that there was serious trouble in the whole of our society. The trouble was that a discourse no longer existed between the Ruling and the Ruled. This, we wrote, was leading towards a catastrophic crisis. What we need to do is to discuss many things, our differences and conflicts of interests and opinion. These things, the Manifesto stated, cannot just be swept under the carpet. This was *glasnost*, although we didn't use that word.

The second aspect of the Manifesto was that we proposed to do things in a legal way. We announced an intention to form an association, a formal organization like a club, which would apply for recognition, according to the prevailing legal procedures, so we need no longer be clandestine. We went into the open, printing our names and our addresses and many people then wrote to us. This was the context of the creation of Neues Forum. I think that an important reason why this Manifesto was so successful (it was extensively copied and circulated all over the country), was that we abstained from political and ideological phrases. It set out, in direct, everyday language what the problems were and stated bluntly that it was no longer possible to live with them – with the exodus to the West, with the ruined economy and the ruined ecology and the double-speak and everything. All these things were said in plain German.

Publication of our Manifesto coincided with the mass exodus via Hungary that occurred a few days afterwards, and also with the mounting demonstrations in Leipzig. These impressive weekly vigils had been taking place at the Nikolai Kirche throughout September, but the scale of involvement and the pitch of political engagement had increased sharply. We became quite unexpectedly a grass-roots mass movement. People copied the Manifesto everywhere, all over the country.

Ten days after publishing the Charter Manifesto of Neues Forum, we were refused permission to constitute ourselves as an organisation. Predictably, they said that we were anti-Socialist and were aiming at the overthrow of the Socialist system in favour of the Capitalist system which, in their book, was anti-constitutional behaviour. In fact, *they* denied *us* constitutional rights. It was the expected reflex reaction. They understood at once what was at stake: that if such a discourse began in the open in the GDR, it spelled the end of their reign. We had also anticipated that they would call us servants of the Capitalist countries. Therefore we were very careful not to say anything that could be construed in this way.

It was the Ministry of Internal Security Affairs that criticised us, banned us, said that our desire to associate was illegal and that threatened us with jail. The Security Minister Mielke was a renowned figure in the Party. He had been a Commissar during the Spanish Civil War when he had harassed the German anarchists in the International Brigade (people serving with the likes of George Orwell): Mielke was a Soviet secret agent at that time. He was known from the Communist Party street riots of the 1920s and 1930s. In short, he was a veteran Party fighter and as Minister of Security he tried to eradicate us.

In retrospect, I do not think that the Honecker regime could have been overthrown by an alternative and formal political party. It could only fall to this kind of popular uprising. A more organised force would have had its head chopped off at once by the Stasi. So how could a regime such as our opponents oppressed us with have been overthrown? Part of the answer is nicely dialectical. Important sources of the anger and the despair which were channelled into revolutionary energy in November 1989 arose in direct reaction to the nature of their oppression, an oppression given concentrated symbolic form in the steel and concrete monstrosity of *Die Mauer* (The Wall).

Reflections on losing the Wall

We used to call it Wall-Sickness. It was a mass epidemic. For years there was scarcely any other topic for the endless evening chats with friends. Uncounted gallons of tea have been drunk in discussing it.

I was a student in East Berlin before 13th August, 1961, before the day of "The Wall". I came to Berlin in 1956, as a boy of 17. I had lived in a rather dull provincial town and after Halberstadt, Berlin was like a revelation for me. Both parts of it, East Berlin and West Berlin. I lived in East Berlin and was a medical student at the Humboldt University, where Robert Koch, Rudolf Virchow and other giants of the discipline had taught medicine decades before my arrival on the scene. My professors were of lesser stature, and we contemplated them with the typical severity and intense criticism of the young. We were also convinced that we would do better than they by adopting advanced Western methodology and knowledge. My dream was to graduate and then to go to the U.S.A. for some time, where the Nobel prizewinners of the day were working, thanks in part to the Nazis who had expelled 80% of the brightest brains in Berlin in the thirties.

And then we had West Berlin. What a thrill! Cinemas, theatres, the Philharmonie. I shall always remember a concert given by the young Glenn Gould on his first recital tour around Europe. Then there was the famous production of Goethe's *Faust* by Gustav Gruendgens, the dubious and flamboyant Hamburg theatre director, who is portrayed in Klaus Mann's novel *Mephisto* (also produced as a Hungarian film in the early eighties). I also remember having seen Jean Cocteau's film *Orphée* at least a dozen times. I took everybody who came to visit me in Berlin. And I remember the coming of The Wall.

I mention all these details, which I remember so clearly, in order give a sense of the shock that we suffered when The Wall came upon us one night. There we were in Berlin, at the crossroads between East and West, at the juncture of two fundamentally different cultures, and suddenly we were locked up like canaries in a cage. Literally from one day to the next, from being a vibrant and cultured city, Berlin subsided into the drowsy torpor of a midsummer afternoon in the provinces. We were imprisoned in a dull, flat country.

In the first years no foreign earth was available to us at all. Czechoslovakia, Poland and the Soviet Union could only be visited by professional people. Bulgaria and Romania opened for tourists in the mid-sixties; but prices were steep and they were holiday resorts rather than centres of European culture. To reach West Germany was a venture that most probably ended in prison for *Republikflucht*, or worse, for the Border Guards shot mercilessly at people trying to climb over "The Wall".

To call it a wall doesn't really do it justice. It was an entire system of watch towers, barbed wire, searchlights, pierced steel plate (to call it "wire mesh" gives the wrong impression of what was called "The Wire" within "The Wall"), strips sown with land-mines, free-fire zones covered by automatic guns, dog runs with ferocious, hungry dogs, armed Border Guard launches on the river to stop swimmers – all this apparatus of containment as well as concrete walls and passages.

There were several places in East Berlin from where you could study this "Wall", for instance from the electric train to the north of the city which passed with firmly closed doors through No-Man's Land. Even as I write in the spring of 1990, although the power and terror that actuated the "Wall System" have evaporated, the brooding wreckage of *Die Mauer*, lying across Berlin like a dead whale and to be viewed as an historical anomaly rather than as an object of fear, still gives a sense both of its enormousness and of the enormity which it represented.

"Wall-sickness" was the eternal, lamenting analysis of our life blighted and circumscribed by *Die Mauer*. It came from being in a cage in the centre of Europe. Wall-sickness was boredom. We felt condemned to utter, excruciating dullness, sealed off from everything that happened in the world around us. Wall-sickness was loneliness, the feeling that you were condemned to die without having ever seen Naples, or Venice, or Paris, or London.

Some people could not stand the prospect of a life of such tedium and literally went mad. People would sometimes do crazy irrational things. You might go to the border, for example, draw your identity card and announce that you wanted "to be rid of this shitty country", a gesture with the guaranteed outcome of years in prison, but done in the hope that West Germany would buy you out sooner or later (often later!). Wall-sickness was the anguish of deprivation of a whole generation born between 1930 and 1950. We knew what we had lost.

Later on, it seemed to me that young people were less scarred and that they also suffered less remorse than did my generation. This was understandable. They had no sharp idea of what life was like behind The Wall except what they saw on TV; and it is never the same to see something on TV as to experience it in the round. For better or worse, America is not *Dallas!* So for them the West lacked the poignancy that our memories gave it for us. For the young, it was not so much attractive as seductive, because of the way in which they encountered western images and sounds.

Western rock and pop music never lost their appeal in the East, and created much unrest and many conflicts between the young and the Communist Establishment, which thought that it knew better what was good for "our people": life in security, with no unemployment, no drug trafficking, no terrorism and none of the other evils of the West. People never finally accepted this tutelage, even if they were "red" or "pink" in their convictions. They sought an outlet. Some of the young found it through rock music, and through rock music they came to politics. A concert at the Brandenburg Gate in June 1988 was one of the first occasions on which demands for the removal of The Wall were voiced openly, while people chanted "Gorby! Gorby! Gorby!"

But before that, and for those who were not rock music performers or fans, there were other ways to seek excitement and some relief. Some went to Siberia, to help with the construction of the oil pipeline. Others tried to reach Africa or South America professionally, through diplomatic or economic or scientific activities. They had to pay through compromise for that, because access to such posts necessitated insincerity or self-censorship in your political convictions, or an outright self-persuasion that socialism was the order of the future, although I maintain that already in the sixties, the evidence was against it. This long-lasting hypocrisy of a generation of the intelligentsia (with a few exceptions of truly convinced people, but this became more and more incompatible with intelligence!) culminated in the late eighties with an increasing feeling of weariness with the state of affairs in our country. This was to be seen even in the Establishment and it eventually helped to bring down the old system.

There was an alternative attitude to submission, an alternative to hypocrisy and to "howling with the wolves", as the German proverb has it. I would call it "inner emigration". One was trapped in the cage, but one's spirit had flown. It was being "contra" and saying so in private, but not in public. Wall-sick, a whole generation yearned for a better future. This time it was a majority (as the sudden breakdown has proved after they broke their silence). My son exemplifies this. He got to University. He was excellent in learning political dogma by heart. He rattled off the lengthy definitions of imperialism as the final state of capitalism, of the socialist economy as being without exploitation of man by man, of the nature of historic materialism and so on without any personal relationship to what he was saying. It was just something to repeat like a litany which was supposed to be your holy creed. It was a sport to him, and a blasphemy. Others had more difficulty in parroting the doctrine. Some have suffered for ever.

I can well understand this feeling, and even its outgrowth: hatred directed against "Them", who treated the country and its people as if they were their private property. I can understand, because I was among those disappointed and cheated. I was in the same situation. After the spring 1990 elections, in the new parliament one saw it. The right-wing conservative MPs from the DSU directed glares seething with hatred in the direction of the PDS (the successors of the Communist Party) members. They felt personally cheated by them in their lives. Cheated of their professional development, their careers, their property.

"They" were guilty for anything that went wrong in your professional career. Indeed it is true that they stopped the development of hundreds of thousands of gifted people. But there also exist other reasons for professional failure. Yet the legitimate and the illegitimate reasons for failure could never be disentangled. As in your professional, so in your personal life. Always the State was to be blamed, even in intimate matters: in peoples' midlife crises. Young people demanded assistance from the State. "They want us to have children, so let Them take care of kindergartens and appropriate flats. They have promised us happiness? They will have to take the steering wheel. Let them do their job before I lift a finger!" There was an all-pervading conviction that "They", the State, the Party, the authorities, were responsible. They had to provide a flat. They had to organize a builder to repair the house or a plumber to unblock the drains. They allocated places at the university to the children who had kept quiet about their true political convictions.

But life was also cosy in Goethe's snail-shell. You didn't need to worry about the next day. Most goods could be obtained eventually by standing patiently in line. The queue for a new car stretched for *fifteen* years, literally, in 1989. I remember a discussion with Eva, my wife, in that year on how to schedule our reservation orders for cars in order to have at least one every eight years. As we talked, we suddenly realized that we were planning for periods that we might not see alive and in good health! It is impossible to enumerate all those situations of daily life and personal planning of family or career which in the West lie clearly within the responsibility of the citizen which the system has taken care of in the East.

Herein lies the poignant irony. Together they had created a population so dependent and reliant on the authority of the State that finally no hand was raised to save the old order when it came into crisis. It was also partly the fault of the old regime in another sense, for in its own terms, it went soft. It lost the courage of its convictions, and as Alexis de Tocqueville said, the most dangerous moment for a bad regime is when it tries to reform itself. There was liberalisation in the last years of the system. They allowed many visits to relatives in West Germany. This was surely a mistake, from their point of view, because the shock of this impression, so at variance with years of official propaganda, must have contributed to the landslide victory of the West-supported parties in 1990. The controlled opening of the Wall did not relieve the pressure, rather the contrary, because again, it was under the capricious control of the State. You had to apply for every occasion. The police decided and had the right to refuse without explanation. You did not know until the last moment whether you could attend the funeral of your aunt or the wedding of your cousin. I have seen people crimson with fury coming out of the police office where the visas were (or were not) issued. So, while creating people that refused to put up resistance for fear of not getting their next travel permit, the old regime also created resentful enemies of the system, because it touched people in their family lives, where they felt and resented it most, even the least sensitive.

How could it come about so quickly?

During October 1989, the refugee crisis had escaped completely from the control of the Honecker regime. He didn't seem to know what to do, and his vacillating actions demonstrated it. He was a victim of what Jan Urban in the chapter on Czechoslovakia called the "Janos Kadar Syndrome": a Communist hard-liner boxed into a corner and unable to use force to fight his way out. In fact, the Kadar syndrome is even more what happened to the grass roots of the Communist Party. They just gave up. They were paralysed. Our Manifesto was so cautiously worded that everybody who read it carefully said, "that's legal, that's reasonable. Why do the Communists oppose it? It's just what we think too." They could only make propaganda against us by not showing the Manifesto. This was the key to its success, because it divided the mass of the grass roots of the Party from their leadership. They then gave up when they realised, like Ceausescu did a couple of months later on the balcony at his last public appearance, that the cheering had turned into whistling and jeering.

On 1st October, 4,000 East Germans who had crossed into Czechoslovakia – the last country to which they could go across an open border – and who had besieged the West German Embassy in Prague were permitted to leave for the FRG on trains. But two conditions were imposed: the trains had to cross East Germany and the Czechoslovak border was closed. The Leipzig and Dresden demonstrations grew bigger by the day. Two days after Gorbachev's visit, 30,000 marched in Dresden, and the day after that, 50,000 in Leipzig. It was too much. The 6th-9th October were the days around the weekend of the fortieth anniversary of the creation of the GDR. The authorities quite clearly premeditated the use of violence.

Threatening articles, warning articles appeared in the Press. There were rumours via the Western media of a impending crackdown and they obviously prepared for counter-revolution. Honecker apparently wanted to use live ammunition against the marchers in Leipzig on October 9th, but lost the vote in his Politburo by a single vote. Krenz reportedly led the opposition to the use of violence and the Soviets reportedly took an active role through the advisers to the Volksarmee. I write "reportedly" because we do not know for certain who took what position. After the event, Honecker, Krenz and the Russians all claimed responsibility for saving the situation. Honecker "resigned" on 18th, but the appearance of a new face didn't stem the tide of opposition. On 30th, 300,000 marched in Leipzig, as if to make that point, and on 1st November the closure of the Czechoslovak border was reversed. A new torrent of would-be *emigrés* flooded through. On 3rd, it was announced that East Germans leaving would no longer have to renounce their citizenship and in the next five days, 50,000 more left via Czechoslovakia. The effect of this exodus upon Czechoslovak opinion is reported by Jan Urban in the next chapter. They seem to have been like heralds, witnessing to the fact that the old regimes could be successfully defied. If ours could be forced down, then so could others.

Half a million marched in Berlin on November 4th. On 7th the entire Cabinet resigned and on the 8th, the Politburo followed them. Then in the afternoon of November 9th, the spokesman Günter Schabowski emerged on to the steps of the Central Committee building to speak to the Press. After various announcements, he glanced at another piece of paper and added that it had been decided that citizens were now free to enter and leave the DDR at will "with immediate effect". "Does that mean today?" asked a journalist. Schabowski shrugged his shoulders and said the fateful words, "I suppose so." It is probable that the Communists and Schabowski only meant that travel permits would henceforth be freely available. The Central Committee had been discussing what they could do to stop the street demonstrations and to stop the mass exodus through Czechoslovakia. The application of force was no longer possible. They had foreclosed that option already. They had opened dialogue and they were struggling frantically to keep control of the terms of the debate. One of the options was simply letting the *emigrés* go to Czechoslovakia. The boil would then be lanced, the pressure would be off. This seems to have been their reasoning. But whatever they meant, it no longer mattered. The rest is now history. Two million East Berliners visited West Berlin that weekend.

One question with which I am often faced is how it could come about that such an iron system of party dictatorship could crumble so swiftly. After all, it was buttressed by the Stasi (the Security Police), who were balefully efficient. It was more ideologically conformist, looked more stable, less surmountable, much more rigid than any other of the East European Communist regimes. How then could such a Leviathan topple so quickly, so precipitously? I see eight factors that played a role.

The first factor lies in the nature of the historical trends which underpinned the situation in the GDR. In physical and biological systems, there exists a well-known phenomenon that the specialists call "catastrophic transition". A system is over-stabilized and by its very structure is difficult to displace from its steady state. Catastrophe theory represents this diagrammatically as a gentle slope advancing towards a fold or "cusp" in the model, where the plane cascades energetically to another stable state. This transition is dynamically like the inception of an avalanche. In the steady state, the snow is very hard to move, but once the avalanche is released nothing can stop it. It is difficult to see direct and sufficient causes for its release; random events play a role here. But the mountain and snow and weather conditions contain the latent potentials. Sometimes something as small as a cough or a shout is sufficient to precipitate it.

The East German situation was ripe for abrupt transformation. It was just such avalanche country. I saw it, although I could not predict the moment of catastrophic transition any more than anyone else. I watched the political weather change, slowly, over time, at the most informal and intimate scale, in my own circle of acquaintance. For example, over the years I have watched colleagues and close friends who were dedicated to the Party and its dogma. Slowly they became more and more detached from the Communist leadership. In the fifties when a political discussion occurred at work, there was always a Comrade who stepped in and defended the position of the Party. In the seventies and eighties such a thing happened far less frequently. They usually avoided this "ideological work" and preferred to walk out of the tea room or to change the topic of conversation. So nobody was really ready to take up the gauntlet on behalf of the Party when finally the crisis burst.

A second factor relates to the management and possession of information. The political information network linking the political leadership and society had been fractured. In a healthy political system, there is information flow up and down, a two-way traffic employing the same channels. In our country the "Down" and "Up" channels were divorced. Information from above descended as commands to be obeyed. It was transmitted down the Party channels, or through the administrative labyrinth. No questioning of commands was possible. The decisions were taken above, "in the clouds".

The feedback information of how society in all its varied complexity reacted, was collected covertly by the security system of the Stasi, its telephone taps, listening bugs and its informers and passed to the top through secret "Up" channels. It was this information flow which became congested and which ultimately seized up. The *nomenclatura* could not digest conflicting evidence. The top did not want to hear critical reports. This was well understood by the news collectors, so they coloured their reports positively in order to get them accepted. Negative reports were dangerous to the messenger, because they were taken as a sign of political immaturity or unreliability and in any case were not taken at face value.

Also this "Up" information flow was not professional, but political in a bad sense. What does a specialist in internal security and subversion report about the economic situation, or the national research strategy in chemistry or in the computer field? They did what their instincts and training taught them to do. They extracted gossip and over-personalized information. Everything was seen through political glasses. In everything was detected the whiff of conspiracy. With such flawed information the leadership could no longer know, and did not want to know, the real state of the country. Conspiracy theories are comfortingly all-embracing.

The burgeoning crisis in the economy illustrates this point. Information about it was suppressed, and the Honecker leadership installed instead a committee that functioned like a fire brigade when something threatened to go seriously wrong. It had wide powers to deal with bottlenecks. Sometimes its members went overseas with suitcases full of Ostmarks and bought Deutschmarks in West Berlin in order to repair an acute breakdown somewhere, or to buy a crucial spare part. This is fine as an emergency measure, but you cannot run a whole economy this way.

So by self-inflicted decision, the leadership was narrowly blinkered and what it saw was systematically distorted. What then of the role of information, especially of Western radio and TV, in stimulating the countervailing actions of ordinary people? It is said that in Romania, for example, the sights from the Berlin Wall and from Wenceslas Square on TV helped to put people into the streets. Was it so in East Germany, at the beginning of the sequence of the three autumn revolutions? Did East Germans make their revolution with a clear image of the West in their minds? I don't know. I think that everyone would have had some image of what the West looked like; but the mass of demonstrators came from the provinces or from regions where Western television is not available or reception is very poor. So they might have lacked a detailed perception of the sort that some analysts seem to presume was universal. Collateral support for my opinion is that when these people came across the Wall after 9th November, clutching their hundred Deutschmarks of "welcome money", they stared into the shop windows on the Kurfurstendamm and at the West Berlin traffic and at the outward signs of life in the West and they were taken by utter surprise. I think it was the shock of seeing something which previously they had only seen in bad photographs. The picture of how the West looks and of how people lived there, was obviously too abstract for the majority. It was a shock to have seen the West as it really was. It was different from the way it had been explained to them and different from what Western television showed. Electronic information is not the same as seeing for yourself. I therefore tend to be sceptical about ascribing too big a role to the Western media in triggering the East German revolution.

However, in contrast, there is no doubt about the role of the third factor. Mr Gorbachev seems to have realised that matters for the Party in the GDR were lurching into disaster and he obviously gave up on the Honecker leadership. During his visit on the occasion of the fortieth anniversary of the creation of the GDR, he made the usual polite speeches to Honecker and his crew, but he took several opportunities which were beyond their power to control, to speak his true mind. He ordered his car to be stopped in the streets and he addressed young people who were waving at him. "Those who come late will be punished by history," was one of the things that he said, a sentiment hardly likely to fall gladly upon Mr Honecker's ear. Again, "If you really want democracy, then take it, and you will get it!" News of statements of this kind spread like wildfire on the grapevine. They convinced us that the Soviets no longer wanted the survival of the calcified East German regime. I think that Gorbachev's second remark is particularly perceptive. Once they realize their situation and exert their will collectively, without fear or hesitation, people can shake off tyranny. Despotism can last only with a certain degree of acceptance.

All three factors mentioned so far served to amplify the effect of the fourth. This was simply the professional incompetence with which the Communist leadership tried to manage the crisis. I mean this in a slightly cynical sense. Their ability to manage any crisis competently had waned, partly because of the self-inflicted damage done to their information channels. Their reaction to the crisis brought on by the exodus of thousands of refugees to the various West German embassies in neighbouring countries was simply crass. What a capital blunder it was to direct trains full with emigrants from Czechoslovakia through the GDR to West Germany! The old regime demanded that this happen as a clumsy face-saving gesture. It was a petulant demonstration of sovereignty which worked entirely counter-productively for them because it served only to underline the illegitimacy of that sovereignty. I can't imagine what they hoped to gain from this stubborn manoeuvre. What did happen was that they were compelled to defend a hundred-kilometre battle front along the railway line through the GDR against people who tried to clamber on to these freedom trains in order to escape as well. In places, the trains were virtually stormed. Another irretrievable gaffe was Honecker's dreadful remark early in 1989 that the Wall was going to last for another hundred years. He added by way of explanation, "as long as the conditions prevail that led to its construction", but no one listened to that. People became furious.

The fifth factor contributing to the speed of overthrow of the Communist regime was more richly ironic than cynical. They overestimated the power and significance of the street protests. These were good Marxist–Leninists who had learned from Lenin's writings that once the united and "entirely justifiable revolutionary initiative" of the masses goes out "resolutely" (another favourite Leninist word) into the streets, it spells doom for the *ancien régime*. Now *they* were the *ancien régime!* Remember Ceausescu's look of utter disbelief when the apparent jubilation of the crowd turned into whistling in Bucharest. In the West, ruling elites have learned long ago that people come and shout, get hungry and bored after a while and return home. You simply have to "sit it out." Happily, Honecker and Co were not cynical enough.

In the event, we escaped bloodshed. But it was not known at the time that we would. There was a real, objective threat of violence. With one part of the mind, one knows that, but – and it's a very strange feeling – in the streets, facing the police and troops, you forget about anxiety. You don't calculate risks any longer, you don't reckon, instead you feel driven. People did what they felt impelled to do. Therefore on the candlelit marches, people made magnificently foolhardy, theatrical and deeply impressive gestures. Marchers went right up to the police cordons and held burning candles to the noses of the helmeted policemen with their riot-shields and batons. The act symbolised our position perfectly. A myriad small, fragile points of light saying, "We are here! In our unity we are invincible because *we are the people!* Individually, we are perilously vulnerable to your weapons, we know. By our defencelessness, we appeal to your humanity. Recognise that your time is past. Go now in peace." People did this, forgetting about the danger that they were in. They were looking ahead, literally and metaphorically. I saw many people on those momentous days in a strange trance-like state, where they did not take anything in any longer. That was the way, finding power from not having fear.

The policemen were not unmoved. The servants of the State themselves turned against the system, or at least became reluctant to defend it any longer. This we saw. In Berlin, I myself and others have been in the streets and saw scuffling around Gethsemane Church. I have seen how uneasy the men making the cordon looked when being verbally attacked by women. The women reproached them. "Aren't you feeling ashamed of yourself standing against your own population? I could be your mother and you stand here with your truncheon. Put it away! Go away!" It is psychologically very difficult for riot police to be forced to recognise the humanity of those whom they are supposed to be controlling. They had to endure the insidious attack of a peaceful crowd approaching them with candles outstretched, offering dialogue. You have to be stone-hearted to stand your ground, to be unmoved and then, when ordered to do so, to wade into those people with truncheons. The authorities knew that it was too much to ask of their troops. Therefore they employed a different tactic. When they wanted to use violence, the men who would apply it were kept under cover and away from sight or sound of the crowd, so that they couldn't be weakened. Then they were unleashed and ordered into action at the double in the hope that they wouldn't have time to think, and in the expectation that their discipline would override their humanity. In several places, it worked. There were several occasions in different towns where riot police beat people severely.

As the revolution continued, the use of violence by the Communist authorities against the demonstrators petered out.

One of the factors is said to have been the refusal of the highest command of the Warsaw Pact – Gorbachev in other words – to leave GDR Volksarmee troops in the towns. I have already mentioned above the different versions of the fateful discussions about shooting on the Leipzig marchers on 9th October. Another factor was that local district bosses refused to co-operate any longer with Honecker's orders from Berlin to employ violence. There is positive evidence of this. We escaped a Romanian or a Chinese solution by the skin of our teeth. It could easily have been the other way around, with a re-established leadership sitting on heaps of corpses, and being ostracised entirely by the civilised world. I think that this was a real possibility.

The sixth factor describes the source of the power which sustained the marchers in the streets during the problematic phase when violence was employed and greater violence threatened. Women played a fundamental part in making our revolution, and it, along with the role of young people, should be recognised. At an early stage, the sanctuary of the Gethsemane Church was the focus and the beacon of our movement. Every evening around the Gethsemane Church, people walked silently in the great ritual of our revolution. Women and young people enacted it, with candles, parading humbly and defencelessly but in awesome unity of purpose in front of the dreadful apparatus of State repression. The riot-police cordon, the armoured trucks, the water cannon. They demonstrated without any sign of fear. They quietly placed their candles on the street, sat down and waited until they were carried away or beaten up or arrested after Neues Forum had been declared illegal and unconstitutional.

We were pleased to notice that the flow of visitors and telephone callers and letters did not diminish after the régime banned us. Usually, our population is very legalistic and if something is declared illegal they won't take any further part. It did not happen with Neues Forum. What we did notice was that the proportion of women who came forward after the banning was much higher than before. Frequently, they said something like, "I disregard the fact that "They" say it is unconstitutional. The Manifesto is so reasonable, so normal. In fact, it's quite what I think and I refuse to be intimidated into not saying so!" Women played a crucial role by showing that special form of courage which is disregard of an actual danger. They simply ignored it. They were without fear.

A very important factor, number seven, was the success of the mass exodus over border fences and through West German embassies. After many years of such crises where East Germans sought asylum, for the first time Bonn refused to settle them by quiet negotiation. In the past, the refuge seekers agreed deals whereby they returned home in return for a promise of emigration a short while later, after things had cooled down. This time, Bonn refused to do deals with the GDR and got its way. This was due to the effect of the principal factor (the third given above), the retreat of the Soviet Union as a Superpower dominating Eastern Europe. Moscow simply did not order the Hungarians any longer to keep their barbed wire intact. Nor could they have insisted upon it if they had and the Hungarians had refused. Was it Gorbachev's insight into the inevitable course of history? Was it preoccupation with more urgent problems at home? Moscow's attitude opened a valve and with a great hiss, the air rushed into the vacuum: a sort of political physics.

The other side of the coin of the successful flight of the refugees was the breaking of the spell of the security paranoia which had enveloped us. This is the eighth and final factor. It is very difficult to describe to those who have not experienced it how this security paranoia used to affect our daily lives: being followed, being overheard on the telephone, being interrogated occasionally, being threatened by subtle means. The Stasi did not use the clumsy methods of the Gestapo but precise sanctions carefully calculated to strike home; for instance, denial of your children's university admission, of your promotion at work, of travel to the West to attend conferences or to see your relatives. On top of this was the knowledge, but never the certainty, that you were somehow under surveillance, overheard, that "They" had got a file somewhere. Read Orwell to understand this. The silly thing was that you did not know when making a call whether you were really being overheard or whether the operator was snoozing! It was an unreal life, in a way, where you never had a certainty of what was going on until finally somebody was taken away and arrested, or expelled from the country. I myself have never been arrested, but people around me have been. I know of cases where people spent ten months and more in custody and were then released without trial or any explanation of the reasons. Read Kafka to understand that.

For them, the speed of the collapse was catastrophe; for us it was salvation. The overthrow could only have happened successfully that way. The future promises to be no less packed with suspense than was that unexpected and amazing autumn of 1989 which threw us, after decades of sleepy calmness right into the pounding surf. The spring tide of History has flooded into our backwater. We are caught by surprise. I hope that we will muster the strength and resolve to swim, and not sink.

This speed of and nature of collapse left us with residual problems. One, common to Czechoslovakia especially, was what to do with the servants of the old régime. The winter revolution was miraculously peaceful. That meant that only the old leadership were ousted and that only those who had committed crimes were taken into custody. At the municipal and managerial level, the old local leadership, more or less, remained in post. In fact, we have a deeply rooted and old administrative structure. A problem soon confronted was how to dispose of those people who had worked in the Stasi. The problem is compounded, because even if they do apply for decent work, like becoming a bus driver or at a factory, they are known, and others refuse to work with them and go on strike if ex-Stasi are hired. One must concede their right to take this view, because they have been harassed by these ex-security agents and understandably, they don't want to co-operate with them. On the other hand, we have an obligation to integrate them somehow, and even more, we must resolve how to re-integrate the much larger numbers of those who were only fellow travellers.

One development which may assist this process is the restructuring of the country during the process of re-unification. The five *länder* (Saxony, Thuringia, etc.) were abolished by the Communists after the war in an attempt to destroy the traditional, regional identities of the population. As soon as they were able to express their views, it became apparent that it was the wish of the great majority of East Germans to re-establish these old federal structures. One can capitalise upon this strong consensus and in so doing rearrange the whole administrative structure and the personnel within it so as to make a fresh start.

Reflections on Losing a Country

"I said, couldn't you describe the kind of shoe, for monsieur's information?"

"It is a lady's shoe. It is a young lady's walking shoe. It is in the present mode. I never saw the mode. I have had a pattern in my hand." He glanced at the shoe *with some little passing touch of pride.*

"And the maker's name?" said Defarge.

Now that he had no work to hold, he laid the knuckles of the right hand in the hollow of the left, and then the knuckles of the left hand in the hollow of the right, and then passed a hand across his bearded chin, and so on in regular changes, without a moment's intermission. The task of recalling him from the vacancy into which he always sank when he had spoken was like recalling some very weak person from a swoon, or endeavouring, in the hope of some disclosure, to stay the spirit of a fast-dying man.

"Did you ask me for my name?"

"Assuredly I did."

"One Hundred and Five, North Tower."

"Is that all?"

"One Hundred and Five, North Tower."

(Charles Dickens, *A Tale of Two Cities*, Book I, Ch.6)

The mass of the East German people were sprung from their prison cages behind *Die Mauer* after the revolutionaries of the first hour, like Neues Forum, had done their job and opened wide the door. They emerged dazed and uncertain of who they were. They were quickly seized by a single, powerful thought: to re-unite at any cost and to forget about the dreadful past behind the Wall. I can understand them. I regret this wholesale break with all our past, all our identity, but I cannot blame them. They have broken their chains, chains that were the more irksome the less you had to worry about bread and butter for tomorrow. Nobody has a right to blame people for seeing no other escape than by submersion within the West German identity after those decades of systematic incapacitation. It is small wonder that our sense of civic life and of its responsibilities and duties had become degenerate and needs some time to recover. We need time to cope with free life; also with the inevitable ugly fringe phenomena which come with it, such as xenophobia, right-wing extremism, stubborn provincialism. Living in shackles for decades leaves its traces on your body. Living surrounded by a barbed-wired wall leaves deep scars in your soul. I would like Europe to be patient with us. We are like Prisoner One Hundred and Five, North Tower of the Bastille, who first sees the sunlight after years in the dark. We need the light, but nonetheless it hurts our eyes. We need time to adjust, but that time we shall not be granted.

In the months after the fall of The Wall and during the first free elections, Neues Forum was swept aside in the stampede towards unification. Other political parties were formed, each with its counterpart in West Germany, and they ran a merciless electoral campaign. In December 1989, they assured us that we would be allowed to develop our own East German form of democracy. It became rapidly clear that we would not. But you cannot stand against a dam breaking. And the political dam broke on 9th November with The Wall. The West German Chancellor, Helmut Köhl was not unhappy at this breakneck pace of developments. His interest was quite obvious. He forged ahead by all means, seeing that if he lost momentum, everyone in Europe would begin to discuss the German question, to enter reservations, demand conditions and slow things down. He therefore tried to exploit the momentum of the moment. Hence his public espousal of monetary union.

Writing now, as reunification approaches, people seem to have lost that intoxicating spirit and energy of the November Spring in Winter. They realise that we are economically more or less in ruins and are therefore in despair and apathy. The only way out, they say, is to appeal to the older brother to help and rescue us. I cannot share this feeling although I am by no means against unification. My concern is rather about the self-assurance that we shall need for the times to come. The rush to monetary union in July 1990 exposes us at once. We shall have hard currency and this will immediately show up the weaknesses of our system and our economy. Most of our factories are not able to compete internationally. Many of them will have to close down very soon, because they are no longer profitable. Profitability was a criterion that was never seriously applied in the command economy. We shall get unemployment, very suddenly, as a shock, on a large scale and without the insurance to cope with it. Old people's pensions are very low. They have accumulated savings for their old age, for luxuries: to be able to continue to have a car, for instance, or to be able to travel overseas, possible only after retirement. Their savings will soon be spent on day to day expenses.

Then we have the problem of single women with children. There are many such mothers in East Germany. They will have grave difficulty continuing to work without the support provided by state kindergartens and all the other social benefits that made it possible to live decently, even if your salary was low. My wife has a friend, a divorcee, who educates her three children alone. Someone like this will be hit very hard upon being thrust into a Western-type society. On the other hand, of course, we need efficiency. It is a dilemma. To resolve it, I think that we should all become aware of our social strength. Together we were strong enough to overthrow a system so fixed that it seemed impossible to topple it. Why should we not now stand together to defend our social welfare? It is a matter of solidarity and of fighting spirit. I hope that we can muster both.

In the first elections, the promise of Deutschmarks was electorally magical and hugely boosted the East German Christian Democrats. The political attraction for Köhl and his allies of going flat out for monetary union as the next objective was dual. They could "bounce" the independent West German Bundesbank, and also exploit an issue that was one of the few which could be progressed in bilateral German negotiations outside the areas of competence of the treaties of the Victory powers (the matters discussed in the so-called "4+2" talks). Köhl's tactic was returning to the immediate post war period, when there was the same situation of a virtually united Germany, occupied by allied troops and covered by international treaties. The tactic during 1990 was to try to tie together both Germanies without violating international treaties by slipping under them.

In retrospect, I think that the first election came too soon. For the forces like Neues Forum, which did not have West German backers, our organisation was too weak. We had immense logistic difficulties. In the old East Germany, you could not buy a typewriter in the shop, you had to be in a queue for months or even years to get one. You could apply for a telephone, but sometimes you had to wait for decades in order to get one installed. Computers and copying machines were unheard of. In the run-up to the 1990 elections, only a few private sympathizers in the West helped us, whereas those parties with West German godfathers obtained all the logistics and the know-how to run a slick campaign. This put us at an obvious disadvantage, but we did not complain about it. Standing as a candidate for Parliament myself, I found it difficult to bring myself to stare into a television camera and say the same short sentence twenty times over. I felt like a chimpanzee.

Neues Forum cannot withdraw from campaign politics, because we are sure that the mood will swing back to deeper matters after a while. It is a long-term process. People will eventually become disappointed with the nature of the grafted-on party system and realise that the political movement of the next decade and the next century must be via direct democracy – people taking their fate into their own hands, not delegating politics to parties or to the government. This is too authoritarian. I ponder the future of Neues Forum and of the parties that are close to us, like the Greens and all those spontaneous political forces. I ponder how to bring them together when they are so dispersed, so separated, so fraught with fights and factions. I think that we need a new approach to politics. We have to interweave politics intimately with the everyday world as we live it and we must learn to interrogate all political questions routinely from the perspective of fifty years on.

The other day a colleague lent me his one year old son because he wanted to go to the shop; he asked to me play with him for ten minutes. The dialogue with the child who was playing with a ball and trying to get my attention made me reflective. He was just one half of a century younger than I, I thought as he crawled about happily on the floor, and in fifty years time he will look back on the nineties of this century. We should make the mental effort to adopt his position now and from it, to ask, "What will last from what we do, what will be praised in fifty year's time and what will be ridiculously obsolete then?" I think there is so much in what we are doing now that they never will understand fifty years hence (hoping that they will be alive then).

It includes the endless ideological wrestling between "Left" and "Right" and bombarding each other with combative phrases, with stickers, with badges about "emancipation" and "human rights", in ways which evacuate such concepts of meaning. I now, and they then will say, "What was their grievance in those days? All their newspapers are full of such rubbish that one cannot understand it." Occupying the imagined vantage point of the future gives a bird's-eye view and it provides much clarity. Use a global, ecological perspective and we can understand at once that the organisational structure of the present industrial system cannot last much longer. It devours the earth and our childrens' inheritance. It must be tamed, which calls for a new politics of global security, far beyond obedience to anything like contemporary conservatism or radical democracy.

We have to live in a different way or we will drown in the mess that we have made in the industrial age, and nowhere more so or more immediately than in the tragic environmental wilderness of Eastern Europe. I think that this is the bench-mark by which we must measure what we do politically, or whether we should do anything at all politically. All the present systems of modern politics are, in my view, old-fashioned and obsolete when viewed in a future oriented way. When this habit grows, the citizens' movement will again come to the fore as it did in spearheading the 1989 revolution. Meanwhile my message to all those who took an active part in the romantic phase of the East German revolution is this. We were in high spirits in November 1989. We saw that our action and our solidarity could prosper, and in the event we achieved things undreamed of. How remarkable was confirmed to me in early 1990, before I was elected to Parliament and while I was still at my Institute. I was summoned by the Director to discuss a professional question. He was deep in the old *nomenclatura* system and he said to me, "I still cannot believe that it really proved possible to eradicate that cancer, the Stasi State within the State." He was much closer to its operation. He knew what it really meant.

Was it really my country at all? We had an ironic paraphrase of the official slogan: "My Fatherland is the GDR", which sounded so odd, so artificial. We said instead "My Fatherland is the Zone", where zone referred to the Soviet zone of occupation after the war, which later on became the GDR. "Zone" was a taboo word, because it indicated imperialistic thirst for revenge and counter-revolution. We were not in favour of the zone, but we never accepted the German Democratic Republic either; only from spite, when the "Wessies" (West Germans) were too arrogant with their rustling banknotes. So was it our country?

There are people who really thought it was their country. They, the *nomenclatura*, regarded it as a self-service shop where you just took what you needed but did not pay. It all began with a noble intention to create a better Germany, after the horror and squalor of the war. But the Communist State suffered from the congenital defect of having been imposed against the will of the majority. Like Stalin, the East German Establishment believed that it knew better than the people did what was good for them, and they carried their intentions out, against the outspoken or silent will of the majority. It could last only as long as Big Brother cast his shadow, as he did in the suppression of the 1953 uprising, when Soviet tanks saved the Ulbricht régime. The Communist régime crumbled like a plaster sculpture in 1989, when Gorbachev refused to send in his troops or even, on 9 October 1989, refused to allow the Volksarmee to interfere with the street demonstrations in Leipzig.

Identification with the GDR as a state never played a dominant role in our society, although in the seventies, when our athletics teams competed successfully with the United States and the Soviet Union in the Olympic Games, there was a widespread feeling that "we are somebody", or at least that "we may become somebody". A wave of recognition by respected nations contributed to that state of mind. But this acceptance declined in the eighties, for several reasons. The main one was certainly the increasing pace of economic failure. It was aggravated by a long-term policy that catered for the present at the expense of the future. This was as true in the wrecking of the natural environment as in the wrecking of the economy and has in the event led to a major disaster for the whole of the state and its socialist ideology. It is difficult to say whether a well-timed reform would have saved this artificial construction. Others tried hard to save some socialism. We wish them success, but do not follow that road ourselves. So, are we happy that this unloved and deformed creature of the cold-war period is now at last dying?

Strange to say, I am not happy and neither are others around me. Now that the state is decaying, people begin to yearn for some of its more sympathetic traits. In a peculiar way, many of us feel homesick for that inefficient and lazy society which is so remote from the tough and competitive society into which we are now thrown. I think that the much trumpeted claim for social warmness of our society (which it was said to share with the other East European countries) is more a cliché than reality. But one cannot deny that it makes a difference whether a young mother, made late for work by her child's sudden illness, can stay at home and afterwards excuse herself without fuss, or whether such a commonplace family event puts her under considerable stress because there is no spare labour capacity at work to cover for her and she knows that she will find little sympathy or understanding of her plight. These were the benefits of laziness. Its costs, however, have destroyed the system.

So we say farewell, but with an oppressive sense of uneasiness. Leave-taking from the GDR is like departure from a small town where you have been brought up and attended the old-fashioned school. You feel liberated and grown up, full of anticipation and longing for the thrill of life in a big city. But one steals a regretful glance backward as well. Perhaps it will transform into a yearning for a past of which you have forgotten the disagreeable aspects? It was the time of our youth, and now we will have to fight for our lives. We cannot and must not shirk our fate. Like Prisoner One Hundred and Five, North Tower, we are recalled to life.

5 Jan Urban

Czechoslovakia: the power and politics of humiliation

Age 39, married, with two daughters, a professional optimist.

His father was a Communist idealist who spent six years in the Czech anti-Nazi Resistance during the War, later becoming a Party official, and ultimately Head of the Department of Culture, Science and Education of the Central Committee of the Czechoslovak Communist Party. He lost his position in the early 1960s for criticising the regime's inability to reform and died in 1988 of a heart attack after three interrogations by the State Police.

Jan followed his father's "remonstrant" path. After graduating from University in philosophy and history, he worked in a theatre, then taught history and civics in a Gymnasium in Southern Bohemia. He was sacked in 1977 for refusing to sign a condemnation of Charter 77, after which he had many manual jobs. Qualified as a bricklayer in 1985.

Signatory of Charter 77, member of the Polish-Czechoslovak Solidarity Group, one of the founders of the Eastern European Information Agency. Chief-of-staff of Civic Forum during the Revolution and since February 1990, its leading representative. He accepted this position at the height of the Revolution on the condition that he would resign it after the June 1990 elections (in which Civic Forum won a resounding mandate). This he did. He is now a journalist and leader writer with the newspaper Lidoviy Noviny.

5

In the course of one week, in November 1989, Winter blossomed into Spring in Czechoslovakia. A non-violent mass movement, led by Civic Forum, triumphed. We are in transition from the negation of the old to the building of the new. It is time to look for the roots.

Czechoslovakia was founded in 1918 on supranational idealist principles. Three nations – Czechs, Slovaks and Germans – together with various ethnic minorities, united in a perhaps historically naive belief in the strength of modern political democracy. In reaction to its intimate knowledge of the great size, but also of the darker reaches of the German spirit, formed during a thousand years of living side by side with Germans, the new state oriented itself within modern world culture, and in power terms, on an alliance with Great Britain and France. The concept of collective security, today generally accepted, was very actively promoted at that time.

Quickly, Czechoslovakia became a democratic state with respectable economic and cultural achievements. But it would soon become clear that certainties built on idealist principles and enthusiasm easily became false myths without substance. The economic crisis of 1929; Hitler's chauvinism after 1933 and the trauma of the 1938 Munich Diktat, successively and brutally made that point. To this very day, in Czechoslovakia, the Munich settlement has been felt to be the failure of the Western democracies and the betrayal of allies. It had exactly the horrible consequences which Winston Churchill predicted. The ease with which humiliated and broken Czechoslovakia submitted to Nazi occupation resulted from, among other things, the loss of faith in democracy which flowed from Munich.

The betrayed Czechs had believed in the strength of parliamentary democracies and in the honesty of their allies. This belief turned to the worst humiliation. For a long time there was no hope for anything more positive. People survived with a "submit, hide or run for your life" psychology. One day before the occupation of Bohemia (14 March 1939), Slovaks formed their own Slovak state. This was felt keenly in Bohemia to be another result of Munich. Humiliation and Despair were also the names of occupying powers. Just a few months previously, a strong state had lost most of its territory, its allies, its independence and its hope. This was simply a terrible ten months. It was only when the World War began that a glimmer of hope returned, at least to some.

The year 1945 came, with mass purges, violent expulsion of three million Germans, and a system of selective democracy that allowed only several specific political parties. In 1948, under the passive gaze of citizens who no longer believed within themselves in the possibility of defending democracy, the Communist Party assumed power.

This episode of betrayal and humiliation forms the essential backdrop to the subsequent history of Czechoslovakia; for humiliation is powerful in politics in two directions. Usually it serves the interests of the oppressor. People live intense, introspective lives, their energies all turned in upon their own miseries and relationships. That is what Milan Kundera has evoked so effectively in his novels, especially in his early books like *The Joke*, but perhaps best known outside Czechoslovakia in his most recent novel, *The Unbearable Lightness of Being*. Yet occasionally, as happened in November 1989, the energy turns again outwards. It pounds upon the oppressor and he simply crumbles. As President Havel writes in the preface to this book, humour as well as honesty had vital roles in the Revolution. So the story of this chapter is about power in the sense of the absurd to shatter the passivity of humiliation and to liberate the energies trapped within. But first, I must explain how we reached that moment. We had to eat a lot of dirt before we vomited.

Why did the Communists succeed so easily in 1948? There were three main reasons. One was the peculiarity of the position of the Communist Party of Czechoslovakia in society. The CPCz had been a legal component of the parliamentary spectrum since 1921. In all other central European states before the war, the Communist Parties functioned underground, illegally. Betrayal by the Western allies, represented by the disappointment of Munich, was followed by the liberation of most of Czechoslovakian territory by the Red Army. This trend towards the Communists was accelerated by the plainly mistaken decision of President Benes to return to Prague with the London Government-in-Exile via Moscow. All this gave the CPCz great popularity. In the parliamentary elections, on a wave of nationalist populism, they attained more than 40% of the vote. They became the most powerful political party in the country. In the struggle for power, they neither had to use force, like Communists in Poland, nor the weight of the Soviet occupation, like the Communists in East Germany. The CPCz had part of the intelligentsia on its side. Industrial workers, profiting from the boom in heavy industry, supported it. Peasants were satisfied with the Communists' land reform and with the redistribution of the property of the expelled Sudeten Germans. The Communists occupied the decisive positions in the Army and Security Services. In February 1948, the Communists seized power without a single shot being fired. With hindsight it is possible to evaluate that event as the failure of an immature, conceited but disheartened democracy faced with threats and force.

Only later we found out that there were two further, important reasons for the ease of the Communist takeover. One was the long-term Soviet (or more properly NKVD) plan to occupy the whole of Eastern Europe in an attempt to build a buffer to a possible Third World War. It meant that already since 1944, and especially in the Spring of 1945, the Soviets were sending paratroop groups to Bohemia with only one task; not to fight, but to organise an information network for the future. Since the end of the war, the Communists were getting more and more important posts in the Security Forces and in the Army so that at the moment of political crisis in Czechoslovakia, the means of power would be effectively controlled by them.

The second reason was a growing political pressure from Stalin's Soviet Union which became visible in July 1947, with a government visit by the Czechoslovak government to Moscow. Stalin simply rebuffed the Czechoslovak desire to receive Marshall Plan aid. Since that moment, even Benes knew that the battle was lost and that Czechoslovakia could not go its own way. Furthermore, we learn from historians that the Truman Administration was actually working on the assumption that Moscow controlled Czechoslovakia *before* the Spring Crisis of 1948 make it a reality. We can never know what might have been the course of events if the West had backed Benes and Jan Masaryk with food and other help, vigorously, during the terrible winter of 1947. Only today, after fifty years of the dominance of ideologically driven and repressive regimes, first Nazi then Communist, we stand, perhaps the wiser, on the threshold of the new era. The economist Milos Zeman described our situation aptly. "We are like emaciated and beaten animals, released from the zoo and looking untrustingly at open country."

The Czechoslovak experience under Communism was bitter for several reasons. A highly industrialised country, like Czechoslovakia, with a relatively developed economic infrastructure, was much more sensitive to the extreme unsuitability of the centralised Communist planning system than were the other East European countries managed by Communist governments after the war. There was also a lot more to squander. In comparison with its neighbours, the economy was not damaged by war. There was the property of three million expelled Germans, the nationalisation of industry and services, the virtual 100% collectivisation of agriculture, the strictly enforced obligatory labour, and the purges. In short, Czechoslovakia started from a higher material base than its neighbours, and so it was possible for decay to proceed for years without people really noticing, because they did not have to suffer an immediate and commensurate decrease in their standard of living.

The years of Stalin's fury left behind them hundreds of executions, tens of thousands of imprisoned, millions of damaged and terrified people. The beautiful dream of equality became a nightmare. The social structure was violently turned upside down with the elimination of the private sector in all areas of human activity, and the destruction or entire subjugation to state control of the church. All citizens, without exception, became state employees, because the state was the proprietor of everything. From the beginning of the sixties, however, it became clear that there was a fault in the system. The economy ceased to function. The intelligentsia, encouraged by the events of the 1956 rising in Hungary, carefully began to formulate a non-ideological culture. The Writers' Congress and the subsequent student protest at the end of 1967 became the prelude to a revolution in the leadership of CPCz, which prefigured the events known as the Prague Spring. But this is to run ahead of ourselves in the story. First we must ask how people organised their lives to survive under this old regime.

Of course, most people collaborated with the regime, maybe only by being passive, but that passivity was very important. In addition there were unknown, but probably large numbers who collaborated actively. The British journalist, Neal Ascherson, in writing on Eastern Europe, has pointed out that if you lift any flat stone, there are many slimy creatures living beneath it, and so it has proven to be under occupation in very many places. The national shame of the French was redeemed by de Gaulle's successful creation of the myth of resistance, a myth which could only be faced squarely and the true scale of collaboration in France revealed, forty years after the end of the war in the famous television programme *Le Chagrin et la Pitié*. Similarly, more poignantly and painfully, the Italian writer Primo Levi, who survived Auschwitz, explained in terms of sadness and without condemnation, how there had been a "grey area" in which victims in the concentration camps were tarnished and compromised, and actually helped to make the Death Camps run. What in Eastern Europe we should do about guilt and its management is something to which I shall return at the end of this chapter. Here I would merely observe that forty years seems to be a decent time to wait before shining bright lights under flat stones which have been lifted only so recently.

For those who did not collaborate in Czechoslovakia, there was only one other choice. This was to live two lives – or a split life. It became a part of everybody's psychology. Children from the age of 12, 13, 14, before they were allowed to go to the High School, had to understand absolutely perfectly that some things could be said at home, but that something completely different had to be said at school, and that they could not be mixed. You could not once make a mistake, because it would be your last mistake. We called this "The one chance psychology", because you were not allowed to make a single mistake. Living like this became a part of a way of life, part of the nation's understanding of the world.

In this system, you were humiliated by the regime. You were humiliated by its representatives down to the very lowest ranks. By every policeman in the street, by every clerk, by everybody who taught in the schools. Everybody who had even the smallest position of power was part of this system of mass humiliation. People learned to live with it. The regime understood that this perpetual humiliation, punctuated from time to time with demands for proof of loyalty, was the best method to keep the people silent. Everybody listened to The Voice of America, to the BBC and to Radio Free Europe and knew what was going on. But everybody also knew the price to be paid for not playing according to the rules and so held silence.

How, therefore did we maintain any semblance of public pride? Historically, the arts and the artists in Bohemia and Slovakia played an important role from the nineteenth century onwards. There was a rebirth of Nationalism in the central European States which were then under German or Austro-Hungarian influence. The Czechs, and to some extent the Slovaks as well, restored their pride in their national attitude to everything through the Arts. So, coming from this heritage, the Arts in Czechoslovakia always ran somewhat ahead of politics. And from that, logically and historically, artists were taken by the rest of the population to be something a bit special: the Nation's pride.

This was one of the most humiliating features in these last forty and, especially, the last twenty years, that hundreds of the most gifted artists – writers, actors, singers – were either forced to leave the country, or they had to be degraded even more than ordinary people because they had to play the roles of good Party members and loyal citizens. Millions who trusted them before, who remembered them from 1968, saw these beautiful people producing absolute rubbish.

The Prague Spring of 1968 was in a way prepared in the manner which I have just described. In 1967, there was a Writers' Union Congress at which they all boiled over. Kundera gave a moving speech about the culture and ideas which play the role of a ping pong ball between West and East. The Communists abolished the Writers' Union and a few months later the students went out in protest. It was enough. In 1968, the artists who catalysed the changes suffered the most in the purges. If you take the Writers' Union list in 1970 and compare it with that of 1968, on both lists are to be found several hundred names; but you find maybe ten which are common to both. The same thing happened in the other Arts, but it was the most extreme in literature. Louis Aragon talked of Czechoslovakia in those years as a "Biafra of the thought". And so it was.

In '68, the Party controlled all aspects of life more or less completely; yet it was from within the Party that the first visible signs of reform emerged. With the abolition of censorship society began to find out about the many political prisoners. Some prisoners had been released gradually during the previous few years. But only in 1968 were the last ones released. The dissemination of this knowledge stimulated people, especially writers and students, to question widely, and for the first time, whether the Party was an absolute and infallible force. This feeling was strengthened by the burgeoning public debate about economic reform, which plainly demonstrated the incompetence of the Party *Apparat* to deliver what it had promised. So in a way, this Czechoslovakian experience prefigured Gorbachev's *Glasnost* by twenty years.

The Party *Apparat* reacted quite logically. It could not cope with public discussion and so it conspired against its own people and its own country by asking for Soviet military intervention to crush the flowering of the Prague Spring.

I remember a great deal of optimism before the intervention. Dubcek and the reformist Communist leadership were solidly and creatively part of this reform; and perhaps naively, perhaps just because we were used to the fact of state power, we tended to believe that if the "Commanding Heights" of the system were going our way, we had made the most difficult part of the journey. We used to joke that, "the water is now only up to our knees!"

Everybody of any public stature in Czechoslovakia, the cream of our intelligentsia as well as a broad swathe of general public opinion, backed the reform movement. Our mistake was simple and fatal. We failed to realise that for Brezhnev's Soviet Union it was impossible. It was unacceptably threatening for our spring-time to mature into full summer. The Czechoslovaks stood as a constant and potent rebuke to their system; and the worst of it was that the Party structure itself was in the vanguard of reform.

August 21 – the arrival of the Russian tanks – came as a complete shock. After the Bratislava meeting there had been a general impression that Dubcek had held, maybe even stabilised the situation; that we could still carry on along our own road. I returned to Prague on the last BEA flight to come from England, on the night of 20 August. I was a student at that time. When I woke up on the 21st, there were tanks in front of my house. Friends telephoned to tell me what had happened elsewhere. I didn't believe it, but it was true. In fury, people tried to block the entrance to Prague Radio with a makeshift barricade of buses and trucks. The tanks rolled over them and drove at the crowd. There were dead and wounded.

We were ready to do anything, but we were told to do nothing. Dubcek and the reformist leadership were kidnapped and taken to Moscow in handcuffs, where they were humiliated and imprisoned. President Svoboda announced that he was going to go to Moscow for "talks". What talks? We believed that it was a victory. We thought that he might convince the Soviets that the occupation had been a mistake. When·they all came back, still in their positions, we still hoped that we would be able to continue somehow.

In the coming months, the leadership proved to be weaker than we might have feared. It was unwilling to use the popular support it had. It lied to the people. It was supine before the attacks of the most hated collaborators and conservatives in the Communist Party. By the end of the year, we finally understood that hope of retaining intact any shred of the reforms of the Spring were dead.

The self-immolation of Jan Palach on 15 January 1969 near the statue of St Wenceslas in Wenceslas Square traumatised the nation. Nothing like this had happened before. He was immediately compared to Jan Hus, the great Protestant martyr who was burnt at the stake in 1415. This was the end of any illusion. We learnt from this that the Party cannot be reformed.

Today, one often asks the question, what is the difference between the Prague Spring of 1968 and the Prague Autumn of 1989? I think that while twenty years ago it was predominately a matter of a crisis of legitimacy within the governing Communist elite in one country of the Communist bloc, in 1989 it concerned a phenomenon of a greater degree. It was the Czechoslovak variant of the crisis of legitimacy of the whole Communist system.

In 1968, only rarely was the leading role of the Party in question in the practice of reform. The party intelligentsia alone led the reform process. It did so with vigour and with genuine commitment. Society, paralysed by twenty years of Stalinism, was unable within a brief eight months, before the August occupation, to generate an alternative programme and movement; there was no power base from which this could have been done. The collapse of the Party elite, around which the nation emotionally united in the days of August, their inability to resist politically and to rely on the virtually absolute support of the citizens, those were causes of the abrupt ending of the Prague Spring. The terrified leadership of the Communist Party of Czechoslovakia could not even partially institutionalise reform; and, without resistance, by April 1969, it had vacated its position for the so-called "normalisation" led by Gustav Husak. In the purges that followed, about half a million Party members were purged and about eight hundred thousand lost their jobs. From that moment on, the CPCz established itself in opposition to the nationalist and humane forces within society, and so aligned itself with the position taken by the other East European Communist parties. This Party could no longer reform. Henceforth, it could only control the people through corruption and fear. The word 'reform' was a curse. The prospect of any solution of basic economic and social problems from that source evaporated.

Humiliation was the watch-spring which actuated Husak's Orrery over the last twenty years. Everybody was at some moment in their life put into a situation of dire choice: to prove their loyalty to the regime by humiliating themselves or to lose everything. Everybody knew what everything meant, for "everything" was defined with a delicate cruelty by the Husak regime. It meant to lose not only your own career, but to blight the future of your children, because they would not be allowed to attend University.

After I was thrown out of my teaching job at the Gymnasium, I had this experience myself. At that time, my wife and I were living in Southern Bohemia. I looked around the town for another job, which of course had to be a manual job – I was forbidden to teach. I did so for a month. Then a Party official told me that I would only be allowed to work outside the town. They intended to drive me out of town, quite literally. So I spent two years as a stable hand in a racing horse stable ten miles from town, riding back and forth on a motorcycle, seven days a week. When my first daughter was born, I wanted to be closer to my family and was allowed to become a fork-lift truck driver, sweeper and general labourer in a factory in town.

After two more years of this sort of life, I began to have problems with the State Police again. I was interrogated and given offers to emigrate. We decided to move to Prague in an attempt to hide in the crowds. It was not easy, and some of our friends did emigrate during that time, given the possibility.

Those of us who were not able to play the game according to the regime's rules, learned not to judge the others, because we found out how easy it is to break down and how easy it is to blow up. I always say that in my personal case, when it came to the critical moment when the other side asked me to prove my loyalty, they simply went too fast and I exploded without thinking of the consequences.

It was at the end of January 1977. I was teaching History and Civics. All state employees (including teachers) were suddenly asked to sign "voluntarily" a petition of condemnation of Charter

77. At that time, no one actually knew the text of the Charter: it hadn't been published (nor was it, until the end of 1989). The whole thing was simply a crude, mass test of loyalty: don't think; don't ask; just sign. The Party Knows Best.

The newspapers carried libellous articles, defaming Charter 77 signatories, some of whom I knew personally. I just couldn't believe those things about them. They were called, "those who poisoned the wells" and "plague disseminators". I couldn't sign their "voluntary" petition. In the evening the Director of the school tried to persuade me that it was not only for my own good but for the good of the school that I should sign. I refused. I defended myself by saying that it was immoral to protest against an unknown text. I was afraid to say that I knew some of the Charter people. Ten days after my refusal, in the middle of one of my lectures, I was summoned to the Director's office where I was handed a piece of paper which informed me that I was to leave the school premises forthwith and not to return. Shortly after that, I was interrogated for the first time in my life, and several times in quick succession, by the State Police on my contacts with anti-state activists.

In retrospect, I think that if they had been calmer, or more intelligent, tried to be a little more friendly .....what do I know? I could have been one of them. Maybe, maybe not. They helped me by being so stupid. They made it so easy. The way they acted forced me to explode and the explosion blew me across to the other side of the barricade. One loses one's work and finds then that it becomes, strangely, very easy. The world becomes black and white. One begins to play one's role on the other side of the barricade.

In the past few years, we have become used to calling our country "Absurdistan". The tradition of Franz Kafka and Jaroslav Hasek has loomed ever larger as the ideological blindness of the Jakes regime propelled Czechoslovakia into crisis. In the years after '68, the problems intensified and the knot tightened. In the course of twenty years, out of a population of fifteen million, almost half a million Czechoslovaks emigrated. According to the then existing laws, they thereby committed a crime and were forbidden to return. The Husak regime offered its citizens a strange contract: you remain silent and we shall worry about a stable standard of living. Don't ask how and don't probe into the future. For very many the split lives and the humiliation went on, especially after Gorbachev came to power. You could see it especially at the beginning of the 1980s. These were for us the most dark and desperate years.

People went to the cinema or to the theatres and they reacted there in a way which was a symptom of occupation. It is how the older generation describe the years of Nazi occupation. In the darkness of cinema or theatre hall, people reacted freely because they were hidden, masked by the darkness. They laughed and reacted to absolutely innocent phrases. Everything was ambiguous and everything was taken in an anti-regime way. When the lights went on, you could see again those grey, closed faces, humiliated people who had been happy for a while. It went on and on with no prospect of an end.

Meanwhile, the Communist regime was finding it increasingly difficult to keep its side of the Faustian bargain with the people. With the example of Poland before its eyes, the Czechoslovak leadership refused to take loans from abroad. Over twenty years, it nevertheless created a painful internal debt. It invested insufficiently, so the structure and equipment of industry became unmaintainable. The transportation system was old, services undeveloped and the natural environment was devastated so that we began to live on a more expensive kind of credit, consuming the time and the wealth which should belong to our children.

The old regime neglected investment in our children as well as in our factories and railways. Czechoslovakia, which always prided itself on the education of its citizens, today has one of the lowest per capita expenditures for education in Europe. In terms of the proportion of the population with a post-secondary school education, we have been surpassed by Nepal. We who, with reason, were proud of the quality of our Health Services, have to admit that the mortality rate is growing and that on the average we have a shorter life span then the vast majority of inhabitants of Europe.

But at the beginning of the 1970s, a focal point of resistance began to coalesce at the centre of the area in which the battle would be fought. After several political show trials, the opposition concentrated itself in the cultural area, which appeared to the regime to be the most dangerous. Given what I have written already, it should now come as no surprise to learn that this was so. It is in the Arts that our deepest politics are played in Czechoslovakia, and out of a battle in the Arts that the movement which mobilised a further generation of Czechs, including myself, came into being.

Under the increasing pressure of the State Security forces, theatre was being performed in private flats, banned rock and roll groups performed in barns in the countryside, and in the cities, *samizdat* (the secret reproduction and illicit distribution of banned texts) was growing. In 1975, Czechoslovakia signed the Helsinki Final Act. This gave the opposition a legal argument for speaking out in public. When the clash came, the pretext was the imprisonment of the musicians of the underground pop group "The Plastic People of the Universe". A broad coalition of people, having the most varied political opinions and beliefs, from former functionaries of the CPCz to Catholics, spoke out in defence of these musicians' right to free artistic expression.

In this way, in January 1977, Charter 77 came into being. It was a historic moment. People, humiliated to the point of desperation about their own powerlessness, were no longer able to remain silent and to hide. They had no other option but to offer themselves to the regime as victims of human conscience against violence.

The inspiration for the birth of Charter 77 was obviously also the Polish KOR (the Committee for the Defence of Workers). The regime unleashed a vicious campaign of intimidation and slander against the signatories of Charter 77: Imprisonment, beatings, and hundreds sacked from their jobs (including myself). At the majority of workplaces in Czechoslovakia, people obligatorily signed a protest against the "anti-socialist pamphlet", whose content no one knew and these signed lists were taken to the Party Secretariats. Political *apartheid* again got the opportunity to test the loyalty of its subjects and made an example of the disobedient. It was the bull-headed crudeness of this tactic which pitched me over the wall into Dissidence, the loss of my teaching job, and everything which has now lead to my present task and responsibilities.

However, thanks to the international solidarity which grew as a result of the Helsinki Declaration on Human Rights, the political trials became uncomfortable for the regime. There could never again be so many of them as to frighten the opposition into passivity. In fact, the trials became the absurd barometer of the simultaneous softening and toughening of the political situation in Czechoslovakia at the end of the seventies and all through the eighties.

Gorbachev and *perestroika* changed the situation in a fundamental way. It accelerated the erosion of the system in all Eastern European countries. The Czechoslovak leadership, however, which took its legitimacy from the Brezhnevite occupation, became increasingly isolated and derided, not least for its attempts to talk about *Prestavba* – our *Perestroika*. It answered in the only way it knew – with increased repression.

In August 1988, on the day of the twentieth anniversary of the Soviet occupation, in keeping with what had already become a tradition, several dozen of the more active dissidents were temporarily detained or kept under surveillance at their cottages. No one believed that anything could happen in a city overflowing with police. But on that occasion, suddenly, the streets of Prague were streaming with demonstrators. I remember the panic at the police station where they were holding me. The policeman didn't want to believe the news coming from their police radios, which I overheard from the neighbouring detention room. All of us, policemen, politicians, dissidents, had simply forgotten that twenty years is enough time for a new generation to grow up.

The opposition left their flats for the streets, and then it was only a matter of time. The demonstrations occurred with clockwork regularity, and the increased violence of the police had as its consequence the acceleration of resistance and international protest. Even hitherto corrupt and silenced groups of scholars, scientists and artists, and increasingly, even the members of the CPCz, openly began to turn against the regime.

Meanwhile, for those of us who were declared dissidents, life was becoming more varied. From the end of 1987, we Czech dissidents had concluded that it wasn't enough to make links with groups in the West, welcome as that was. We had to develop a broader context, and even co-operation, with dissidents in other parts of Eastern Europe. From 1988 we had occasional contact with the Polish dissidents. But now we understood that we had to think about joint approaches. So we began to meet regularly with the Poles – Adam Michnik, Jacek Kuron and others – in the mountains on the border. We filmed our woodland picnic and sent it to the Western media, who screened it on television, because we wanted to show that we were now starting a new phase of co-operation.

I myself had gone to Moscow in December 1987 for the First International Independent Human Rights Seminar, organised by Press Club Glasnost. I met there with Lev Timofeev, Andrei Sakharov and other prominent Soviet human rights activists. By participating together with the Soviets in such a public manner, we presented an insoluble conundrum for the Husak regime: not to arrest me for such a flagrant defiance was a mistake; but equally to arrest me for meeting with Andrei Sakharov at a time of Gorbachev's *Glasnost*, would be an even bigger one!

To increase the effect of our activities, we launched a so-called "Eastern European Information Agency" which immediately became a great success. We were hated and quoted everywhere, even by the official Czechoslovak mass media. From now on, whatever happened in Eastern Europe, we consulted with our friends in the neighbouring countries and were able with them to publish joint comments on events. In all these ways we gradually fused our different efforts into a joint struggle.

In January 1989, we had a demonstration in Prague and some people including Vaclav Havel, were arrested for attempting to lay flowers at the place where Jan Palach had immolated himself in 1969. Both the immolation and the honouring were symbolic for Czechoslovaks. I think that it was at this moment that it became too much for the people of Art. They started to cross the shadow line. They started to enter the new era: not becoming dissidents, not wanting to take risks; but they couldn't go on being silent. They started to sign petitions against Havel's trial. There was an explosion of petitions. Thereafter, we dissidents were absolutely confident that in the moment of crisis, when it came, they would be on our side. Close personal links and friendships were formed at that time.

The open co-operation between dissident groups from various East European states were transformed in a dramatic and incongruous way by the other revolutions of 1989. From illicit forest picnics, we moved to open collaboration between Czechoslovak dissidents and representatives of the Governments and Parliaments of Poland, Hungary, and the Soviet Union. Adam Michnik and Zbygniew Bujak came to Prague in July 1989 as representatives of the Polish *Sejm* (parliament). The StB (the Secret Police) could only stand by and film the meetings! Andrei Sakharov telephoned us from Moscow. The Polish and Hungarian Parliaments condemned the participation of their military units in the occupation of 1968 about which even some Soviet newspapers began to write critically. In the late summer, two waves of East German refugees came through a shocked Prague.

Twice in one month, the streets of the Mala Strana district, near the West German Embassy were clogged with East German cars. Rows of Trabants and Wartburgs, many of them with the ignition keys left in them, were just abandoned. Remember that these cars were prized possessions of people many of whom would have waited and saved for ten years to get one. Hundreds of people also streamed from the railway station to the Embassy. For us locals, it was very moving. They walked with fixed intent, those East German refugees, quite uninterested in the beauties of Prague; and there was nothing we could do for them except to try to show them where best to cross the Czech Police lines surrounding the Embassy building. They were climbing over the walls of the Embassy gardens, handing up their children to others above. Many people cried in the streets.

Very soon the Embassy was full and hundreds of them had to sleep outside. The Czechs gave them hot tea and blankets and allowed them to use their toilets. That was all that we could do for them; but we understood that if they succeeded in escaping to the West, it would be the end of the illusion of impregnability of the system in which they, and we, then lived. Twice in one month, train loads of East German refugees left Prague for the West. The buses which transported them from the Embassy to the railway station were cheered by hundreds of Czechs in the streets, showing them the "V for Victory" sign.

Poland, Hungary and now East Germany were moving. What about us? On the 9th November 1989 the Berlin Wall was breached. Now it was completely clear that Czechoslovakia would be the next on the list. I returned to Prague on the 14th November after three weeks absence. It was to a completely different city from the one I had left. The atmosphere was electric. We knew that the Husak regime was desperate enough and isolated enough to contemplate the use of force which, we knew, Honecker had wished to do, but had been restrained from doing, in October in Berlin.

There were two small demonstrations in the streets on the 15th November, one about environmental issues and the other commemorating the second anniversary of the Brasov massacre in Romania. Both ended with minor clashes with plain-clothes police who behaved with considerable individual brutality. But many of us expected the 17th to be a crucial day. This was because on that day an officially permitted student march, commemorating the fiftieth anniversary of the Nazi crushing of the Czech student movement in 1939, would take place. We thought it might be a turning point. For the Husak regime, it would present another and more critically insoluble conundrum: to forbid the march would be to invite direct comparison between themselves and the Nazis. To allow it, it was already clear, would run the risks of thousands protesting against them in the streets. What would they do?

On the 17th November special units surrounded a part of the student demonstration in the middle of Prague. After an hour's wait, during which no one was permitted to leave, the marchers were atrociously beaten. There was blood in the streets. During the night of the 17th, rumours about deaths spread through the city. It will never be proven for certain whether there were deaths on that day. But there are eye-witnesses claiming to have seen up to three corpses lying in the street.[1]

1 Editor's note: More information on this matter has come to light since this chapter was written. The report of the new government Commission investigating the

But whatever the truth, the rumours hugely inflamed public anger against the regime. On the following day, students of DAMU (The School for the Dramatic Arts) suggested to other University faculties that they should initiate a strike. This was joined unexpectedly in the afternoon by an absolute majority of Czech theatres.

On the 18th, an actor friend took me to their meeting in one of the Prague theatres. When I got there I was astonished to find four hundred actors, maybe more, from all parts of the country. They had been telephoning throughout the night of the 17th. They had

---

activities of the StB, chaired by Milan Hulik explains some of the questions in this paragraph. Not everything is yet explained, but interviews with former senior members of the StB were among sources which together propose the following, remarkable account. The Hulik Commission suggests that the course of events on 17th November was carefully planned and orchestrated jointly by General Lorenz, Head of the StB, in collaboration with the KGB. Their plan was to create the violence in which the marchers were beaten in Narodni Street. To this end, *agents provocateurs* who were actually StB officers but posing as student leaders led the demonstrators into the confined space where the beatings took place. One of the StB officers then impersonated a mathematics student, Martin Smid and a further conspirator, Dragomira Drazska, carried the news of Smid's supposed death at the hands of the security forces to dissident sources. Reports, authenticated by photographs and by many eye witnesses, of the appearance of a mysterious ambulance which removed one of the "corpses" seen in the street were, it is suggested, observing the removal of one of the StB lieutenants faking the death of the student. The purpose of this elaborate charade was then later, the next day, to be able to discredit the dissident news agency run by Petr Uhl, one of the leaders of Charter 77, by demonstrating that in fact the student was not dead. Indeed, two "Martin Smids" were produced on State television on 19th November. But this was only a secondary purpose. The primary purpose was to cause the overthrow of the Jakes and Husak regime as a result of popular fury and to open the way for the installation of a moderate reformist communist, Zdenek Mlynar as president in place of Husak. If this was the intention, it certainly bears marked similarity to the substitution of Krenz for Honecker in the DDR. At the time of writing, the degree of Soviet involvement in either case is not known, although the BBC report on Mlynar asserts that he went to Moscow where Mr Gorbachev, with whom he had been a student and friend in the 1950s, failed to persuade him to take office. The conspiracy failed firstly because Mlynar did not wish to take on the role and secondly because the popular revolution developed its own momentum and found its own authentic presidential candidate in Vaclav Havel. The story of the involvement of the StB and KGB, based on the Hulik Commission's preliminary findings, have been reported in *The Independent*, especially by Edward Lucas 15 May, and broadcast on BBC Television in a programme written by the BBC Diplomatic Correspondent, John Simpson on 30th May 1990, entitled *Czech Mate*. The basic facts of the Smid story were published in *Facts on File*, 24 November 1989, p.879.

told the others that they had all to come to Prague to decide what to do. After two hours discussion they had decided to go on strike. It was a crucial moment, because not only in Prague, but also in twenty five cities in Bohemia and Moravia there were immediately theatre buildings with great posters on them: "We Strike". Everyone knew why.

In a country like Czechoslovakia where, as I have tried to explain, actors and people of Art have great moral authority, when they choose to exert it, no government can survive. So in all of those places, the actors' strike and the students played the role of the nuclei of the uprising. Different University faculties in different cities did the same. Within twenty four hours, the uprising had several dozen points of support across the entire Republic, and another twenty four hours later, it had its own political representation, for in one of Prague's theatres, Civic Forum came together.

Thousands of students and hundreds of actors rushed in cars from Prague everywhere, talking to meetings. I am certain that frightened people in towns somewhere outside Prague were changed into an organised and concentrated party, nerved at the moment when a famous actor stood in front of them and said to them, "Listen people, enough is enough. Now we go against the regime!" So they went.

I ran from the theatre meeting with two declarations: one from the students and one from the actors, each announcing their strikes. I telephoned the texts to Radio Free Europe and the Voice of America. There wasn't time to do more because we heard what turned out to be three unmarked State Police cars roaring towards the cul-de-sac where we lived. I quietly slipped away over the roof-tops. Eight friends who remained in my flat were detained upon leaving. Two Poles were immediately expelled, not even given the chance to collect their belongings.

I crossed the river and went at once to another theatre (in fact, the one where Vaclav Havel began his career as a stage-hand). I explained in Russian and in English from the stage to the audience the reasons why the actors were going on strike. I did this because it was supposed to be the tourist performance of a pantomime. To our surprise, none of the foreigners protested! Then began a long period of sleeplessness for us all. That night we discussed the means of co-operation with the student leaders.

On 19th November, Havel having just returned to Prague, we discussed in his flat the genesis of what later that evening became Civic Forum; for in yet another of Prague's theatres (the reader will by now really understand the centrality of the life of the theatre in our culture, and how important it is to have many theatres!), about four hundred people spanning the entire spectrum of political opinion, formed a united opposition of that name. I myself was not at that founding meeting in the evening, although I had been at the flat in the morning. I was trapped in another theatre, which was surrounded by the State Police. Again, this time with the help of the actors, I was able to escape. They blocked the entrance to the passageway and I sprinted down it and away to hide. This was the last time that I saw them face-to-face.

After two days of constantly changing the headquarters of the newborn Civic Forum, we realised that the Art Galleries which we had been using were not suitable. One was too small and in another, we couldn't control the entrance. So we ended up, again, in a theatre. This time, it was called "The Magic Lantern." We chose it because it was right in the centre of Prague, near Wenceslas Square. It had many small rooms suitable for offices and a huge stage for meetings and daily press conferences. The name "The Magic Lantern" has become something of a short-hand for what was done during those crucial days. Somehow it seems very appropriate that from a place with such a name we negotiated with the collapsing Communist regime, which had so prostituted democracy that Prague people commonly described the Parliament as "something between the Theatre and the museum" (the buildings which flank it). We used to meet them on neutral soil in *Obecni Dum* - the building where in 1918 the original declaration of independence was signed.

To stay in a place like The Magic Lantern was a desperate but very logical move. We knew perfectly well that a few dozen riot police could have taken us in five minutes: we were not barricaded in. But from the first moment, we wanted to be aggressively non-violent in our stance – to make a power of our lack of weapons. It worked, even during the mass demonstrations when a quarter of a million people were in the streets. Someone invented a slogan: "He who throws the first stone is a provocateur." There were no stones thrown. It was magic in the streets.

Meanwhile, down in The Magic Lantern, sixty to eighty people were working twenty four hours a day, divided into groups and conducted by a steering group around Vaclav Havel. Some people were preparing for the General Strike. The objective of the Strike had been set in the very first student declaration. Others were preparing the opposition programme, later called, "What we Want."

There was also what was called the Crisis Group. This was the busiest group and the one with which Havel spent most of his time. It was located in "Number Ten Wardrobe". This wardrobe room was the real heart of the revolution. The Crisis Group had the responsibility of analyzing the intelligence coming into The Magic Lantern and of taking tactical decisions.

We also had a Media Monitoring Group and a Liaison Group for the students, artists and actors. We had printing facilities and (which was rather important) a Catering Department. To co-ordinate all these different groups was the H.P.V. Department (*Holka Pro Vsechno* – literally the "Girl Friday" Department). This is what I ran. We had to do whatever was needed. So we negotiated with the Soviet Embassy one moment and we found clean shirts for people, another.

All this we had in place within two days of entering The Magic Lantern. On 24th November, Alexander Dubcek, who had made his first major public speech since 1969 at Bratislava two days before, appeared in Prague with Vaclav Havel. Before they went on to the balcony Marta Kubisova, the singer who had been the voice of '68 and who had been forbidden to sing since then, preceded them and sang "The times, they are a changin'".

Just after seven o'clock that evening the Politburo resigned. Havel and Dubcek were in the middle of giving a press conference on the stage of the Magic Lantern when the news came. I was wearing a T-shirt. The slogan was "I'm Czechoslovak and proud of it!" I leapt on to the stage with a bottle of champagne and we all celebrated in front of the world's press.

The streets of Prague now took on, for the first time, the spirit of Carnival. People now dared to believe that the regime really would not use violence. The latent fear of the previous week was lifted like a cloud. The two-hour General Strike on the 27th was a pure celebration of the victory. It was amazingly successful, mobilising an entire cross-section of society across the country.

On the 3rd December, President Husak named the new Government, appointing fifteen Communists out of twenty. For him, this was the last throw of the dice. Civic Forum immediately announced the threat of a further General Strike unless the Government became properly representative. On the 9th December, Husak and the Communist Party leadership agreed to all our demands. The One-Party system ceased to exist. The absurdity of the situation became even clearer next morning when Husak, still President, had to appoint a Cabinet composed of those whom he most despised, including several freshly released political prisoners.

Shortly after that, Husak resigned and the Old Parliament abolished Clause 4 of the Constitution (on the "leading role" of the Communist Party). Husak and the Party leadership had fallen victim to what we in Eastern Europe call the old János Kadar syndrome. In the West, people tend to think of Kadar as a hard-liner who turns liberal: what the Americans call a "dovish hawk", like Nixon. But that is a misplaced analogy.

For us, Kadar was the first to demonstrate the inability of a Communist hardliner to manoeuvre in a tight situation when confronted by popular sentiment and unable to have resort to armed force. In this predicament, he lapsed into apathy and then just gave up. (Soon after being ejected from power, he died.) The same happened to other hardline leaders in Eastern Europe, most conspicuously to Honecker. It was evident that during his recuperation from surgery, his will to live collapsed.

With Husak gone, who would be President now? These were days when we had to re-think and change our strategy constantly, sometimes with a few hours' grace, sometimes only a few minutes. The entire political structure collapsed in front of our eyes. We didn't want to allow the state to collapse with it, so we had to act. There was no one else to do so. There were even moments when we had to support some Communist Party officials against whom we had just fought.

It was this sort of reasoning which eventually caused Havel to overcome his own deep reluctance and to accept that he had to go to the Hradcany Castle, as the crowds demanded ever more insistently, in chanting and in posters: "*Havel na Hrad!*" It was very risky. He was the symbol of hope for those who had made the revolution, but, because of twenty years of hostile propaganda against him, he was for many people who had read the old regime's newspapers or watched TV, the symbol of evil. But within a few days, it was plain that the positive symbol would prevail. On the 29th December, in St Vitus's Cathedral a Celebration Mass was held following Havel's installation as the President of Czechoslovakia.

I write this before the June 1990 election. In it, the Communist Party will, according to the most recent opinion polls, have great difficulty in surpassing the obligatory five percent threshold. In January 1990, only 8.7% of the voters would have voted for it, and its influence is constantly declining. The principal obstacles to the development of Czechoslovak democracy have now become on the one hand, the difficulties about introducing a market economy and on the other, the necessity of arousing interest in civil politics from below. The difficulty of this second problem must not be underestimated in a country where for so long the habits of participation in politics have been stifled.

In the remainder of this chapter, I shall turn my attention to the legacy of the Spring in Winter Revolution: possibilities and problems in creating afresh a legitimate civil society in Czechoslovakia. But before I do so, as a way of introducing the political and ideological context created by the 1989 revolution, it is useful to look for a last time at the comparison with 1968. That year, Czechoslovaks created spring in spring, and it was followed by winter in summer. In 1989, we created spring in winter and we must ask what our chances are of regaining a normal European cycle of political seasons hereafter.

It is, in a strange way, true that '89 was just '68 turned upside down, as one of the poster slogans put it; for the biggest difference between the Prague Spring and the Spring in Winter was on the place of reform in the rhetoric of dissent. In 1989, it just wasn't there.

I might be mistaken because I don't know much about China, but my understanding is that even the Tienanmen movement tried to use and incorporate the vocabulary of the regime within its own. That was the mistake of 1968 in Czechoslovakia. What was clear in 1989 was that this system could not be reformed. Its ideology could not be reformed. No one discussed doing this. It just didn't appear in any of the discussions about abolishing the leading role of the Communist Party. It was outside discussions. So this was the biggest advantage.

Loss of belief in any ideology has brought a renewed respect for facts. We feel that we have to pay attention to the facts and one has to try to be a realist. But that's not to say that ideas don't matter. In the building of our new perception, we have a playwright for a President who likes to use expressions like "velvet revolution" and "new beginning" and "prosperous Czechoslovakia". Sometimes it sounds funny. But the point is that no one is forced to believe it. No one controls you. This gives the possibility of being flexible, of trying different alternatives. Now, after the revolution, when we are not successful, we won't lose everything. You can say, "this was the wrong choice, let's try another way." Therefore we have a completely different situation.

You might on the one hand need a strong state as a tool and a referee. On the other, you have to wake up people to take their share of the responsibility. We don't feel that this is incompatible. But maybe it will be one of those wrong choices? We don't know, we have to try. We must find the mistakes in our history and in the history of the system we have lived through, and we must strive to avoid them in the future. We must find the sources of our recent victory as I have tried to do in this chapter so far and finally we must ask ourselves whether this victory is really definitive. We may have reached the end of Communist domination, but we must ask whether this means the end of the domination of totalitarian thinking in our country.

Civic Forum came into existence as "a self-defence task force". The phrase has a military ring and that was what we sought in so describing it, deliberately. There came a moment when we had to react and we were desperate enough not to count the cost. In a few hours we had created, from the far Left to the far Right, a coalition with only one goal: to get rid of Husak. No one would have believed it hearing a prediction that it would take us only one week. So there we were. We did it ourselves, and having done so, we found out that it was not enough. Now we had to change the whole system! We decided that the best way to achieve this was through free elections. This is the primary reason why the Civic Forum coalition continued to exist after the revolution had passed its first phase.

The second reason is that people in Czechoslovakia were not only fed up with politicians of any ideological stripe, but with politics as well. Politics were disregarded as a normal way of behaviour. Only morally depraved people went into a political career under the old regime, and so according to opinion polling in the spring of 1990, three quarters of the people supporting Civic Forum did not want it to become a political party. At the time of writing, we want to keep it a political movement, what I call a sort of "primary school" for politics and for politicians. We have eight small political parties within Civic Forum entering the June 1990 election on our canvas's list. We will help them to survive the elections, to get their people to Parliament and to give them time, in those two years of constituent assembly which we think will come from this election, to grow up, to build nation-wide stature and to go on. Then, from June to November 1990 we shall concentrate on municipal elections. We think Civic Forum will have to change tactics and to concentrate much more on regional politics. What comes after that, who knows? It depends on people and it depends on the political parties which will grow in the meantime.

To achieve this change we built a nation-wide network of what we called Civic Forum Election Campaign Centres. There are forty electoral regions in Czechoslovakia and the aim has been to create at least forty of these centres before the June 1990 campaign. Their purpose is to foster discussions with trained people, professionals skilled in organising elections, able to teach these techniques to other people. In these "primary schools" for politics will be offices with Xerox machines, fax machines and publicity means open to all the new political parties for their use. In this way they can recultivate their grass-roots political lives to permit the growth of local and regional politics and of local and regional politicians. We felt that it was not enough to destroy the old system from above by having a president and a few other of the active dissidents as ministers. Even more important was to destroy the system from below by destroying the fear and feeling that politics was abnormal.

This leads to an obvious question. What sort of society, what brand of politics do we want? I notice that many people in the West are full of advice to us on these subjects. I would make three observations. First, John Kenneth Galbraith is quite correct in his chapter earlier in this book to disabuse those who think that because we have thrown off the chains of Stalinism, we wish therefore to embrace naked, uncontrolled free-market Capitalism. As he says, rightly I think, very few, if any, Europeans, Western or Eastern, want that.

Personally I prefer to put it the other way around. There is much that we want and need from the West but there is one thing which I do not want: carelessness with people. The best that I took from those sufferings in my country; the best that I took from the Spring in Winter Revolution last November and the best that I took from meeting people like Andrei Sakharov was that they cared about others. I would like this caring to remain in my country. I would like society to care for its weak, its socially weak, its economically weak, its disabled. I would like there to be tolerance. I wish to be proud of having my gypsy friends. I do not want to be afraid that my neighbours would mind them visiting me.

So this raises the second question. Is Socialism viable in a country such as ours after Communism? In a country like Czechoslovakia, and especially in Bohemia, which at the beginning of this century possessed 60% of the total industry within the Austro-Hungarian Empire – a region which was often compared to the British industrial regions at that time – it is nonsense to think that Socialist thought or concerns for social welfare would disappear just because of forty years of Communism. Of course the idea of Left-Wing thought is compromised. But I am convinced that when it comes to economic difficulties, we shall find that feelings of social equality, the feeling that the state has a caring role to play and that society should take care of the weak, are still very strong.

I don't know what name it will be given, because the problem is that in Czechoslovakia after forty years of Communism we are really fed up with any "ism" at all. We like to do things; we like to change things; but we don't like to give names to things. So it might be called a Democratic Party; and viewed from outside it could be called a Social Democratic Socialist Party. A problem with names is that there is a Socialist Party hanging about which was, or it used to be for forty years, a lackey of the Communist Party. It now spends most of its time showing its anti-Communist attitude! Aside from this Socialist Party, there are other groups which are Left-Wing. But I must observe that before, or until we meet the real problems, the economic problems, it is much easier for them, and for all the forty parties that we now have, to speak about democracy, human rights, free market economy and not to specify their policies!

My third observation is that in so far as we can see a new sort of politics forming in Czechoslovakia, it is being driven by newly important issues of ecological and global security; and so none of the old rhetoric or language about "left" or "right" may be appropriate to describe it. However, to this matter I shall return towards the end of my chapter.

Havel writes in the preface to this book that honesty was a potent weapon in all the 1989 revolutions. It certainly was in our case, and the Playwright/ President embodied it both in his earlier sufferings under the old regime and in his refusal to become trapped in the trappings of office. Civic Forum was able to use his portrait in the election posters with the simple slogan, "Vaclav Havel Guarantees Free Elections". That promise from that man was powerful.

But honesty is not an unmitigated political blessing. Indeed, bureaucrats and corrupt politicians everywhere can hide in secrecy just because there are some issues which people prefer not to bring out into the open. Well, for better or worse, in Czechoslovakia, the Government created by the Spring in Winter

Revolution could not do this even if it wished it! It would deny everything that we stood for. So in consequence we must face the problems that were previously silent. Of these, the most entrenched is that of the national relations between Czechs and Slovaks.

In 1918 Czechoslovakia combined three major nationalities. The Sudeten Germans have now gone and we have two – Czechs and Slovaks. But still about 10% of the population is made up of smaller national minorities: Hungarians, Poles, Ukrainians, Gypsies. The latter had become for the first time in our history a racial problem. We have no experience of this, and it already becomes quite visible. It is logical that after forty years of pretending that there is no problem at all, problems appear on the surface and surprise a lot of people.

All kinds of things are possible. The ethnic violence seen in the USSR in Ngorny Karabakh is one extreme. We may expect anything from that extreme to the other and everything in between; for the situation in which we find ourselves is like that of swimmer who has swum too long under water. You feel as if you can't go on for another second. Your lungs feel about to burst. You kick and thrash your way to the surface and before you start breathing, you cough. You don't swim elegantly, you just cough. This was the experience that we have had as a consequence of the November revolution. For forty years we were taught that the Czechs and Slovaks were brothers, that all people were equal; that it was just the imperialist tradition that caused the nations to hate each other. When there were some small problems, it was either the fault of provocateurs or of uneducated people who still had the remnants of capitalism deep inside them. This was the reason why the gypsies were forcefully displaced and scattered among the majority populations in an attempt to educate and civilise them, not taking into account that theirs was simply a different culture.

Now the old regime has gone, but the new one is not established. We have surfaced; we cough; and all sorts of racial animosity comes up. We are horrified at how easy it is to inflame national feelings. We have no experience with these things.

The only positive result of 1968 was the so-called Federation System, which gave many more rights to the Slovak Republic than it had had before. Still, the Slovaks are not satisfied with the Federation and ask for much more equality, which is again quite logical and normal. It is combined with different historical and cultural experiences than those of the Czechs. Slovaks are traditionally much more deeply connected with the Catholic Church, while the Czechs feel the Catholic Church to have been the tool of German ambitions; so they tend to be either atheist or Protestant. Seventeenth-century German baroque churches in Prague are a witness to the attempts by the Jesuits to proselytise and Germanise the Czechs.

There is furthermore a problem with seven hundred thousand Hungarian minority people in southern Slovakia who have, strangely enough, had better relations with the Czechs in Bohemia than with the Slovaks, their nearest neighbours. To complete the ethnic picture, there is a problem in Moravia which is geographically and historically part of Czech-land; the people speak the same language, but with a slightly different accent. Following the Revolution, the Moravians all of a sudden demanded a three-part federation which very much annoyed the Slovaks and made problems for the Czechs too. It was something like Yorkshire asking to have equal standing with Scotland, Wales and England in the United Kingdom. But nevertheless, we are trying to co-operate by moving some state institutions like the Supreme Court to Brno, which is the capital of Moravia.

When economic difficulties come, as they surely will, the first social groups who lose their positions are women and ethnic minorities: unqualified labour which, in Czechoslovakia, means principally gypsies. We could have up to one hundred thousand unemployed gypsies. This is alarming because the state cannot destroy itself by allowing such potential unrest. We have already had early signs of such danger. In the winter of 1989 there was something close to a pogrom in Slovakia. The only thing that we, the new government, could do, was to ask the Church to talk to the people and to convince the heads of Slovak television to show the film "Gandhi". We then tried to convince our Slovak friends that we had to hold a conference on these matters; that they had to have open and frank talks about all of these differences. We asked Havel to go there and use his moral authority, not to tell people "come, you are brothers", but to tell them to talk about their differences.

I have written at length, and frankly, about this question. It may be the first time in recent memory that a public figure in Czechoslovakia has done so in this manner. But I do it deliberately because, looking around, we see that to leave these problems unsolved, not to speak about them, would be the biggest mistake. So we try to be absolutely frank and open about our ethnic and regional differences in order to avoid violence especially tragedies like Ngorny Karabakh in the Soviet Union.

In fact, I am not pessimistic about solving the problems of the nationalities, because Slovaks played an active and early role during Spring in Winter, in contrast to the situation in 1968. The Western press sometimes gives the impression that the revolution was all Czech. This was not so. That impression came from the fact that all the Western journalists were concentrated in Prague and were too lazy to drive the four hours to Bratislava!

As I have already observed, the fact is that Slovaks, to a certain extent, were quite happy with the results of 1968 because they got their Federation. There were virtually no purges in Slovakia because we always say that in Slovakia, "everybody is everybody else's cousin". It is a joke, but to a certain extent only. So there were very few dissidents in Slovakia. But things started to change in 1987. In that year, there was an upsurge in the Catholic Church because of Poland. The Jakes/Husak regime was stupid enough then to beat some of the Catholic demonstrators. And again, the people of Art became "oppositionary".

In November 1989, everything began in Prague because of the concentration of dissidents and because of the theatre strike. We understood that is was impossible to play this game without the Slovaks, yet we were astonished by the speed with which that happened. It took only one day and the Slovak theatres were on strike as well; it was three days after the foundation of Civic Forum in Prague, Public Against Violence was organised in Slovakia. The Slovaks achieved tremendous things in a very short time. At some moments they went even faster than Civic Forum because, "everybody is everybody else's cousin"! There was co-operation even in the revolutionary days because at those most important round table talks, we always had spokesmen from Public Against Violence with us. This co-operation has continued. I think that relations between Czech and Slovak democrats have never been better then they had become by early 1990. I think that the present reality is very good for Czechoslovak co-operation.

Honesty demands that we are open about our ethnic and nationalist problems. It also demands that we face squarely another issue, a common inheritance of all the post-Communist governments of Eastern Europe. What are we to do with the servants of the old regime; and, equally interesting, what will they do with us? That in turn is linked to another common worry. Could Soviet tanks again restore the old regime?

One wondered at the time whether our new government was brilliant or whether it was foolish to give the State Security Police two months notice before abolition in February 1990. Giving them two months meant that the really tough hardliners had time to hide, to run from the country or to prepare for conspiracy. No doubt there were some of them who were sufficiently unrealistic to do so. But they had no chance. It would have made sense if they had believed that the pre-Gorbachev Soviet Union could bring back all the old guard of the Communist Party, riding on their tanks. This fear was widely common in the first two months after November 17th. As time went on, it seemed more and more unrealistic. So sometimes I think, with a smile, about someone sitting, hiding somewhere in a flat, and dreaming about conspiracy. I don't exclude that there might be someone like that hiding somewhere; but the longer he stays there, the less chance he will have of a decent job afterwards, for we shall, very soon, face some kind of unemployment. It will not be the best of qualifications to have been a Secret Policeman.

I wrote above quite firmly that the fear of a repetition of August 1968 had evaporated. Not least, this is because even in the event of the worst outcome within the USSR, we believe that neither the will nor the means exist to reconquer Europe – even us. We see it in our interests, however, to maximise the chances of the *best* outcome. This is the reason why Havel himself, a person who lost a lot because of the Soviet occupation, said in the US Congress on the 21st February 1990, that the best way to help Czechoslovakia was to help democracy in the Soviet Union. It may sound absurd, but it is the central European way. This is the reason why we use our contacts from the past with the Soviet dissidents to try to get as much information as possible from there, and to get as much information about our experience to them. We wish to tell them how easy it is in some parts of the world to get rid of a Communist regime when you wait for the right moment and when you use no violence to provoke violence on the other side.

The other part of our tactic is to strive not for the extinguishing, but for the normalisation of economic relations with the USSR. We think that it is in the powerful interests of the Soviet Union to show its goodwill to world opinion. This may be done by letting Eastern European countries do what they want. Gennadi Gerasimov has famously named this the "Sinatra Doctrine" ("I did it my way...!"). I think we all in Eastern Europe are realist enough to understand that at the very least for economic reasons, it is unwise to get rid of such a good and huge market as the USSR for our goods, which are still of low quality by world standards. Who else would buy them? This is the reason why we have agreed to conduct trade with the Soviet Union in hard currency. Believe me, it is very hard to trade in hard currency when you don't have it! But it is the only way, and by this we put our context economically and politically on a normal basis, a visible, countable basis; and we suddenly become partners.

Such a policy has a military security dimension also. On the removal of Soviet troops, we agreed immediately with them that they were to withdraw. Later on we believed it when the Soviets proved that it was technically impossible to send seventeen hundred trains with military equipment and personnel to the Soviet Union before the end of December 1990 using one railway station at our Eastern border. There we had to re-load everything because the Soviet railway has a different gauge to ours. Our experts calculated matters and it is indeed impossible to re-load more than four trains in one day. The Hungarians are also removing Soviet troops from Hungary, using partly this same railway station, which leaves only three trains a day for Czechoslovakia. Then it is a matter of simple arithmetic. So in a time when we are sure that the Soviets want to remove their troops, not only because of our bilateral contacts, we can be generous and wait a bit longer. Furthermore, since we count our trade in hard currency, the USSR has to pay for the upkeep of their soldiers in hard currency.

So if, for these reasons, we did not fear what the servants of the old regime might dream of doing to us, the question remains of what we did with them. The short answer is that we used them. No one had anticipated the speed with which the old regime collapsed. We had to take power. We didn't want to participate in taking the ministries and taking a share of power before the elections, but the old regime collapsed so fast that we had to. So, as we say, we had to "parachute" our people to the top posts in the ministries. Remember that for forty years those ministries were deliberately filled with Communists. Thus we had Jiri Dienstbier, a dissident, becoming the Foreign Minister. A few hours after being named in the afternoon by the President, he had to run to his former working place to stoke his boiler, because they had not found a replacement for him yet. Dienstbier was alone in the Ministry with about twelve hundred Communists, Communists who were perhaps the worst sort because they were intelligent servants of the old regime.

He called all of them together and he said to them, "We all know the rules. But I want to tell you that from now on, I will count only your results. We all know that the State Security people have had to leave this Ministry. There is no hesitation about that. But for the rest of you, I want proof of your loyalty to the new government shown by hard work. Again, let me say that I will only count results." As a consequence, the inherited civil servants work harder than ever to prove that they are solely state employees, purely professionals. It happened in Portugal in the same way after 1974, and in Spain after Franco. If they can do it, why can't we? Always the young officers were the most loyal to the regime because they wanted the higher positions of the really compromised dismissed officers; and it has happened in this way in Czechoslovakia as well.

In Czechoslovakia, as in much of the rest of Eastern Europe, we have inherited an industrial Rust Belt and a natural environment ravaged from forty years of scornful and systematic abuse. Earlier, I raised the question often put to us of what sort of politics we wanted. I postponed until now a fuller comment on the "New Politics" which I think will follow from the Spring in Winter Revolution.

Pollution in our country is appalling. In parts of Northern Bohemia, parents are obliged to sign an undertaking when removing a newborn child from the hospital. This is an undertaking not to allow him or her to drink tap water for one year. Imagine! We accepted and bureaucratised such poisoning. In Northern Bohemia (along with Silesia) there is said to be worse pollution than in any other part of Eastern Europe. According to opinion polls, the situation is so bad that the majority of the people, 62%, think that ecological problems are *more* worrying than economic problems; and close to the same number think that ecological problems should be solved *before* economic problems. It gives you an idea of how broadly informed on ecological problems the population is.

We have high infant mortality. This becomes a very direct political problem because we do not have the resources to solve it. We have to get the people to understand that the Government is trying to help them, but our situation is extremely alarming. We have to make choices about how we shall improve our industrial sector. The choices will not be easy, nor will they be easily accepted – for people want both an improved standard of living and action on the environment, simultaneously.

Vaclav Havel is amazing. But we have a lot of problems with him, because he sometimes doesn't count the consequences. He is very fast. Coming to the most polluted area of Bohemia, he was greeted by crowds of people in the streets. It was at a time of very heavy air pollution, and they said, "Listen Mr President! It is splendid! For the past few months now we have been informed about the environmental situation here, which we were not before. That's fine, but the information is horrible. We are told that the children should not leave the houses; that people should not open their windows; that workers should not work too hard outside. What should we do, we who are paid for hard physical labour outside?" Without hesitating Havel replied, "If I were in your place, I would go on strike!"

Three days after that Mr Pithart, the Czechoslovakian Prime Minister came to the same area. The people said to him, "Listen Mr Prime Minister, you have thirty days in which to do something about this pollution. If you don't, we will go on strike, or we'll leave this region in droves." They were serious about it and we know perfectly well the situation. No, on second thoughts, we don't even know the situation. British producers of monitoring systems have complained to us about Eastern Europe and Czechoslovakia in particular. They say that their equipment is too finely calibrated for such levels of pollution! We simply don't have the money to pay to solve this.

This anecdote gives both the shape and scale of the challenge which the global and environmental security problems pose in political as well as in physical and economical terms. This is where I think we need specific and extensive Western aid. The aid is not just of money; indeed, unattached money we do not need anything like as much as we require "know-how" and specific technology which will help both abatement of pollution and cleaning up of poisoned land, water and air.

However, we are not just supplicants in this matter. We in Czechoslovakia are about to be, at least in this one point, pioneers for the whole of Europe. The Spring in Winter Revolution undermined a tired totalitarianism which fell in upon itself like an empty eggshell, once we pushed. So we have inherited the closest thing to a political *tabula rasa*. The Husak regime was peculiarly obnoxious and illegitimate in the eyes of Czechs and Slovaks for reasons I have explained. It humiliated us, and we struck back. Nowhere else in Eastern Europe has the old regime gone, leaving behind a country in a position and possessed of such a general will to construct a new society. So this is where we are ahead of the whole of Europe.

At the very moment when the new general agenda of global security is moving to the centre of international politics, Czechoslovakia is, in a way, and partly by chance, conducting the first great experiment in the politics of the twenty-first century in Europe. We are trying to create a new political discourse and to promote new political structures responsive to the new agenda. Our people have suffered much and this gives them a depth and a political maturity in which Civic Forum has confidence. So a major lesson of the 1989 Revolution has been the need to combine appropriate Western "know-how" and technology with a fierce desire for an ecologically sustainable improvement in material well-being and a proper grounding of our intellectual life in honest soils.

From this mixture, we may produce a model upon which other Europeans, West and East, may reflect. A slogan of Civic Forum in the June 1990 election was "Come with us back to Europe!" Czechoslovaks feel that they return home to Europe not as beggars, but with suffering and experience to offer. Quoting the economist Zeman at the beginning of this chapter, I wrote that, "we are like emaciated and beaten animals, released from the zoo and looking untrustingly at open country." This time, however, we know precisely what we do *not* want. Therefore we have a chance.

We changed it! We all have changed it! For the first time in the history of Czechoslovakia, we have escaped from that complex of being told by others that the Czechs are always given their victories, always given their liberation. This time it was completely our own victory. Because of the problems in our economy and ecology that we will be facing in the near future, we may safely predict that we shall have to pay a price. Punishment is the wrong word, but the price has an element of punishment within it. It is the price for forty years of silence, and it is fair to pay it. It is very fair that for the first time we all pay the same share. So I do not think that there is a need to investigate everybody's soul and everybody's personal history because this would cause only more stresses and more humiliation. Almost everybody became corrupted under the old regime because it was impossible not to be. There were a few hundred of us dissidents in a population of fifteen million. We knew the moment would come. The longer that it took, the more dramatic the change would be. It happens as it happens. We know that there are hundreds, perhaps thousands of deeply compromised people. Should we purge them? For what? This is the not the best way for our society to begin its new life.

Real problems are before us. It is the end of the simple role of dissidents. It is the end of secret meetings and of spectacular escapes along rooftops. Economic difficulties are awaiting us, clashes with dissatisfied workers, the challenge of environmental destruction. There will be nationalist frictions and the passion of the unsophisticated beginnings of a parliamentary democracy.

Sir Winston Churchill once said to Britons that he could not promise them anything other than blood, sweat and tears. Czechoslovakia was able to avoid the blood during the Spring in Winter Revolution; but the sweat and tears will obviously attend us for a long time yet. We cannot avoid them. It is necessary to pay the price of too long a silence. If Czechs and Slovaks accept this price without complaint and lamentation, it will be possible to admire them. Not sooner.

© Gabriella Bollobas

6 Jonathan Eyal

Why Romania could not avoid bloodshed

Dr Jonathan Eyal was educated at London and Oxford Universities. Aged 33, his initial training was in international law. He has also completed a Masters in international relations and a Doctorate at Oxford on ethnic relations in Eastern Europe.

After having taught students at Oxford for several years, he was appointed Research Fellow at the Royal United Services Institute for Defence Studies in London. His recent studies are on Warsaw Pact Military Expenditure (published by Janes *in London 1988) and Soviet Policies in the Balkans (to be published this year).*

He has contributed many articles to the Institute's publication as well as other periodicals such as The World Today, The Financial Times, The South Slav Journal, Janes Soviet Intelligence Review *and* Soviet Analyst.

Dr Eyal has given evidence to the House of Commons Foreign Affairs Committee on British Policy towards Eastern Europe and was recently appointed a member of the UK delegation to the CSCE follow-up conference in London (the London Information Forum).

He is currently Assistant Director (Studies) at the RUSI, a position which entails supervision of all the research activities of the Institute. Dr Eyal is also a frequent contributor to the BBC's World Service Programme.

6

A year of peaceful revolutions throughout Eastern Europe, ended with violence in Romania. For the first time in history, a communist regime was violently and successfully overthrown and the world rejoiced in the removal of a particularly odious dictatorship. How could a regime which maintained such tight control over all walks of life collapse so swiftly? What were the reasons for the revolt and what are Romania's prospects now? The crowds which stormed the Presidential palace – in scenes reminiscent of the French Revolution – only began a process of change, whose future is still unpredictable. In essence, the rebellion merely removed Ceausescu, but it has yet to provide a framework for the country's future.

Throughout the long years of Ceausescu's rule, Western observers noted the paucity of internal opposition, the absence of social dialogue, the disappearance of a 'civil society'. And, since all these factors were inherently unquantifiable, general analysis increasingly relegated Romania to anthropological and clinical disciplines: Ceausescu was equated to a latter-day Dracula and his people were regarded as traditionally fatalistic and meek; the dictator was assumed to be far too cunning and his forces of coercion were considered invincible. The reality was far simpler: the President offered a solution to Romania's deep-seated problems of historical development, underpinned by a none too original system of rewards and punishments.

The greatest source of Ceausescu's strength was his ability to capitalise on his country's history in general, and on the process of nation-building in particular. Every nationalist movement seeks to unite people on the basis of the lowest – and most acceptable – common denominator. In the case of the Romania this could only be a common language, for otherwise Romanians were subjected to four administrations, operated three different currencies and practised two different faiths until 1918. Romanian nationalists, however, sought to offer more by reviving their people's feeling of pride in their long historical connection with the Latin world. This connection promised many advantages: it comforted the oppressed with dreams of a glorious past; it differentiated the Romanians from all their Slav and Magyar neighbours and it promised a glorious future. In effect, Romanian nationalism sought to create a country whose feet were in the Balkans, but whose heart was in the West, a state which discarded a wretched present in favour of a rosy future. The concept of the country's Latinity was, in itself, neither reprehensible nor very different from other nationalist myths. However, in the Romanian case it remained particularly potent, precisely because the reality of the country's situation could never be squarely faced.

Nineteenth-century Romania was a nation–state, but not a state for all Romanians, for millions remained under the control of the Habsburg and Russian empires. As a result, most questions of national formation were merely postponed; the country's administration evolved into a peculiar mixture of Western (mainly French and Belgian) democratic structures, coupled with Ottoman traditions of corruption and nepotism. It was governed by a King who balanced two political parties, supported by a small group of large landowners but few urban dwellers. The significant Jewish minority was excluded from political participation, precisely because its control over the national economy threatened to upset the carefully constructed fiction of the country's nationhood. The unification of all Romanians at the end of the First World War broke this political stalemate, only to institute another unsatisfactory arrangement. Culturally and economically, the Transylvanians (ruled until 1918 by the Austro-Hungarian empire) were more advanced; politically, however, they were no match for the politicians of old Romania. It is wrong to suggest that Romania did not evolve strong political institutions: two main political parties (one of which was formed by Transylvanians in the 1920s) retained the loyalties of most citizens until the communist seizure of power and parliament was at the centre of all social and political life. Nevertheless, between the wars Romania was continually beset by its neighbours' territorial demands (in this century alone the frontiers shifted five times: in 1913, 1918-19, 1940, 1941 and 1944) and by every conceivable economic problem. More importantly, unity could only be achieved through the incorporation of many other ethnic groups. Thus, if before 1918 the Romanian state was not a country of all Romanians, after the First World War, it became a nation–state where only one in every three citizens was ethnically Romanian. The paucity of established channels for political discourse, economic decay, the fear of the outside threat, the lack of a solid middle class which could bridge regional and sectional interests ultimately coalesced into fascism and royal dictatorship by the end of the 1930s. Therefore – and more than many other nations – Romanians remained obsessed with national unity, tending to view regional autonomy and ethnic diversity as a constant and very real threat to their independent existence. The frustration generated by this condition reverberated throughout the country's political life: Romania's parties continued to argue not merely about tactics: everything, from the monarchy to the 1923 constitution and from industrialisation options to the maintenance of an agricultural economy, was constantly challenged in the knowledge that political power entailed not merely the ability to govern, but also the opportunity to refashion the country from scratch. This was the ultimate result of a stunted growth of the nation–state, of the tendency to impose institution from above, rather than adopt institutions grown from below. As A. D. Xenopol, one of Romania's greatest historians remarked, his country experienced constitutional settlements that 'taught us freedom, rather than constitutional contracts born out of the exercise of freedom'.[1] This historical inheritance provided a fertile ground for what followed under the Communists.

[1] A. D. Xenopol, *Opere Economice*, Bucharest, 1969, p.181.

The specific features of Communist rule

The absence of a wide, popular participation in democratic institutions and an unfinished process of nation-building were not, however, the primary reasons for the establishment of Communist control. Nevertheless, they facilitated the creation of a particular type of dictatorship, which did degenerate into Ceausescuism. The Romanian Communist party – established in the early 1920s – had little place in the country's political life before the war.[2] Advocating the dismemberment of the country, guided by leaders appointed, dismissed or murdered on Moscow's behalf and claiming to represent the 'workers' in a country which was overwhelmingly agrarian, fervently nationalistic and devoutly religious, the party had a slender chance of winning power through democratic means.

Similar problems were experienced by communists in other East European states. However, the Bulgarian and Hungarian parties claimed, with some justification, credit for having organised rebellions in their own states, while the Czechoslovak and Polish parties could at least point to some serious parliamentary activity before 1945. The Romanian Communists, on the other hand, had nothing: their party failed to benefit from the substantial economic and social dislocation which followed the achievement of Romanian unity[3] despite subsequent efforts to exaggerate their role in some industrial disputes.[4] The feeling of detachment from the nation which they ruled had important consequences: it spurred Romania's Communists to pursue their social engineering policies with a speed rarely encountered among their counterparts.

At the beginning, the lack of national roots mattered little, for the rule of Romania's Communists was overwhelmingly based on the employment of terror, backed by Soviet control. However,

[2] For an extensive debate on the origins of the party, see R. R. King, *History of the Romanian Communist Party*, Stanford, California, 1980.
[3] E. Weber, 'The Men of the Archangel' in *Journal of Contemporary History*, Vol. 1, No. 1, 1966, pp. 101-27.
[4] See S. Fischer-Galati, *20th Century Romania*, New York, 1970, p.35; Gheorghe Tutui, 'Dezvoltarea Partidului Comunist Roman in anii 1944-1948' in *Analele de Istorie*, Vol. 6, July 1970.

once the interests of the Romanian party started diverging from those of Moscow, the establishment of a truly national base became a question of political survival. All East European Communists experienced a split between a 'Muscovite' faction formed by those nurtured and propelled to power by Stalin in 1945 and an 'internal' faction comprising those who – for one reason or another – remained to fight for their cause in their own state. The Romanian party had no less than four factions and only one, entitled the 'Workers' Group' led by Gheorghe Gheorghiu-Dej was relatively homogenous, for it was formed by industrial workers of Orthodox religious background. Most shared a similar experience, and most served many years in jail, usually in the same prisons.[5] The fact that this group of home communists succeeded in wresting control from the 'Moscovite' faction well before Nikita Khrushchev's de-Stalinisation policies were imposed in Eastern Europe ultimately decided the future of the country. When the clash of interests with Moscow took place, the Romanian party, ruled by a tightly-knit circle of leaders who were very much aware of what was at stake, managed to resist any change.

Romania therefore continued to apply Stalinist policies of economic development and social control right up to 1989. Indeed, the country's rift with Moscow started precisely because of its leaders' refusal to accept any digression from industrialisation at all costs. For the Romanian Communists, pursuing heavy industrialisation was perceived as not only a matter of sound economics and ideological rectitude; it was seen as a question of political survival, for there was only one other option: the perpetuation of the country's agricultural base. Like most urban-based political movements, the Romanian Communist Party equated the peasantry not merely with economic backwardness, but also with superstition and opposition to 'progress'. If the transformation of society was to take place at all, it could only come from the breakdown of rural communities, from the dismantling and reassembling of a new Romania. The small clique of Ceausescu supporters who fought with their leader until

[5] For an analysis of this group, as well as for the first period of the Communist rule, the best work is still G. Ionescu, *Communism in Romania*, Oxford, 1964.

his death last December, experienced the period of the 1940s and never veered from this course. Again, similar policies were pursued elsewhere in Eastern Europe, but the Romanian Communists distinguished themselves by the sheer scale and speed of implementation, which was the direct result of the conviction that – isolated as they were from their society – they had only two options: success or utter oblivion.

Most investment was diverted to vast steel mills and heavy engineering projects and, due to the exceptional haste, little attention was paid to the country's industrial infrastructure or, indeed, patterns of capital formation. As early as the mid-1950s, it was clear that Romania's electricity supplies, raw material reserves and transport could not keep pace with such a growth, but the priorities never changed. However, the disappearance of Moscow's explicit support presented the Romanian party with grave difficulties. Most East European Communist regimes ultimately had to face the question of some accommodation with their own people. They usually opted for two alternative paths: 'consumerism', the deliberate attempt to buy popular acquiescence through the maintenance of a steadily rising standard of living, and nationalism, the effort to anchor an essentially alien ideology in their country's historic traditions. The mixture between these two approaches varied from country to country, but both consumerism and nationalism were used in this process of legitimation. Romania's example remains however unique, for there, the Communist party under Ceausescu relied almost completely on only one ingredient: nationalism. Given the clash with Moscow and the priorities of the party, this could have hardly been otherwise: consumerism meant the diversion of resources and consumption to 'non-productive' sectors; in short, it could have resulted in the postponement of the radical transformation of the state. A revolutionary party – such as Romania's Communists claimed to represent – clearly could not seek legitimacy through what Max Weber classified as 'rational-legal' means. Instead, it sought to rely on 'traditional' and 'charismatic' methods. The appeal to nationalism was an appeal to the former; Ceausescu's cult of personality (begun in the 1970s) answered the latter legitimation method.[6]

The pillars of Ceausescu's regime

The vulgar cult of the leader and the faintly ridiculous traits of Ceausescu's character should not obscure the fact that Romania's President was, essentially, a brilliant tactician whose skills went further than the mere consolidation of power, a task he achieved through the time-honoured method of purging opponents, rehabilitating potential supporters and blaming former leaders for all misdemeanours. Unlike his predecessor who initiated the policy of differentiation from Moscow, Ceausescu was not content with merely responding to Soviet moves (usually by attempting to limit their impact on Romania), but initiated his own aggressive foreign policy of opening up to the West, a policy which served many needs. The first need was obviously very practical: access to Western technology, raw materials and markets, in order to supplant Soviet ties. The second reason was strategic: Ceausescu calculated that burgeoning ties with the West would raise the price which Moscow would have to pay should it ever consider whipping Romania into compliance. But the third, internal reason for better ties with the non-Communist world was equally important. The implicit aim of Romania's historic founders was the rejection of their country's place in the Balkans and its transformation through the imposition of Western institutions. To this day, this 'westward yearning' remains potent and nothing was more resented by Romania's intellectuals that the Communists' subservience to Russia, an explicit connection with an inherently 'inferior' East. Ceausescu's flirtation with the West in general promised a change in this predicament and, as such, was initially very popular with most Romanians. Thus, a westward orientation in foreign policy was also part and parcel of the President's strategy of achieving internal legitimacy through the subtle manipulation of nationalist symbols.

This is not how it was perceived outside Romania at the time, and in the West the President was fêted as a brave defender of his

---

[6] A useful discussion of these points is contained in M. E. Fischer, *Nicolae Ceausescu: A Study in Political Leadership*, Boulder, Colorado, 1989, pp 83-85.

country's independence. He was offered large financial credits and trade benefits: alone and without the aid of any Congressional lobby Romania retained pride of place in America's commercial ties with Eastern Europe right until the end of the 1970s. No matter what conflict – in the Middle East, China, the super-powers, Africa – the Romanian President offered mediation and his offers were not always derided as a mere diversion. In multilateral negotiations, Ceausescu was praised for advancing arms control proposals which were often different only in wording from those of his Warsaw Pact allies. This did not matter in the West, where the simple fact that Romania was perceived to be in a conflict with Moscow was considered the best recommendation.

At home, the Romanian President revealed additional talents of control. He was an experienced manipulator of the party *Apparat*, a man who predicted that his country's rapid industrialisation would result in a vast expansion of professional cadres. As Romania's society became more diverse, as sons of peasants migrated to the towns and flocked into factories, it was clear that the party had to accommodate their interests and articulate their aspirations in some way. Ceausescu's response was incorporation without representation: during his first years in power, almost half of university professors and academics carried a party card and, in the armed forces, 80% of all officers were co-opted into the party.[7] Most of these people were attracted by the image of change which the President projected, but many would ultimately be disappointed, for the small clique of 'professional revolution-aries', trusted aides and family members remained in complete control: skilled working personnel and other professional people were brought under the wings of the party, but not admitted into its counsels.

Throughout his rule, the constant enlargement of the party served two particular aims: the penetration and neutralisation of any alternative power base and the increasing equation of the state with the party. Yet Ceausescu's control techniques went even further: he did not merely neutralise alternative power bases, but actually perpetuated a conflict between them, a constant state of

[7] *Yearbook of Communist Affairs*, Stanford, California, 1986, p 308.

tension which assured his position as supreme arbiter. The treatment which Ceausescu meted out on the armed forces, Romania's biggest alternative source of power, is particularly instructive. From the start, he appealed to their patriotism and professionalism by assuming the nationalist mantle. This allowed him to sever the umbilical cord between Romanian and Soviet officers and strengthened Ceausescu's security against any foreign challenge. The very fact that the President's initial arch-enemy was Alexandru Draghici, the head of the internal security service – the Securitate – also reinforced Ceausescu's image as a man who would rely on the armed forces rather than the party's own instruments of coercion. Nothing could be further from the truth. Having secured his power base, Ceausescu moved to control the armed forces through a method which he applied throughout his life: their deprofessionalisation. Immediately after the invasion of Czechoslovakia, Romania adopted a military doctrine of territorial defence which envisaged that the entire nation would repel any invader. The doctrine allowed for the creation of a parallel military body, the Patriotic Guards, which was placed under the control of the party, rather than the General Staff. Having established two levels of command, Ceausescu then proceeded to unify them under a Defence Council which was intended to supervise all military and economic activities.[8] In practice, Patriotic Guards officers (promoted from party members rather than military personnel) were put in command of the armed forces and the army – whose importance was automatically reduced by the formation of additional paramilitary organs. The army ultimately ended up as nothing more than a vast pool of cheap labour, digging canals or helping with the agricultural harvest.[9] The Securitate, however, was allocated vast resources and large investments also went into the air force and the navy. Ceausescu therefore perpetuated a four-cornered fight: between the armed forces and the Securitate; between the army and the navy and air force; between the Securitate and the Interior

[8] *Conceptia politico-militara al tovarasului Nicolae Ceausescu*, Bucharest, 1983, p.123.

[9] J. Eyal,'Between Appearances and Realities' in his (ed.) *The Warsaw Pact in the Balkans*, London, 1989, pp.102–8.

Ministry which was supposedly in charge of most paramilitary forces and between the Patriotic Guards and the regular troops.

The same tactic was applied more generally to the party's cadre promotion policies. A territorial reorganisation in 1967 promised local party officials enhanced freedoms and greater decentralisation.[10] In fact, precisely the opposite happened: as Ceausescu's economic priorities became more and more unrealistic, the party officials at the county level were increasingly squeezed between the need to provide for the people under their responsibility and the fulfilment of the central plan. This was Ceausescu's precise intention: the imposition of draconian measures ensured a perpetual conflict in the countryside and therefore prevented local leaders from assuming too much power. At the national level, the policy was reinforced by a system of rotation of cadres with the explicit intention of preventing the promotion of professionals. Some officials were dismissed in order to take the blame for failures of policies which they did not elaborate; other were replaced without any reason at all. The sheer pace of this musical chairs game defied most Western experts, yet it served a purpose: it isolated personalities and set up party officials one against the other. Demotion did not necessarily signify disgrace or permanent oblivion either, for Ceausescu was also aware of the dangers inherent in the creation of a large pool of discontented officials. Army generals who swapped positions with Central Committee secretaries and county officials who donned the hat of a scientist or a planner were often reprimanded and punished for misdemeanours but they usually reappeared, sometimes within a matter of months, under different guises. Blind loyalty to the leader and the readiness to perform any task was the only requirement, just as important in a position of power, as it was during a period of temporary disgrace. The result was an utter atomization of society, the complete deprofessionalisation of all Romanians.

The system was ultimately underpinned by two additional levers of control: the President's family and the security police. No less than fifty members of Nicolae and Elena Ceausescu's relatives controlled the most strategic positions in the state: central planning, the capital city, the army, security services,

[10] M. E. Fischer, *Nicolae Ceausescu: A study in Political Leadership*, Boulder, Colorado, 1989, pp. 123-6.

foreign intelligence, the party cadres and its youth movements. The placement of family members probably accorded with Ceausescu's personal and very Romanian belief that – at the last resort – only members of one's own family are actually completely trustworthy. Yet the promotion of the family also created a sophisticated advance warning mechanism quite outside party institutions and the security services: the Ceausescus and the Petrescus (Elena Ceausescu's maiden name) saw to it that threats to their Godfather's survival were located and eliminated well before they became dangerous. In practice, members of these families established their own royal courts. Elena supervised the promotion of professionals within government authorities; one of the President's brothers supervised promotions in the armed forces and another checked the credentials of Securitate officers.

It is important to note that Ceausescu's aim was never to rely on sheer terror for his survival. Instead, he sought to control Romanian society through the encouragement of nationalism, the fusion of the state and party and the destruction of any alternative power base. The Securitate remained, therefore, an instrument of last resort, rather than the first line of the system's defence. Many stories were created around this organisation, and most of them remain untrue. It appears that Romanians actually believed that one in four of their co-nationals co-operated with the Securitate, and that the organisation listened to every telephone call, intercepted every correspondence and followed every citizen. It hardly needs stressing that a country which ultimately proved unable to distribute a loaf of fresh bread could hardly control a network of more than 5 million informers and keep track of millions of telephone lines with any degree of efficiency. The truth was much more banal: the Securitate certainly employed informers and intercepted communications, but its main strength was the very fact that it operated in a complete legal void, in a country where capriciousness ruled. Throughout the last two decades, most East European dissidents who dared speak their mind, usually knew what to expect from the authorities: loss of employment, perpetual harassment, imprisonment, exile. In Romania, however, this was never the case. The country's few dissidents were almost never put on trial: some escaped unmolested for many years, while others disappeared or experienced fatal 'accidents'. The Securitate's tactic was therefore one of perpetual deterrence through the very unpredictability of the potential punishment. Had it been otherwise, Romania's post-revolutionary rulers (most of whom disagreed with the dictator at one time or another) would have never lived to tell their story.

Given the fact that all the instruments of control were in place by the late 1970s, how is the demise of Ceausescu's regime to be explained? Essentially, through four cardinal mistakes. The first was the belief – implicit in all of the President's policies – that his Romanians would bear any suffering, however great, without a murmur. The second was the mistaken assumption that the geopolitical interests of both East and West would remain immutable. The third was the conviction that nationalism was an infinite commodity and the fourth was Ceausescu's miscalculation in assuming that the perpetual conflicts which he created within Romanian society would neutralise any opposition to his regime. With the benefit of hindsight, it is clear that the roots of the Romanian revolution are located in the early 1980s, when the policies of the Communist party started unravelling one by one. And, with a nice twist of irony, the process followed a neat sequence: the first to fail was the country's economic experiment, which was the first to be put into place in the early 1950s; then followed Romania's foreign policy, the employment of nationalism and, ultimately – in the fury of the December rebellion – the party's coercion *Apparat*.

The failure of the economy

During the 1970s, Ceausescu had the best opportunity of modernising and integrating his country's economy in world trade. Romania had a vested interest in moving away from COMECON's specialisation plans and benefited little from cheap supplies of Soviet raw materials. The West was, however, willing to help with financial credit; the country enjoyed preferential trade agreements with the United States and the European Community and was the first East European state to adhere to all the major multilateral financial institutions. Yet Ceausescu's aim was not integration in the world economy: in a curious way, he forged closer co-operation with the West in order to pursue precisely the same autarkic policies of import substitution which other East European states strove to achieve through the much more modest technique of foreign borrowing. The result was, therefore, the same as elsewhere: the squandering of hard currency in vastly inefficient projects in complete ignorance of world market trends, proper pricing and prospective demand. And there was worse, for Ceausescu's follies – such as the continued build-up of the country's steel industry and the creation of a gigantic petrochemical capacity – relied on imports of oil and coal and therefore compounded the country's exposure to those world market forces which the President never understood. The steel mills at Galati, for instance, (by no means the only ones in the country) currently employ 50,000 workers and daily devour more than 6,000 tonnes of coal, in order to produce goods which no one will buy.[11]

When Western credits dried up in the aftermath of the Polish crisis in the late 1970s, Ceausescu resolved to repay his $10bn worth of foreign debt as quickly as possible. This move was not dictated by economic necessity but, rather, by the President's determination not to accept any of the strictures which foreign creditors regularly impose on defaulting debtors. As a result, exports were maximised and imports strictly forbidden even when they entailed the purchase of new machinery. More importantly, investment in the agricultural sector was squeezed even further in order to allow for the unabated pace of industrialisation. A vicious circle therefore set in. Antiquated machinery produced goods which failed to find markets. This forced Romania to rely more and more on exports of food and semi-finished products in order to gain hard currency. But, since resources devoted to agriculture were minimal, exports of food could only be sustained through the further reduction in local consumption. By 1982, rationing was introduced; by 1985 most food products were persistently unobtainable and by 1987, the population was subjected to serious malnutrition. Worse still, every industrial branch continued to

[11] *Adevarul*, 18 January 1990.

apply Ceausescu's 'precious indications', as a gigantic machine spinning out of control. Steel production outpaced power generation and the electricity grid collapsed; coal extraction exceeded transport facilities and the rail network disintegrated. Unable to increase productivity, the President continued to resort to extensive growth: Romanians were forced to produce more children in order to satisfy the thirst for labour in unautomated factories and, since agricultural production failed to live up to the President's hare-brained targets, Ceausescu resolved to erase thousands of villages, partly in order to destroy the last vestiges of private agriculture, partly in order to eliminate the peasants as a group and partly simply in order to increase the surface of arable land. All these policies were pursued with the instinctive knowledge that Romanians could be whipped into harder work and would stomach every privation. In reality, however, a veritable social time bomb started ticking. Even after repaying most of its foreign debt, Romania's economy was in such a state that shortages continued as industrial branches were outgrowing everyone's control. This ultimately had an impact on employment as well. Between 1966 and 1976, Romania produced 40% more babies than might otherwise have been expected.[12] Yet, even with the highest infant mortality rate in Europe and the most inefficient employment policy, a labour market of such a magnitude simply could not be absorbed. The heirs of this baby boom were the first to man the barricades of the Spring in Winter revolution.

The importance of Gorbachev

Ceausescu's foreign policy represents yet another case of missed opportunities, grounded in the man's fundamental inability to perceive the difference between a mere tactic and an immutable reality. Baiting Moscow and enhancing Romania's independence could only succeed as long as the Soviet Union chose to rise to the bait and as long as the West was prepared to encourage such wayward behaviour. Yet tactics, however brilliantly executed, could not change strategic facts: tucked away in a corner of the Balkans, Romania was only important as long as Europe remained

[12] *Time*, 29 January 1990.

a chessboard between East and West. Thus, despite Ceausescu's yearning to be recognised as a universal peacemaker, his interests always resided in the continued existence of a bi-polar world. Mikhail Gorbachev's policies changed the situation in three different ways. The Soviet Union's interest in disarmament and a relaxation of tensions automatically reduced Romania's importance for the West. Secondly, the Soviet leader's tolerance of diversity in Eastern Europe transformed Ceausescu's objections to Soviet hegemony from an act of defiance into an historical irrelevance. The traditional game of cat and mouse game between Moscow and Bucharest simply outlived its usefulness. Finally, the political and economic reforms which the Soviet Union instituted threatened the control of Communist parties throughout the region.

At the beginning, Ceausescu responded in the only way he knew – by ignoring the Soviet reforms. However, once it became clear that the thaw in East–West relations would last, Romania proceeded to complicate the process of disarmament and multi-lateral negotiations as far as possible. Just as Moscow accepted to separate nuclear and conventional arms in disarmament negotiations, Ceausescu insisted on linking these weapons in one major conference.[13] And, just as the Soviet Union proved ready to accept additional human rights obligations, Romania not only publicly rejected such obligations, but actually delayed the conclusion of a new agreement under the Conference on Security and Co-operation in Europe framework. Additionally, Ceausescu hinted that his country could produce nuclear and chemical weapons,[14] in a clear attempt to contradict the disarmament priorities of his Warsaw Pact allies.[15] Neither East nor West paid much attention.

Yet by mid-1989, Ceausescu's main threat came from the gradual collapse of Communist regimes elsewhere in Eastern Europe. Again, the Romanian President attempted to apply his well-worn recipes of nationalism in order to limit the impact of

[13] *Scinteia*, 15 April 1989.
[14] *Scinteia*, 15 April 1989.
[15] J. Eyal, 'Romania: Looking for Weapons of Mass Destruction?', in *Jane's Soviet Intelligence Review*, Vol 1, No 8, August 1989, pp. 378-82.

this collapse on his own country. His first target for criticism was Hungary, whose reformist leaders were equated with 'fascists' in an obvious effort to capitalise on traditional animosities. However, this policy of 'xenophobic Communism'.[16] failed to elicit any response among Romanians who – courtesy of the broadcasts of Western radio stations – followed East European events closely. In the second half of 1989, therefore, Ceausescu suddenly abandoned all claims to independence and, instead of opposing the Warsaw Pact's designs in the region, actually called upon this military alliance to 'close its ranks' in order to defeat 'imperialism' and 'renegades'.[17] When even this failed to persuade Gorbachev to intervene with force in Eastern Europe, Ceausescu simply retreated into the existence of a hermit. He renounced trade agreements with other countries, launched vicious attacks against both East and West and instituted a clear policy of *Abgrenzung*. The tactic of 'fortress Romania' could have worked many years before, when many Romanians still believed that their leader, however reprehensible he may have been, at least saved his country from the even worse fate of Soviet domination. Yet in 1989 the threat of Soviet intervention looked remote, and years of near-starvation rendered the supposed choice between independence and subservience less important: Ceausescu could offer an endless supply of tricolour flags, but he could not make these flags edible.

Revolution and the future

With hindsight, it is clear that by the end of 1989 exasperated Romanians were ruled by an exasperated President. The economic crisis could only grow worse, the appeal to nationalism fell on deaf ears and foreign policy diversions produced no results. The Soviet Union was transformed from a threatening bear into a beacon of hope; the 'golden future' of socialism which Ceausescu predicted turned into a hasty and unedifying flight of East

[16] On the traits of this policy, see M. Shafir, 'Xenophobic Communism – the Case of Bulgaria and Romania', in *The World Today*, Vol 45, No 12, December 1989, pp. 208-13.

[17] *Scinteia*, 29 June 1989.

European dictators. Precisely because he was aware of this impasse, Ceausescu never contemplated even the simulation of political and economic reforms. By observing the developments in neighbouring states, he realised that such exercises merely opened the floodgates of further demands. More importantly, the President was ultimately paralysed by the lessons he drew from his country's history: in the context of Romania, any talk of 'reformist' Communists, of 'socialism with a human face', of power-sharing agreements with a non-existent political opposition were entirely meaningless. As the transcripts of the party meeting which decided to meet the Timisoara riots with force indicate, Ceausescu went into battle convinced that the confrontation with his people would ultimately decide the future of Communism in his country. Those who followed him down this path did so out of an instinctive belief that, having ridden a tiger for so many years, they could hardly afford to dismount.[18] Ceausescu's overthrow could only be accomplished by force: the absence of a coherent opposition, the perpetual conflicts between interest groups, the social and economic decay and the atrophy of a leadership which went down seriously believing that it was a victim of a plot concocted by both East and West guaranteed this outcome. Essentially, the atoms of Ceausescu's Romania ultimately split in a bowl of fire.

The fact that the spark for the rebellion was provided in Timisoara on the 16 December 1989 hardly seems to matter very much. The miscalculations which followed were, however, important. The first miscalculation was to assume that Romanians would remain insulated from the events in other East European states. They were not: the demonstrators who chanted 'We Are the People' copied the crowds in East Germany and those who tore the Communist symbol from the national flag were following in the path of the Hungarians in 1956. The second miscalculation was Ceausescu's belief that the judicious use of force would contain the uprising to Timisoara. It did not: the cruelty of the massacre in that city simply fuelled opposition throughout the country. The President's third mistake was to rely too much on

[18] The transcripts were published in *Romania Libera*, 10 January 1990.

the Securitate to control his population. In the context of the challenges which Ceausescu faced in the Jiu Valley in 1977 and in the city of Brasov in 1987, the Securitate proved sufficient for the task but, once the riots spread to other Romanian cities in the days following the massacre at Timisoara, the deployment of troops could not be prevented. It thus happened that the army, that body of conscripts and officers whose professionalism Ceausescu denigrated throughout his career, was called upon to save the President's position. Not surprisingly, they proved reluctant and, once army units stopped firing, Ceausescu's fate was to all intents and purposes sealed.

Yet it is important to remember what the Romanian revolution signified. It was not a movement with a political platform and – despite the claims of Romania's present rulers – it was led by no-one. Essentially, it was a violent revolt against a man and his system, born out of sheer despair, followed by a swift (and probably pre-planned) takeover of power. As a result, the Romanian revolution became, from its inception, a prime candidate for reinterpretation and modification. On the 22 December (the day the President fled his capital) no less than three different groups vied with each other to claim the mantle of leadership and the group which ultimately won was that which seized the radio and television stations, persuaded the military commanders that it was worthy of support and projected a clear sense of purpose and determination. Given Romania's conditions, this group could only be composed of former Communist party members, of people who were at one time or another part of the system and therefore knew how to operate it. The Front of National Salvation, the body which took over the country on that day, was precisely such an amalgam of former officials. The Front's President, Ion Iliescu, was Ceausescu's party youth leader in the late 1960s; his deputy, Dumitru Mazilu, served as a Securitate officer and as a diplomat; their senior partner on the Front, Silviu Brucan, was at one time deputy editor of the party daily and subsequently served as an ambassador. They all had one thing in common: a quarrel with Ceausescu at one time or another.

Yet these were not the dissidents which came into prominence in other East European states during the same year. Silviu Brucan is a lifelong Communist who helped the party to power in the 1940s; President Iliescu and Prime Minister Roman were born into families of professional revolutionaries and benefited from a system which pampered such former 'illegals'. They all belonged to a ruling elite, a caste which sought redemption simply by eliminating a wayward member from its midst. That member was Ceausescu, a man who – in their opinion – distorted the 'humanistic' values of socialism and 'seized' a party of 'honest' workers. Romania's revolution therefore represented a paradox from the beginning: the first successful and seemingly complete overthrow of a Communist regime, produced leaders devoted to the resuscitation of Communism as an idea and a principle of government. It could have hardly been otherwise: Ceausescu's rule was such an aberration that most people were inclined to place blame for all failures on his shoulders. Furthermore, the control of Dej and Ceausescu over the party during the last 40 years was so complete, as to preclude the emergence of a 'reformist' Communist group in any form. Those who quibbled with the leader did so out of personal considerations or because they objected to particular features of the regime; they did not, however, question the basic premise of the ideology and did not agonize – as other East European Communists did – over the future of the ideas which they sought to implement. The inherent conflict between the achievement of the people and the aspirations of their new leaders ultimately led to one of the shortest periods of post-revolutionary euphoria: Romania's democratic dawn lasted precisely two weeks.

Within that period, ordinary Romanians learnt that their leaders, who considered themselves 'broadly to the left' of the political spectrum, persisted in talking about twenty four years of dictatorship, rather than forty five. They also refused to discuss the fate of the Securitate (which was officially incorporated into the armed forces) and employed familiar tactics of government. The Front was supposedly formed out of 145 personalities from different walks of life. The full list of their names was never published and some were included in the Front without their prior consent. The full body of the Front had no powers, just as Romania's 3.8 million Communist party members were merely a abstraction. This Front delegated most functions to a Council which also did nothing, just as Ceausescu's Central Committee never supervised party affairs. The Council, in turn, established a executive body which was the real power in the land. Yet, just as happened with Ceausescu's own Political Executive Committee, control remained concentrated in the hands of the few: Brucan, Iliescu, Roman and, initially, Mazilu.

More disturbing was the fact that these leaders decreed the separation of powers but continued to hold both executive and legislative powers. Government ministers were made responsible to the Front, rather than to the Prime Minister, and 'decree-laws' were issued without any reference to the cabinet. It was Mr Iliescu – and not Prime Minister Roman – who solved industrial disputes, and it was Brucan – and not the government – who expounded on the country's new policies. The Front talked about the independence of the media, yet it appointed the head of radio and television as its spokesman; it promised that all political parties would be allowed to function freely, but at the same time suggested that the very notion of a political party was 'surpassed by history' and no longer relevant to Romania's present conditions. Ultimately, the Front – which claimed to be a temporary revolutionary administration – turned itself into a political body determined to rule Romania for a long time.

Was the revolution hijacked by a team of Communists, as most Romanians fear? Did the sacrifice of the people ultimately result in the replacement of one unrepresentative clique with another? The answer is probably no, simply because the revolution resulted in a diffusion of power, the reassertion of the role of the army and professional institutions and the temporary disintegration of the centralised state. In effect, what seems to have happened is that the uprising merely returned Romania to 1945, and reopened the country's historical wounds yet again. All the issues which were debated immediately after the end of the War, are subject to scrutiny today: the place of agriculture in economic development, the pace of industrialisation, the rights of ethnic minorities, the system of government; in short, the remaking of the Romanian state. The country's post-revolution leaders certainly acted in an autocratic manner which did not inspire confidence. However, they were essentially functioning like any other Romanian politician did for more than a century, by attempting to refashion the state according to his (and, incidentally, never her) priorities. They did this without a national consensus, partly because they instinctively suspected that such a consensus did not exist and partly because they believe that a consensus is unrealisable. In the process, members of the Front denied the heritage of former generations; everything, from the restoration of the monarchy to the bloody repression of a 1907 peasant rebellion were subjected to intense debate. And just as passionately, the Front is challenged by the National Liberal and National Peasant Party, the two political formations which dominated Romania's life before the War. The fact that the debate about the character of the state is conducted from above rather that from below, between politicians rather than between all Romanians, is also entirely in keeping with the country's history. In that respect Romania's Spring in Winter revolution was merely an outburst of anger, a spurt of violence which became unavoidable given the nature of Ceausescu's regime. The future of the country will ultimately be decided not by this revolution, but by the political confrontation currently unfolding. That political confrontation may bear some resemblance to the peaceful revolts in other East European states during 1989, or it may disintegrate into renewed violence and an authoritarian regime. Everything is still in the balance. But then, that was always Romania's experience.

7 Andrei A. Piontkowsky

The Russian sphinx: hope and despair

Andrei A. Piontkowsky, born 1940, graduated from Moscow State University with a PhD in Applied Mathematics in 1963. He has worked in the Institute for Systems Studies, Moscow and is currently Senior Researcher of the Soviet Branch of The World Laboratory. A Member of the American Mathematical Society, he is the author of more than 80 papers on optimal control theory, on strategic stability and on global modelling, of which he was one of the first practitioners in the USSR. He is an active participant in the "Democratic Russia" movement and acts as Adviser to several Deputies who are members of the Inter-Regional Group of progressives in the Congress of Peoples' Deputies. Dr Piontkowsky has broadcast extensively on Western radio and television, commenting upon politics in the USSR. In 1990/91 he is Quatercentenary Visiting Fellow at Emmanuel College, Cambridge, and an FCO/British Council Visiting Fellow in the University of Cambridge Global Security Programme.

7

In his famous poem, "The Scythians," the great Russian poet Aleksandr Blok wrote hauntingly in January 1918:

> *Russia is the Sphinx. Rejoicing and grieving,*
> *and steeped in black blood,*
> *she gazes, gazes, gazes at Europe,*
> *now in hatred, now with love!*

The question of Russia's uneasy relationship with its neighbours to the West has remained central ever since.

I remember that in the early stages of *perestroika*, many of us in the Soviet Union dreamt that there might come about some movement in Eastern Europe like Solidarność had been briefly in Poland in 1980 or like the Prague Spring in 1968. We felt that if such developments occurred, it would greatly influence our own chances. This, we thought, would push the USSR very strongly towards a democratic solution and that might precipitate things.

Spring in Winter in 1989 brought much more radical events than we might have dared to contemplate, not only in Poland and Czechoslovakia, but all over Eastern Europe, even – indeed first in the historic sequence of November 1989 – in East Germany. What really has happened in Eastern Europe? Plainly, the current Russian Revolution, which is still unresolved as I write, but which is clearly fully engaged, is related to the events of 1989 in Eastern

Europe. It was related in two ways: as *cause* and as *effect*. In this chapter I wish to explore both.

Professor Galbraith is correct earlier in this book to emphasise that whatever the Spring in Winter was, it was neither the simple transition from socialism to capitalism in Eastern Europe, nor the wholesale adoption of rampant "free market" ideological principles. Professor Ziolkowski, Professor Hankiss and Jan Urban all, from their different national and ideological perspectives, have made the same point. I think that these terms "capitalism" and "socialism" are now obsolete. I have always shared the old-fashioned British empiricist scepticism about "-ism" words: they are too easy to use and too easy to abuse. Viewed in 1990, when the new global security agenda is rapidly advancing across the general international agenda and is specifically active in the emergent politics of Eastern Europe, we must set these terms in historical context. I see them as concepts akin to phlogiston and ether.

In eighteenth century physics, people sought to explain the nature of fire. At that relatively early moment in modern analytic chemistry, the vital element (never actually isolated, but usefully and generally hypothesised and assumed) was named phlogiston. A similar concept was that of ether. This was the view that space was filled with a hypothetical substance through which electro-magnetic waves propagate, like sound waves through air. These were popular and popularised paradigms. Ordinary, informed people believed them to be true. They played an important role in scientific conception at that time, but later in the development of science, as we learned more and more, they were superseded. The concept of ether lost its former meaning as a result of Einstein's Special Theory of Relativity in 1905.

So I believe it to be with the terms "capitalism" and "socialism" in the late twentieth century. In both systems, there is impressive convergence at the large scale in the application of power to economics (a point which Professor Galbraith has made elegantly in the past). But now I think that these terms can't explain anything fundamentally useful in the world today. In large part, this is because I believe that the *motive power* in contemporary social transformation is *decreasingly* fuelled by local material circumstance and *increasingly* fuelled by control of knowledge and information.

The role of the electronic media in the 1989 revolutions has been much, and in my view correctly, remarked. They transformed not only time and space for millions of captive East Europeans, they also gave hope to those masses of people, to each privately, in their own homes, watching the TV or listening to the radio. I write this with special feeling as one who has, for many years, relied on the BBC World Service as a lifeline. So I would argue that the process which has happened in Eastern Europe is better described in socio-political than in socio-economic terms. In country after country (but not yet my own) it was not so much the transition from state socialism to capitalism as the transition from a Party State to civil society that best describes the essence of the experience.

In 1903 Vladimir Ilich Lenin founded what he called then *The Party of the New Type*. George Orwell called it more directly the "Inner Party". Stalin used to call it "The Order of the Sword"; and now it is often called the *nomenclatura*. All these names are different names for one and the same phenomenon: a Party constructed as a self-appointed society for the purpose of obtaining and retaining forever for itself (Orwell's "Inner" group) absolute power.

This Party State has disappeared in Poland, in Hungary, in Czechoslovakia and in East Germany, I think irretrievably. The chapters of my colleagues in this book generally concur with this opinion, their views arising from rather different combinations of domestic circumstance. I can't say that it is so in Romania in spite of all the dramatic character of events there in December 1989 and January 1990 because it appears to me increasingly that the National Salvation Front is just another name for the previous Communist Party.

But while domestic circumstance and history differed across the Continent, one factor was constant: The role of the USSR. What was the role of the Soviet Union in producing this situation? It was axiomatic, yet remains paradoxical; the same Gorbachevian Government simultaneously lifted the threat of armed intervention from Eastern Europe, thus permitting spring to flower in the winter of 1989, yet refused to accept the logic and moral imperative of liberalisation at home.

The contradiction became inescapable on May Day 1990 in Red Square. Elsewhere in Eastern Europe, this was the first occasion for the classic public holiday of Communism to be stripped of its old rags and dressed anew. In Moscow, the parade of the people was permitted to be more representative of the whole range of society. That was, for Gorbachev, the problem. He has chosen, boldly and correctly, to let *glasnost* loose into Soviet society. Standing on the reviewing balcony, he saw it displayed before him and felt its sharp edge himself.

First, the speakers from the official Trade Unions were not obsequious. They spoke directly and harshly of the failure to stimulate the Soviet economy since 1985. Then the Communist leadership was subjected to a storm of criticism and abuse from the broad cross-section of the Democratic Russia bloc (stretching from progressive Communists, through social democrats to western-type liberals.) Flags of independent Lithuania, of pre-revolutionary Russia, and the Red Flag with the Hammer and Sickle ripped out, paraded before a grim-faced Mr Gorbachev who, after fifteen minutes of constant heckling, left the podium of the Lenin Mausoleum. I return to the consequence of this contradiction later in this chapter.

Here, however, we must note only that this grave act of political theatre indicates that the motives for letting Eastern Europe go by removing the latent threat of military intervention may have been other than a commitment to ideas of freedom, self-determination, human dignity and democracy. Indeed, in my opinion, so it was. A changed Soviet view was a prerequisite external determinant of the 1989 events in Eastern Europe. This changed view arose not from ethical but from pragmatic sources. It was a new conception of the Soviet Union's western border security, a conception which has plainly been accepted in Moscow.

It is difficult to locate the precise moment when this new conception took hold. Many, especially strategic analysts, tend to seek evidence in doctrinal strategic declarations. The so-called Budapest Declaration of the Warsaw Pact in May 1986 was in my view rather ambivalent, but is taken by some to be that signal; or the later Berlin Declaration. I tend to look to other sorts of evidence. For me, the most convincing came towards the end of August 1988. There was a strike in the Gdansk Shipyard, the same where Solidarność was born. But unlike in 1980, this was comparatively mild. Rather unexpectedly, the Polish Government yielded to the demands of the strikers on the convening of Round Table negotiations between the then still outlawed Solidarność and the Government. I do not think that this would have happened without the Polish Government having concluded that Soviet military intervention was no longer to be taken for granted.

It is an interesting fact that historically this new security conception might have been accepted even by Stalin after the Second World War, although that opportunity was lost. It is natural that after such terrible ordeals as Russia has periodically endured at the hands of prospective western invaders, it was necessary for us to secure our western borders; and since 1945, there have always been two models for doing this.

In fact, both models were implemented immediately after the war. One model was Finland: a country independent in its internal affairs, clearly part of the world economy but a state connected with the Soviet Union by a defence treaty. The other model was implemented in Eastern Europe. This was the imposition of Stalinist regimes on the peoples of each country across our security perimeter. Events have shown that as well as being more humane, the first model is much more secure and much cheaper from the USSR's point of view. It is now clearly accepted in the military and foreign policy community of the Soviet Union as the preferred situation for Eastern Europe, *irrespective of our own internal development* which I will discuss below. This reappraisal of the approach to security was an integral part of the new political thinking which accompanied Mr Gorbachev to power. It is more subtle, more realistic and comparatively free of ideological blinkers.

The experience of the Afghanistan war was crucial in stimulating this rethinking. Afghanistan showed the limitations of military power very clearly and convincingly. Even the most hard-line generals and political and military analysts in the Kremlin understood this message. So it would be fair, if a little surprising to

Europeans, to say that it was not so much thinkers in the corridors of the Kremlin as the *mujahadin* in the hills of Afghanistan who were the real liberators of Eastern Europe.

The impact of the Afghanistan experience was at the most fundamental level in the hierarchy that governs the Soviet military apparatus. In my view, the dramatic changes at the level both of military doctrine and of conventional arms control in western Europe, events which have been much more centrally the concerns of western analysts, were *subordinate in importance* to the fundamental reassessment which arose from the Afghanistan experience. The potential military confrontation in Europe was fundamentally what the Cold War had been about. As I have argued elsewhere, military stability is a multi-level problem and to change the terms of confrontation (by changing the military-political objectives) at the conventional level in central Europe was, by definition, to force a reassessment at all the super-ordinate nuclear levels of strategy.[1] This has all occurred. Some of the consequences are to be seen in the positions adopted by the USSR in the CFE (Conventional Forces in Europe) and other arms control negotiations; but my point is that they arose from causes *external* to central Europe.

The changes in the status of the military variable in the Soviet equation of security had a decisive influence on the course of events in Eastern Europe. The fall of the imposed regimes of "barracks Communism" was long overdue. As Ziolkowski observes, except for the presence or threatened presence of Soviet troops, they would have been swept away in the 1950s. The 1989 revolutions revealed startlingly the concealed bankruptcy of these unloved regimes. But their simultaneous disintegration during the autumn of 1989 occurred *only after it became obvious* that the Soviet Union would not use its military power to save them.

It is known now from various sources that the Soviet military advisers in Berlin were instructed to dissuade Honecker on 9 October 1989 from using force against the 50,000 demonstrators in Leipzig that day; in fact, they took Krenz's position when

[1] A.A.Piontkowsky, "Stability as a multi-level Problem", in Reiner K. Hüber, Hilmar Linnenkamp and Ingrid Schölch (eds), *Military Stability – Prerequisites and Analysis Requirements for Conventional Stability in Europe*, NOMOS Verlagsgesellschaft, Baden-Baden, FRG, 1990.

Honecker wished to authorise the use of live ammunition against the demonstrators. Some sources believe that they were even ordered to prevent by intervention a repetition of the Tienanmen Square massacre in East Germany. This may explain somewhat the subsequent respect and even popularity of Soviet troops in East Germany, in stark contrast to their ostracism in Czechoslovakia and Hungary, an attitude which may ease for them the transitional period immediately after German reunification. The withdrawal of the Brezhnev doctrine from Eastern Europe has been accepted by all sections of public opinion in the USSR, some with enthusiasm, some with reluctance, but none with active opposition. No one would now dare to raise the possibility of using Soviet military forces in Eastern Europe.

The speed of social transformation taking place in Eastern Europe following the 1989 revolutions is certainly a consequence of impatience, most clearly so where a precise alternative is perceived, as in Germany, to which the results of the spring 1990 elections in the GDR stand as eloquent witness. Yet in addition to these domestic causes, they are urged forward by the uncertainty of the East Europeans about the policy of any possible successors to Mr Gorbachev. This lies behind the desire to hurry as much as possible, "while Gorbachev is in power". A shadow skulks in the forest. In apprehension, the coachmen whip up their horses.

Such was the course of events in Eastern Europe. Certainly they were indebted to the great intellectual influence of Soviet *perestroika* and to the example of Soviet new political thinking. But now, after influencing greatly this process, the Soviet Union is self-evidently lagging behind. Why?

Russia is – and always was – a very special case. A poem of Fyodor Tyutchev, the great nineteenth-century Russian poet, stated the problem in an apt and well-known aphorism:

> *Russia cannot be understood with the mind and measured by a common yardstick. She is a special case. Russia one can only believe in.*

Nevertheless, let us try to understand something with the mind. What are the substantive differences between the situation in the Soviet Union and in Eastern Europe? First of all, the Soviet population has been much longer subjected to totalitarian indoctrination. For example, a crude egalitarian mentality is very widespread amongst Soviet people and it plays into the hands of the conservative element in the Communist Party. Second, for seventy years we have experienced the reverse of Darwinian natural selection of the fittest, rather an "anti-selection" militating against the brightest and the best of the population. It was a gigantic and perverse experiment upon the whole nation.

Those in the West who have cared to investigate have known for a long time what for the first time Soviet citizens in any number only recently learned: that during the last seventy years of Soviet history at least seventy million people died by violent means. Thirty million of them died during the Great Patriotic War and another forty during the civil war after the Revolution, the collectivisation of farms, the extermination of the *kulaks* and Stalin's purges. (The easiest way to remember the magnitude of this tragedy is that it comes to a million violent deaths for each year of the Soviet State's existence.)

Herodotus tells the story of how Periander, son and successor of Cypselus, the Tyrant of Corinth, sent a herald to Thrasybulus, the Tyrant of Miletus, to ask his advice on how to rule. Thrasybulus took the herald into a cornfield. With his cane, he proceeded to lop off any ears of grain that stood above the general level of the crop. Then, without a word, he sent the herald back to Periander, who interpreted the message by initiating a policy of extreme cruelty against the citizens of Corinth. In the USSR, mostly those who were out of line were killed first. So we have a very special kind of personal and public psychology which strongly favours passivity and silence and collaboration with the powers-that-be. The political consequence in our society of such repeated and perversely efficient anti-selection has been the survival of the most coarse, brutalised and unprincipled in the *nomenclatura*. The "Inner Party" is stronger in the USSR than in Eastern Europe. Besides, in Eastern Europe this *nomenclatura* was alien to the nation; it was imposed on it from outside. In our country it was also imposed, but it was imposed from inside and has more organic roots in our society and history, which it penetrates pervasively.

This has a frightening, yet sociologically interesting consequence in the context which is developing during 1990 in the Soviet Union. During the 1988 election to the All-Union Congress, right-wing conservative forces (i.e. orthodox Marxist–Leninists) had practically no popular base in the Soviet Union. They were isolated in their Party palaces and there was a confrontation of Party and society. In 1990 they have acquired some popular base. They are appealing, sometimes successfully, to the nationalist sentiments in Russia.

It must not be forgotten that during the history of Russia it was a tragic separation between the democratic and national movements, between "Slavophiles" and "Westerners" which has repeatedly frustrated attempts to break through to freedom. Due to the imperial nature of the Russian state, people with noble and patriotic feelings were often swept away by an overriding imperial consciousness, which deflected them from the democratic road. Even today, some nationalists argue that democracy is a Western conception, alien to the Russian mentality. I disagree strongly.

It is sufficient to remember that the first Russian Parliament, *Novgorod Veche*, ruled the city–state of Novgorod very efficiently in the fourteenth century, during a time of French absolutism (and, incidentally, was elected on a more democratic principle that the First Congress of Peoples' Deputies in 1989. There were no special quotas for a "Party of the New Type" in the fourteenth century.) This Parliament was destroyed by Ivan the Terrible in the same way that the Constituent Assembly was destroyed by Lenin and Trotsky in January of 1918. But it only shows that there were always two tendencies in Russian history.

So what is the secret of success of the Eastern European countries, and even of the Baltic Republics, in their method of democratisation? It is that the democratic idea and the national idea are combined together in their cases. When the democratic idea is separated from the national idea it lacks energy, strength and excitement. The situation is rather like that facing a coachman with a heavy load and two horses. The only way forward for him and his carriage is to catch and to harness successfully the two horses, so that they may pull together.

That is what happened in Eastern Europe and to some of the national republics of the USSR, Baltic ones first of all, but it has *not* happened so far in the ethnic Russian heartland. Rather the reverse has happened. The national horse has not only failed to team up with the democratic one; it has found a different partner.

A bizarre alliance between Russian ultra-nationalists and the Communist Party bureaucracy is forming. It is bizarre because Party conservatives see themselves as inheritors of the October revolution of 1917, and guardians of its spirit, whereas ultra-nationalists consider the October Revolution to have been a Judeo–Masonic conspiracy. Nevertheless, they are united more and more closely in a political struggle against the democratic forces.

I think that it is possible to explain this phenomenon, for in spite of their apparently diametrical differences, both groups have common totalitarian archetypes of consciousness underlying their thinking. This is not the first time in our history that this unholy alliance has occurred. One recalls the Hitler/Stalin Pact of 1939. But precedent is not explanation. I believe that this odd teaming is not to be explained only by the political expediency of the times, in 1939 or now, but that it has very deep roots. Unless we expose those roots, we shall not understand the contradictions historically exposed in Red Square on May Day 1990: neither the extent of the political courage of Gorbachev in releasing *glasnost* into our society in the first place, nor the pent-up frustrations of those using the new-found freedom of expression to criticise him. Unless we expose these roots, digging deeper into our recent history, we shall not understand why revolution in the Soviet Union is necessarily, predominantly and paradoxically socio-political and moral in the midst of economic ruin, when common sense might seem to suggest that a good dose of capital and consumer goods could fix things well enough.

This marks one of the most fundamental differences between the situations in Eastern Europe and the Soviet Union. In truly Russian fashion, we must pass through repentance and the exorcism of old ideological demons which have tormented our minds and our souls for so long. Our East European neighbours do not share this predicament. The totalitarian ideology was always a superficial element of their social structures and never penetrated their inner selves as it did ours; and they did not commit our sins. That is why for us the process of disposing of our ideological mythology is much more tormenting and inflicts such pain. But without enduring this patiently now, when the 1989 revolutions of Eastern Europe offer us an example, hope and our best chance, we are fated to be thrown back again and again, as happened with the first Khrushchev *perestroika* of the 1950s and early 60s.

The Outpost of Ilich by M. Khutsiyev was a very popular film of the early 1960s. In one clip, the children of the 20th Party Congress, the children of Khrushchev's "Thaw", sing of "the commissars in the dusty helmets ... at that long ago time, in the Civil War ...", their hands firmly clasped together, with democratic enthusiasm shining in their eyes. Both in the romantic words and the children's earnestness are to be seen all of the contradictoriness and limitation of the first *perestroika*.

Romanticisation of the "commissars in dusty helmets" – true Leninists, knights without fear and above reproach, who later became the victims of Stalin's Terror – entered as a necessary element into the mythology of the liberal wing of the Soviet intelligentsia of the 1950s and 1960s. (We should remember that a young law student from the provinces, Mikhail Sergeyevich Gorbachev received his first lessons of political education at that time.) Of course their position differed from the official one, with its inarticulate mumbling about "the mistakes, especially in the last period of the life and activity of that prominent Marxist–Leninist I. V. Stalin," but in essence I think that it was just as immoral and shallow.

This formula "especially in the last period" is instructive in its naive cynicism. Stalin's former lieutenants who were responsible together with him for the destruction of tens of millions of people, only refer to this last period because it was only during this period that they found themselves personally under threat as he turned his paranoid and murderous suspicions upon them. For this error, in contrast to all the previous ones which "the Communists fully tolerated", Comrade I. V. Stalin, apparently paid with his life. He may have been poisoned by his entourage; he was certainly left alone to die without assistance for over twenty-four hours. It is interesting that this formula to this day retains its official and mandatory status for Party members. The CPSU Central Committee Resolution of 30 June 1956, "On the Cult of Personality and its Consequences," which contains it, has not been repealed to date and the CPSU Committee has not made any new official statements in this regard.

It is a hard and bitter thing to face unpalatable truths. Others in this book have noted that it seems to take about a generation before a society can engage in frank, public retrospection, repentance or forgiveness. In the USSR it has certainly required almost four decades in order, only in 1989 and 1990, to begin to approach a public understanding of the obvious conclusion that in a civil war there can be no victors and no heroes. There can be only the vanquished, the victims and the executioners. A civil war is always a tragedy. It is the fault and crime of politicians who were unable (or who did not wish) to foresee and prevent the consequences of their actions.

On 25th October 1917 (the day of revolution), on 5th January 1918 (the day of the dissolution of the Constituent Assembly) and on 6th July 1918 (the day of the liquidation of the last party in opposition to the Bolsheviks, the Left Socialist Revolutionaries, marking the installation of the One-Party system), V. I. Lenin and L. D. Trotsky each time methodically chose those options which favoured the accretion of absolute power to their party, but which also led inevitably to the catastrophe of a civil war which cost the lives of millions of people. I will not discuss here the responsibility of the politicians of the other camp. Enough has been said about this in the last seventy years.

The three-year slaughter, which devastated Russia's land and people, eventually ceased. On 2nd October 1920, the Third All-Russian Congress of Communist Youth convened. The young enthusiasts were ready to hang upon every word of their charismatic leader. V. I. Lenin's speech on that occasion, "Tasks of the Unions of Young People," is frequently cited but usually in connection with one admonition: "Study, study and study more". But he also spoke there in detail about other much more important things. Lenin spoke of the Communist understanding of morality and he spoke about the attitude towards the peasantry (i.e. towards the huge majority of the Russian people.)

V. I. Lenin explained to his young Komsomol listeners that we Communists do not believe in fairy tales about God and classless morality:

We say that our morality is entirely subordinated to the interests of the class struggle of the proletariat. Our morality derives from the interests of the class struggle of the proletariat. And what does this class struggle consist of? The class struggle continues, it has only changed its forms. This class struggle of the proletariat is so that the old exploiters cannot return, and so that the splintered mass of ignorant peasants are united in a single alliance. If a peasant sits on a separate parcel of land and appropriates excess bread to himself, that peasant is already turning into an exploiter .... It is necessary that everyone work according to one common plan, on common soil, at common factories and plants, and according to a common routine.

Ten years later the delegates to that conference, now grown up, evicted entire *kulak* families and deported them to Siberia under conditions of appalling privation. On the way, millions of children died of hypothermia and of hunger. Yet did they not act precisely upon Lenin's analysis in identifying the *kulaks?* Was not their action then quite moral, by Lenin's lights?

We are amazed today at such massive, pathological cruelty. One can understand the logic in the behaviour of the professional murderers – Stalin and Molotov, Kaganovich and Epshteyn, Postyshev and Kosior. Perhaps one can also understand a liberal Communist, N. I. Bukharin, whose wife recalled that he lay sobbing on his couch out of pity for those dying of hunger, but who, in strict accord with the resolution of the 10th Party Congress on the unity of the party continued to praise Koba (Stalin's nickname).

But how is one to understand the tens of thousands of Davydovs, Nagulnovs and Pavlik Morozovs[2] willing to deny natural warmth, loyalty, personal feeling in their subordination to Lenin's higher purpose? Was it not the consequence of a revered leader explaining to them that "there is no God" and that what is

[2] Davydov and Nagulnov were heroes in Mikhail Sholokhov's novel *Ploughed Virgin Land*, which praised Collectivisation. Pavlik Morozov was a real boy who betrayed his father to the OGPU [Secret Police] for having helped *kulaks* to escape deportation to Siberia from his village by issuing them with papers to show that they were not wealthy peasants. This little snitcher has been presented thereafter as a role model for Soviet children; there is even now a statue to him in Moscow.

moral is not reverence before the absolute values of human life but, "uniting the splintered mass of ignorant peasants into a single alliance"? In its destructive consequences, this moral sermon can be placed on a par with the appeal of only one other charismatic leader: "We may be inhuman... We may work injustice... We may be immoral, but if our people is rescued we have once more opened up the way for morality!"[3]

Overall, the perverse and conscious moral blindness and ideological fanaticism of the original leaders of the Bolshevik Party are still striking, viewed from over seventy years later. In the balance of historical judgement, I believe that it was their attempts to implement from as early as the beginning of 1918, primitive Campanellan Communist utopias about the "common factory" and the common labour camp that caused the civil war to occur on such a destructive scale.

But then, in October 1920, V.I.Lenin called for everything to begin all over again. Only the Kronstadt uprising and a real threat of the loss of power in the fire of a peasant rebellion forced this flexible tactician to make a temporary retreat. It is true that his deathbed papers contain a note about the need for a "fundamental re-examination of our views on socialism". However, as his companions-in-arms explained, correctly in my view, "this was not the *vozhd'* (leader) speaking, but the *vozhd's* illness".

Having recovered a little, and well fed at the expense of the peasantry, the Party, now headed by I.V.Stalin, resumed its pitiless civil war against its own people. In not a single official Party document, including Gorbachev's Kremlin speech on the occasion of the 70th Anniversary of the October Revolution, have collectivisation and dispossession of the *kulaks* been condemned as crimes against humanity. Moreover, they entered and remain in the canonical listing of the historical services of the Party to its ever grateful people. Therefore the question which is posed with increasing frequency of whether a civil war in the USSR is possible is incorrectly posed. The right question is *the reverse* of this one: Will we be able to stop once and for all the civil war in

---

[3] Speech on "Politics and Race: why are we Anti-Semites?" by A.Hitler, 20 April 1923, translated in N. H. Baynes ed., *The Speeches of Adolf Hitler*, April 1922-August 1939, Vol. I, Howard Fertig, New York, 1969, p. 60.

Russia, which has lasted, in hot and cold phases without interruption, for seventy three years and can we finally establish civil peace in this country?

All of the problems that are breaking Russia's heart – national, social, political and moral problems – are fraught with the possibility of an uncontrolled explosion. All, in my opinion, stem from two interrelated sources: the philosophy of "the victors" of the Hot Civil War as preached by the ruling elite, and the political immorality of this power, as formulated, sanctioned, taught and advocated by V.I.Lenin. "What is moral is that which serves the interest of the class struggle of the proletariat" teaches Vladimir Ilich. And what serves the interests of the class struggle of the proletariat is defined by the "Owners of the Ideas", a narrow group of rulers who are not burdened either by a profound education, or by serious moral reflections.

As I write this, I hear immediately indignant objections on two main points ringing in my ears. First, did we really neither condemn nor disassociate ourselves from these old ideas; and did we not change? Have we not proclaimed the priority of human values? Yes of course we did change. For example, I do not exclude the possibility that these words will be published in the Soviet Union. But in the main, I fear that our society and especially its power structures have remained fundamentally unchanged, defining morality in Lenin's way and therefore fundamentally immoral in normal, human terms. Under pressure, in any crisis situation, this is consistently and vividly apparent.

The catastrophe at the Chernobyl Nuclear Power Plant was terrible. But no less terrible was state policy after this ecological and technological catastrophe. A secret instruction existed, unknown until recently, which prohibited doctors from making the obvious diagnosis of radiation illness in any person who was connected with the accident.[4] This government instruction

---

[4] "To all military commanders. Explanation." Central Military Medical Commission of USSR Ministry of Defence, 7th July 1987, by Surgeon Colonel Baksutov. Point 2: *"All acute somatic conditions of people participating in the liquidation of the consequences of the accident must not be connected with exposure to the effects of ionising radiation."* The existence of this instruction was publicly revealed just before the Parliamentary Hearing on Chernobyl in April 1990.

dooms millions of people – the "liquidators of the accident" and the residents of the affected *oblasts* – to a slow and agonising death. Contrary to elementary human morality, but to the benefit of a perverse high state and ideological interest which apparently cannot bear to admit either the true and horrendous extent of contamination or the powerlessness of the state to mitigate the effects of what its power station had done, people *are not allowed to be resettled* (except in an unrealistically tight zone). Instead, they are forced to fulfil and to overfulfil agricultural plans on their irradiated land. Then their contaminated products are disseminated throughout the country, mixed with food from uncontaminated sources and sold to all. Such a Kafkaesque mixture of the absurd and the cruel is possible only where public consciousness is in the grip of a dominating and distorted ideology, captivated by a conviction of the omnipotence of the State.

In the USSR, the source of this ideology is clear. It comes from that inhuman relativism in Leninist morality which is derived from the absolute predominance given to ideological and class (i.e. "Inner Party" defined) expediency and from the arrogant conviction that everything is permitted to the "commissars in dusty helmets" and their successors, because they know what must be done better than anyone else. When Andrei Dmitriyevich (Sakharov), a saintly man, appealed to their conscience, what hatred those in the hall breathed at him during the First Congress of Peoples' Deputies and at the Presidium of the Second Congress, three days before his death. With justice, his widow Yelena Bonner blamed that hatred, coming on top of his earlier and long suffering, as one of the reasons for his premature death.

The slaughter on 9th April 1989 in Tbilisi, Georgia, which took away young lives was terrible. But no less terrible was the reaction of the state, which includes the members of the new Congress of Peoples' Deputies, to what took place. At the time of writing, already more that a year has passed during which Generals, Cabinet ministers and Politburo members have continued to weave and dodge. Not only has not one of them repented (this word is simply absent in their Party dictionary) but not one of those immediately responsible has even expressed sympathy to their victims' families. Up to 22nd April 1989, they denied that any poison gas was used in the massacre. Then they conceded that one type of gas had been used. Up to 3rd May 1989 they maintained that only one type of gas was used, but then they admitted that another, more lethal, was also employed. On 31st May 1989, during the Congress of Peoples' Deputies, they applauded the bloodstained General Rodoniov, who had commanded the operation.

On 24th December 1989, the delegates applauded General Katusev, the military investigator whose report on the Tbilisi massacre whitewashed the armed forces and who tried to deny the findings of the Sobchak Commission of Inquiry established by the Supreme Soviet (I served as adviser to one of the Commission Members). Katusev's lies (for so they were) were only rejected by the Congress and the Commission's report accepted after the Georgian and Baltic delegations and members of the Inter Regional Group of Deputies walked out during his presentation. Fearing that if the Georgians walked out they would never come back, but declare independence unilaterally, Gorbachev stopped the proceedings and asked them to return. After this high drama, the report was accepted and Katusev implicitly rejected. Then on 6th February 1990, Gorbachev, Ligachev and Shavardnadze engaged in a fishwives' brawl at the Central Committee plenum, shifting the blame for ordering the massacre from one leader to another.

Just before the bickering over blame for Tbilisi, a fresh demonstration of the continuing power of Lenin's morality occurred. From 11th to 13th January 1990, a pogrom of Armenians took place in Baku. People were thrown out of windows and publicly set on fire. Yet the local and central authorities were strangely inactive. There were troops located in the city, but they did not intervene to stop the mayhem. However, on 19th January, a real prospect appeared that power would shift from the local Party apparatus to the organisation of the Popular Front. On the night of 19-20th January, additional troops entered the city, not sparing the lives either of the civilian population or of their own soldiers. Why? Why did they not intervene on 11th January when they might have saved the Armenians? The

Minister of Defence, General G.T.Yazov answered with admirable frankness. The troops were deployed, he explained, "to smash the structures of the Popular Front in all enterprises". It is Lenin's logic again. The lives of Armenians were of less value to the Communist authorities than the preservation of their local feudal-Communist structures, which were rotten to the core and had lost all legitimacy in the eyes of the people.

It was the publication of Aleksandr Solzhenitsyn's *Gulag Archipelago* which made it inevitable that in the end our society would be required to reassess the role of V.I.Lenin in our tragic history. Perhaps not surprisingly, we encounter strong resistance as we approach the hard core of the Communist mythology. Any attempt to probe in this direction evokes withdrawal and resistance. Through *glasnost*, we have learned much about the Civil War and this is to the great credit of the grass roots publicists and investigative journalists who brought these things out. Yet while some "liberal" journals and papers attempted to canonise the political and military leaders who fell victim to Stalin in the Purges of 1937, documents and testimonial reveal to us what butchers these victims of 1937 were from 1917 through the 1920s.

The appalling directives instructing the extermination of the Cossacks, the mass shooting of hostages, the destruction of entire villages, the first labour armies and first concentration camps were, as a matter of simple historical fact, signed by L.D.Trotsky, Ya M.Sverdlov, G.Ye Zinovyev and I.V.Stalin. This is now openly known in Soviet society and these people are universally regarded as butchers and murderers. Even the clearly anti-democratic Russian ultra-nationalists, such as those associated with *Pamyat* (the best known of the Russian ultra-nationalist groups), can easily join in this condemnation, since three of them were Jews and one a Georgian.

But these men were the closest associates of V.I.Lenin. Could they have carried out their inhuman policy without the knowledge and approval of Vladimir Ilich? Even the boldest investigative journalists balk at this point. They reason that either Vladimir Ilich did not know or if he did, was not able to stop them. But this just isn't true.

Here we read a document reproduced in an historical maga-
zine, the *CPSU Central Committee News* of August 1989. It is a
telegram directive written to Comrade Zinovyev in Petrograd:

Comrade Zinovyev! Only today we learn in the Central Committee that in
Piter the workers want to respond to the killing of Volodarsky with mass
terror and that you held them back. I protest resolutely! You are
compromising yourself. We threaten mass terror even in the resolutions
of the Soviet of Deputies, and when it comes to deeds we hold back the
entirely justifiable revolutionary initiative of the masses. This is impossible! It is necessary to encourage the energy and massiveness of the terror!

The telegram is dated 26th November 1918 and this striking
document is cited without comment. The cruelty and cowardice
of Zinovyev in Petrograd during the Civil War is well known. But
apparently even Zinovyev's mass terror was insufficient for Ilich.
Nor can it be said that this telegram is selectively quoted, out of
context. Hundreds of such documents can be cited.

Herein lies a paradox. Judging by all of the testimonies of his
contemporaries, on a personal everyday plane Vladimir Ilich was a
modest and decent man. He, having consigned thousands of
families to the furnace of "massive terror" by his telegrams, could
touchingly and defensively take offence for his own wife. "I take
an insult to my wife as my own," he said when Stalin insulted her;
and in an entirely un-Marxist way he feebly wrote to Stalin,
"Would you be so kind, dear sir, as to bring me your apologies?"
This makes his ideological fanaticism all the more fearsome. He
would not kill you directly, but would without flinching order the
deaths of thousands for the sake of ideological consistency. He did
not hate his victims in a personal way, as Stalin did. He just
eliminated them purely mathematically as a nuisance to his
conception of an optimal social structure. He was himself a victim.
First, he was an irredeemable slave to the ghastly proposition of
the primacy of ideology over people. Later, after suffering a
stroke, it was black irony that he became a physical prisoner also,
held incommunicado in Gorky village, near Moscow, by Stalin
and his other close collaborators during the last year of his life.

History has already shown on all continents that everywhere
that the utopian ideology of Communism has seized power it has
led to civil war and genocide. Like mythological Uranus,

Communism seems condemned to eat its own children. So why continue this experiment which has already been supplied with such vast and mainly Russian human fodder? In order to end the Civil War once and for all, this ideology must be removed from power.

It is futile to try and extinguish it. That, in any case, is to be trapped in a mirror of Communism's pitiless absolutism. In any society there will always be some portion of spiritually impoverished people who may be attracted by what I consider to be primitive and morally alienating totalitarian levelling utopias. I guess that given free choice, this portion will never rise above twenty per cent of the population; and that is *precisely* how much support the Bolsheviks received at the elections to the Constituent Assembly in 1917 when they had just seized power promising everything and not yet having discredited themselves. So let these twenty per cent unite, struggle and try to turn others to their fanatical faith. Only this aggressively obedient minority must not be allowed to establish its dictatorship, as took place seventy three years ago in Russia.

There can be no civil peace in a country where absolute power is held by an ideology that has always considered that in order to sustain its rule it is moral to kill children – the children of the Tsar at Yekaterinburg in 1918, the *kulak* peasant children deported to Siberia in the 1930s, the children of the Crimean Tatars in 1944, the children of Tbilisi in 1989, and the Belorussian children from the orphanage in the town of Slavgorod, Mogilev *oblast*, who for four years have lived on territory where even today the level of radiation fall-out from Chernobyl exceeds all permissible norms.

Is it not time for us to say at last with Ivan Karamazov that, "higher harmony is not worth the smallest tear of even one tormented child," (and Lenin would have found such an equation preposterous) "... What kind of harmony is it if it's Hell?" Shall we not agree with Karamazov that, "...too high a price has been set on harmony," defined in Lenin's terms, and that, "it's not at all within our means to pay so much"? Therefore, following in the footsteps of Ivan Karamazov, is it not time to say that, "we most respectfully return our ticket"?

To return a ticket to the Communist Paradise does not mean that we can renounce our obligation to travel. We have no choice but to travel a hard road. The ticket of the Democratic Russia movement tries to present a new route. I will not write about economic proposals except in passing; for basically, it advocates transition from an administrative economy to a market economy and Professor Galbraith has elaborated that issue extensively in his chapter here, as in his other recent works. I wouldn't add anything significant to his analysis and would concur that he is absolutely right to warn that such a transitional period is very difficult. Also, it must be controlled to a sensible degree by the government. It must be a transition from an administrative system to a modern welfare state. Professor Galbraith gave many recommendations on this subject and mainly they are already included in the "Democratic Russia" economic platform.

The obstacles to be surmounted on the road which the USSR must now travel on the democratic ticket are many. They are spiky with contradictions: for example, to obtain economic efficiency, we need social differentiation (but on just criteria, i.e. that hard workers get higher wages); but there is an extremely strong ethos of egalitarianism, of the duty of common suffering, which makes that differentiation difficult to accept. Again, in converting to a market economy, the existing political elites are against it because they fear that they will lose their existing privileges, perks and power. Thirdly, in the initial stages of real economic restructuring, the living standards of a considerable part of the population will inevitably decline; but the current standard is so low that further lowering would probably incite social unrest. So, paradoxically, society as a whole needs the changes urgently, but individual social groups do not want them. For the first and third problems, the lower and middle classes are against change; for the second problem, the elites are against change.

Unfortunately, the obstacles exist not only at the level of personal resistance. National and regional aspirations can unintentionally work against economic reform. We need a big, national market, but each republic is trying to create a separate economy, isolated from the rest of the country, in order to provide what its public wants as well as to assert its autonomy. Yet even when we do have a national market, it is weak in relation to the world economy. The USSR only enters the world market on any scale to sell products with low added value, such as raw materials or oil. Here again, contradictions abound. We need a comprehensive technological restructuring of the economy, to escape from our obsession with smokestack industries. But this is impossible without a skilled and motivated workforce; and stimulation of workers is difficult because there is an inadequate supply of goods to satisfy their demands. People want goods, not money, because money seems to be useless in getting them what they want. Consequently, higher wages are ineffective in motivating greater effort and productivity. As we say, "They pretend to pay us and we pretend to work." Arching over all these obdurate obstacles of the traditional sort are the insistent imperatives of newly visible global security problems which, in the USSR as in much of Eastern Europe, are most immediately pressing in the natural environment. Nature, as well as Man, has been scorned and abused for seventy three years. Ecological catastrophe has been caused by our grotesquely over-developed smokestack industries, by mono-maniac monoculture agriculture and by intensive irrigation which has ruined the Aral Sea and large parts of central Asia. Finally (as if this catalogue of gloom were not enough) we must note the synergistic nature of all these problems. All are occurring at the same time.

Let me turn now to the political part of the "Democratic Russia" ticket. It is often said that to make democratisation irreversible the Soviet Union must pass from a one-party system to a multi-party system. I would put it slightly differently. I would say that we must shift from a *zero-party* system to a multi-party system. As I explained earlier, the Communist Party is not a social political union; it is just a structure of power.

I, myself, am not a Communist, but I know that millions of people in my country don't share my views and consider themselves to be Communist, and it is necessary for them to have a real political organisation to express their views, not a semi-secret society for power and privileges. Yet it is not after all very difficult to undo the omnipotent *nomenclatura* and to transform this organisation into a real Communist Party. To accomplish this, no violent revolution, nor storming of any Bastille is necessary. It is necessary only to change one or two paragraphs in the CPSU election regulations because since 1903, when this "Party of the New Type" was created, no person has ever been elected to a leading post within it. They were always appointed. This was the system of election "by acclaim", and the secret of the power of the *nomenclatura* lay in this system because it was self-appointed, self-assigned from above. The demand of many ordinary Communists now, all over the country, is to have election to the Party Congress in a different way: specifically, to have direct election chosen from alternative candidates from the Party districts. This seems rather simple, but today in the Party, election to the Congress and to all leading posts is multi-staged: ordinary Communists must elect District Assemblies, Regional Assemblies and so on and so on; and so in this process, genuine election is erased. This change of election instruction will change the CPSU dramatically. Not only will another kind of person be elected, but the nature of the power of this person will be quite different.

A multi-party system is not necessary for us as an aim in itself. It is necessary for us to ensure peace in a situation where we are threatened by civil war. Only when all three mainstreams of contemporary political activity in the Soviet Union – Social Democratic, Communist and Nationalist – shall be presented in civilised forms by political parties, only then will there be a possibility of constructive dialogue between them, and only then will extremists in all camps be isolated.

The nationalist problem in the USSR is very different from that in Eastern Europe. We have about one hundred and thirty nationalities in our country. The Democrats' point is that the only way to save the Soviet Union – and "Democratic Russia" wants to save the Union – is to dissolve it immediately and to conclude a new Union Treaty, voluntarily subscribed. This was Andrei Sakharov's proposal. We think that in this way, the political dignity and national aspirations of all republics will be satisfied. They will see that there are many reasons of an economic, historical, cultural and demographic nature for preserving the whole confederation. There is scarcely one republic with a uniform national population.

There is also a security reason for trying to preserve the Union. For example, I remember that in the midst of the Georgian crisis during the summer of 1989, I was talking with one of the leaders of the Georgian National Liberation Movement. He said, "We are speaking all the time about Georgian independence, but basically this idea is self-contradictory. If in Moscow there remains an authoritarian government, they will never give us independence; but if in Moscow there comes a democratic government, Georgian nationalists could not dream of a better friend than a democratic Russia." (Georgia and Armenia are surrounded by the Muslim world and certainly they have a natural inclination to preserve some kind of union with Orthodox Christian Russia.)

So far I have examined many Soviet problems and have not mentioned the one which most excites people in the West: the question of Gorbachev. For heuristic reasons, I find it helpful to distinguish two main Gorbachev (or "Gorby" as he is often called) models. *Gorby Model One* is that he is a convinced liberal democrat who is doing the maximum possible to reform his country and to integrate it into the world community under tremendous resistance from the conservative forces. *Gorby Model Two* is that he himself has grown up in this Communist *nomenclatura* environment, that he shares all the prejudices and all the restrictions of this closed society and that he has already reached the limits of his democratic potential. I don't think that either model is true. The truth is a mixture of both. Physicists know that in quantum mechanics the wave function of an object is the superposition of different contradictory states, and only a definitive macro-experiment leads to wave function reduction and makes the real state of the object manifest.

In 1990 Gorbachev faces this crucial test. All his political effort of 1987-1989 was concentrated upon balancing in the middle of the political spectrum: scaring conservatives by the threat of the Left and the Left by the threat of the Right; keeping to one side, keeping to the other. Trimming always. I think that in the final analysis the only course which promises political survival for

Gorbachev is to unite with the democratic forces. He is hated by right-wing conservatives for all that has already happened in the Soviet Union and Eastern Europe since 1985 and they will never forgive him for this. For them he is a traitor to their *nomenclatura* interests. Certainly, the Left is disappointed by his performance on many occasions but is always ready to accept him as its leader and to fight with him against a possible conservative overthrow. (For example, in the December 1989 Plenum when Gorbachev was strongly attacked by conservatives on the Lithuanian question, he was defended by Boris Yeltsin who was regarded widely as his opponent from the Left).

Gorbachev's predicament was analysed in the celebrated article by Z, entitled "To the Stalin Mausoleum".[5] I think that it was misunderstood in the West and in the Soviet Union; for example, Shevardnadze made some very negative remarks about it. The article was regarded as anti-Communist and anti-*perestroika*. But in fact, Z dismissed completely the western hardliners' theory that *perestroika* was a ploy for making Communism stronger and more dangerous to the West. He showed convincingly that this system could not become stronger in any way without making the transformation from Party State into civil society. Z does not believe that Gorbachev is capable of securing this transition. So in my classification, he shows belief in Gorby Model Two, and I think that Z has some reasons to hold this belief. Z was accused of advising the West not to help Gorbachev. Not at all. He advised the West to be co-operative in disarmament and to make investment in the Soviet economy in ways to strengthen a new market-orientated structure. But Z believes that *perestroika* will fail because Gorbachev is not capable of securing it. In the end, Z thinks, he will be overthrown by the right-wing conservatives.

I must agree that this is a rather reasonable scenario; on trends crystallised by the contradictions seen in Red Square on May Day 1990, it is even, I think, the most probable. By alienating democratic forces, by expelling from the Party the most progressive and independent minded people he is isolating himself

---

[5] Z, "To the Stalin Mausoleum", *Daedalus*, January 1990.

and literally paving the way for the right-wing coup. If Gorbachev makes more and more compromises with the Right, some day the conservatives will not need him any more and will overthrow him. The other possible scenario, and in my opinion the only hope for the survival of Gorbachev and of *perestroika* is, as I wrote above, for him to unite with such people as B. Yeltsin, Yu. Afanasiev, N. Travkin and other radical democrats in fighting the party bureaucracy together, hard as he may find it personally to have to make such alliances. It is impossible to sit on two chairs at the same time. It is impossible to be the head of Government and the head of the Opposition. It is impossible to be the Pope and Luther. He must choose.

What would these two scenarios mean for the West? I think that the first and negative scenario would be terrible for us Russians but would not be very dangerous for the West. Even if conservatives took power, they would have no ability to intervene in Eastern Europe. They would be too preoccupied with National Liberation Movements in the Soviet Republics and in preserving their power in Moscow and in Russia in general. There has been in 1989 and in 1990 rather convincing confirmation of this assessment. During the Azerbaijan troubles in January 1990, the Minister of Defence called up reservists; but the indignation amongst people was so great that in three days this order was rescinded and the reservists went home. The Afghanistan syndrome is so strong in Soviet society that in the worst scenario and under the worst leader, the Soviet Union cannot use force outside its borders, even if the leadership wishes it.

It is not to be excluded that under certain, not inconceivable circumstances, we may face another neo-Stalinist cycle in our history. But it will be comparatively short. The potential right-wing regime would have no solution to any Russian problem other than blood and more blood. They couldn't hold power for long.

In the long run, I believe that democracy will win. The essence of this victory would mean a conclusive transition from the Party State to civil society and the end of civil war which in various forms, Hot and Cold, has been devastating my country for seven decades. It will demand *perestroika* of a much deeper character than hitherto achieved. We must reconstruct not only the political and economic but also the moral and spiritual foundations of our society. And never again must we permit any ideology to gain the saddle and reins of our State and to ride us roughshod across the faces of the people, like the horsemen of the Apocalypse.

8 James Eberle

Understanding the revolutions in Eastern Europe: a British perspective and prospective

Admiral Sir James Eberle GCB, served in the Royal Navy which he entered as a Midshipman at the Royal Naval College, Dartmouth. He continued his studies during his Service career at the Royal Naval College, Greenwich and at University College, Oxford where he undertook a Defence Fellowship.

In 1976 he became a member of the Admiralty Board. He was subsequently appointed Commander in Chief Fleet, Allied Commander in Chief Channel, NATO Commander in Chief Eastern Atlantic, and Commander in Chief Naval Home Command. He retired from the Royal Navy in 1983.

Upon leaving the Navy, he became Director of the Royal Institute of International Affairs in January 1984. He takes a particular interest in East–West, especially Anglo-Soviet, defence including European defence cooperation. He has written extensively on international affairs. He is a member of the British Königswinter Steering Committee and of the UK–Japan 2000 Group which seeks to promote better relations between the United Kingdom and Japan. He leads the British contribution to a British–American group concerned with the development of UK–US relations for the 'Successor Generation'.

Sir James Eberle is Chairman of the Editorial Advisory Board of Naval Forces *and Chairman of the Committee and Trustees of* The Naval Review.

8

This chapter, in seeking to understand the Spring in Winter revolutions in Eastern Europe, starts from a different position than that of the other contributors. For I am a practitioner, not an academic. I am not a politician, nor now a government servant. I have a naval background which spans the invasion of Normandy in 1944 to the recapture of the Falkland Islands in 1983. I am in many ways 'a child' of the US relationship and of NATO. Since 1983, as the Director of The Royal Institute of International Affairs, I have been able to have widespread contacts with the Soviet Union and Eastern Europe; yet I am not a specialist. I am one of that great army of those who might have predicted – but did not – what has probably been the most fundamental, rapid and non-violent period of change in Europe's history.

Yet when I think back, there were clues to what was about to happen. I was aware of an underlying sense of change. But like so many others, I failed to read these clues correctly. My view will be a rather personalised one, because it seems to me that the value, in terms of perspective, that I can be now, when the events of these last remarkable months are still so close upon us, is as one informed source which may help in a very small way to mould the theories, the ideas, the lessons that should in due course be drawn from the rich seam of history that this unique period is providing.

There are two hypotheses that form the basis of my perspective. The first is that the changes in Eastern Europe and the Soviet

Union have been as much the triumph of communication, as the failure of communism. The second is that the existence of nuclear weapons, and the increasingly powerful and destructive capability of modern conventional weapons, have made a major contribution to an awareness that the high cost of pursuing *national* interests by war greatly outweigh the benefits from the peaceful pursuit of common interests between nations. These *common* interests span the fields of economic interdependence, of political cooperation, of security and of environmental concerns.

The first experience which frames these hypotheses for me was on one of my early visits to Moscow in 1983. I recall three incidents. The first was in speaking to the Deputy Director of one of the major Institutes of the Academy of Sciences on the subject of the future of international relations. He remarked that, as we moved into the next century, the Soviet Union would remain a superpower in military terms, in that it would retain the power to destroy the world – but that in every other sense the Soviet Union would become increasingly irrelevant. I did not know then either whether he meant it, or if he did, whether to believe him.

I went on to a meeting at which I listened to a Soviet General describe why the Soviet Union felt threatened by the United States. The United States, he said, had an offensive global strategy, was expanding its defence budget, was extending its worldwide network of bases, was increasingly exploiting technology for military purposes and so on. As I listened I realised I could hear exactly similar words being spoken by any NATO General as to why we in the West felt threatened by the Soviet Union. Here was a case of total mirror imaging. The discussion moved on to economic issues. We discussed the workings of the Soviet economy. Two Soviet economists from the Institute gave a reasoned and apparently coherent view of how certain functions of the Soviet economy worked. Subsequently, a senior official from GOSPLAN (the elephantine state planning organisation) inter-vened to comment that he had listened with interest to his two Soviet academic economist friends. They may indeed have believed that the system in theory functioned in this way. In practice, however, it was very different. There followed a considerable internal argument. Gone was my belief that there was a single Soviet 'line' to which all adhered.

My second experience was at the time of Gorbachev's first visit to London shortly before his appointment as General Secretary. I travelled in a car with a Soviet colleague who knew Mr Gorbachev well and had personal experience of work at the top levels of the Soviet Government. He told me that when Mr Gorbachev, as Soviet Minister of Agriculture, visited Canada, Mr Gorbachev underwent a strong political and emotional experience. For the first time Mr Gorbachev saw the reality of what had been achieved in the standard of living of the West compared with that which had been achieved in the Soviet Union. He also described his own experience of how the Politburo worked – how because unanimity was required in decision-taking, it was very easy to get through small changes which had little impact – but how difficult it was to achieve more meaningful changes.

My third experience was of a visit to Hungary. Here was a country under Communist rule which seemed to be beginning to show the acceptable face of socialism. The availability of food and consumer goods in the shops, the atmosphere of relationships between the Communist party and the people, the way of life, and the openness of discussion at both the official and private level was in remarkable contrast to the situation that I had observed in the Soviet Union. So much for the homogeneity of the "Eastern bloc", which was then part of the then accepted Western wisdom.

Thus it was that in the mid 1980s when addressing audiences in both East and West, I started to express the feeling of a growing sense of pan-Europeanism. I put it this way. If you had asked me fifteen years ago 'Are you a European?', I would have answered, 'Certainly not, I'm British'. If you had asked me ten years ago 'Are you a European?' I should have said 'I'm British of course; but yes, I suppose I am a European too'. If you had asked me five years ago, I should have responded 'Yes I am a European,' though adding that I was also British. But I would have had no sense of a Europe that extended beyond the boundaries of NATO and the European Community. Now if you asked me 'Are you a European?', I would respond 'Of course', and I would clearly recognise that Europe did not end at the inner German border.

This then raises the question "Where does Europe end?" In her Bruges speech, Mrs Thatcher described Warsaw, Budapest and Prague as being as much European cities as Bonn, Paris and London. But what about Bucharest – and Vilnius – and Leningrad? It would be difficult to deny the European character of St Petersburg in the early years of this century. But should Europe be defined in such historical terms? Should we attempt to describe Europe as embracing a set of particular cultural or religious values? Europe can be defined in so many ways. Yet "What is Europe?" is no longer an academic question for historians. It is a political question for policy-makers.

Let me return to the first of my two hypotheses – that what we have seen in Eastern Europe is as much the triumph of communication as the failure of Communism – and begin by considering the changing relationship in the economic field between the factors of production, materials, labour, energy, and knowledge. We have only to look at a modern pocket computer, as compared with the size and complexity of a computer of similar power only a few decades ago, which would have filled a small room, to see how much the material, labour, and energy inputs to its manufacture have reduced; and how the knowledge or information element has increased. We use a shorthand for this process by talking of our modern industries as being "knowledge based"; and we speak of the revolution that has been brought about by information technology. We are right to talk in these terms although we should be careful not to associate knowledge based industry with 'service' rather than 'manufacturing' industry. Our failure however has been that we have not sufficiently noted that the impact of the Information Technology Revolution, which is the basis of improved communication, has been as strong in the political field as it has been in our economic, business and personal lives.

The value of communication was well recognised by Lord Callaghan who, as Foreign Secretary, proposed the setting up of an Anglo-Soviet 'Round Table' Group, whose establishment was formally agreed in a joint statement signed in Moscow on 17 February 1975 by Prime Minister Harold Wilson and General Secretary Brezhnev. The purpose of the Round Table was to provide a forum, outside the framework of inter-governmental consultations, for a fresh approach to the consideration of important European and global problems. British and Soviet representatives at the Round Table meetings were to be drawn from various walks of public life. The Foreign and Commonwealth Office and the Soviet Ministry of Foreign Affairs were entitled to send observers from their Embassies, but they did not take part in the discussions. The Round Table has continued to meet annually. It has been paralleled by some other non-official groups such as the 'Edinburgh Conversations'. But the Anglo–Soviet Round Table has remained the most influential element in the UK/Soviet relationship, not least because, on the Soviet side, two of its leaders, Alexander Yakovlev and Evgenii Primakov subsequently became members of the Politburo. Similar 'round table' groups were established with the countries of Eastern Europe. We can never know with certainty what role these groups may have played in helping to promote a climate in which the conventional wisdom of the supremacy of Marxist/Leninist doctrine could be challenged. I only know that I myself was continuingly exercised with trying to understand how, when visiting for round table meetings in the west, the Eastern bloc members could reconcile what they seemed to believe, with what they heard and saw. This problem was, I believe, even more acute for those diplomats that were living in the midst of our western societies. In this way at least, the groups certainly acted as an important channel of communication.

As communication improved at the elite level, so gradually, through the spread of sporting and cultural contacts, through the reinforcement of Western radio by the visual impact of Western television, and through the pursuit of knowledge that knows no national boundaries, there developed a widening understanding in all the Eastern bloc countries that the rest of the developed world was leaving the Communist world behind. The legitimacy of the Communist monopoly of power rested on its ability to satisfy the reasonable expectations of its people in improving their living standards. Increasingly in the West, the improvements in material standards in our way of life were based on the acquisition of knowledge. Where once the basis of political power was the acquisition of basic resources, and thus of territory, the new basis of power was knowledge. Knowledge could not be acquired by military might or by territorial conquest. The appreciation of knowledge required the free flow of information; and the free flow of information was inimical to the maintenance of a Communist system.

Whilst communication provided an underlying climate of the need for change, so it also provided a mechanism which allowed change to take place. Once it was clear in the autumn of 1989 that the Soviet Union did not intend to use military force to support the legitimacy of the old order in Eastern Europe, it was the nightly television screens showing scenes of mass protest that brought to all in the East and the West the confidence that peaceful "people power" could prevail. It was the computer and the photocopier that allowed large numbers of leaflets to be quickly produced. It was the fax machine that allowed these to be widely and rapidly distributed.

The process of change was different in every country, as it continues to be today. This was itself a vindication of British policy towards Eastern Europe that had been amongst the first to be based on differentiation in the treatment of the various 'bloc' countries; and which had sought to provide support to the legitimacy of reformist groups without being seen directly to threaten the established order. As we continue to observe and to react to the process of German unification and change as the other Eastern European countries struggle to build democracy and to rescue their economies and their environment from the ravages of forty years of Communist rule, there are a number of basic questions that we need to consider.

What for instance now constitutes action which can reasonably be considered as interference in the "internal affairs" of another state? What are, for example, "internal" environmental affairs? Pollution respects no borders. What role should the armed forces of a modern state play in the internal political balance between continuity and change? Are the changes in Eastern Europe and the Soviet Union symptomatic of a wider process of change that is taking place on a global scale? What are its implications for the future world order? I flag these questions and will come back to the last when I return to consider "prospects".

My second hypothesis relates to consideration of whether from the changes we have observed during the Spring in Winter Revolutions, we can deduce any fundamental change in the likely political behaviour of the nation-states in Europe. I believe that the answer is yes. I believe that what we have seen is, at least in part, an indication of the fallacy of the MacNamara doctrine that the existence of nuclear weapons only deters the use of other nuclear weapons; and the bankruptcy of the charge of the so-called 'Peace Movement' that nuclear weapons had changed everything other than our thinking. I believe that there is an ever-widening consensus that war, as an act of organised inter-state violence, is no longer an effective or acceptable means of settling international disputes. After it had become apparent that the Soviet Union would not repeat the savage excesses of 1956 and 1968, there was at no time in this process of remarkable change any apparent possibility that war would break out, even though a network of bilateral security guarantees existed throughout the Eastern bloc. At no time was there a stage when the use of nuclear weapons appeared even remotely relevant to the crises through which we were passing. At no time did the existence of the high-technology weapons of the Warsaw Pact, or of NATO, seem likely to play a significant role in the changing structure of real power. Such weapon systems that were relevant were the armed foot soldier, the 'look-alike' tank and perhaps the helicopter. Here was confirmation that the utility of armed force has changed; that the existence of nuclear weapons has changed our thinking about war; that the destructive power of modern conventional weapons is now so great that they are becoming increasingly unusable as a means of achieving long-term political advantage. This is of course not to say that armed force, at the nuclear or conventional level, no longer has any part to play in international relations. It is to say that the perception of the utility of military force is indeed changing and that its effectiveness as a means of achieving long-term national objectives has been called to account and found wanting. There were all those modern arms and nobody on any side could think of any way of using them to their advantage.

Let me turn to *prospects* and the future. I wish to address three issues concerning Europe – the problem of Germany; the future of NATO; and the transatlantic relationship. I will then turn to a global perspective and end my chapter with some thoughts on what I see to be specific British interests.

The disintegration of the Eastern European bloc has occurred at breathtaking speed. But the process of building established democracy will take very much longer than has that of dismantling Communism. There should therefore be time over the next decade to achieve an orderly transition from the two military blocs, NATO and the Warsaw Pact, which have confronted each other for the last forty years, into a new European security order founded on East/West cooperation. In this way, German unification would take place as part of, and in concert with, the wider unification of West and Central Europe.

The unification of Germany might be seen in three stages. The first stage, in which we are already engaged, would see the development of closer economic links and political links. The security of the Federal Republic would remain, as now, firmly anchored in NATO. The GDR would remain a member of the Warsaw Pact. Soviet troops would remain stationed in the GDR and Allied troops would remain stationed in the FRG.

The second stage would involve consolidation of the economic and political links, leading to confederation and the absorption of the GDR into the European Community. It would see the withdrawal of Soviet troops from East Germany and a reduction of Allied troops in the FRG. By the end of this period it should be possible to determine the outline of a future new security structure for Europe which could be evolved perhaps through the framework of the CSCE (Conference on Security and Co-operation in Europe) process. The form of such a new complex of guarantees of mutual security is not yet clear. It must, however, involve all the countries of Europe and include the United States. With a new security structure in place, Germany could become a fully unified state.

However, time is not now available for such an orderly transition. Despite efforts from political leaders in East and West to check pressures for precipitate unification, it had become apparent after the March 1990 elections that early unification with the FRG was most likely. The unification that the people urged was more likely to be that of Hans Modrow's "One united Fatherland", than that of a confederation. Whilst with the possibility at the time of writing of 'all Germany' elections taking place before the end of 1990, it should be possible to put in place the requisite political and economic structures, including German monetary union, to support 'One Germany'. But it is not easy to see how the existing security structures could be adapted to meet this time-scale. Not only is 'German time' running faster than 'European time', but the security clock is not running as fast as the political and economic clock. We are faced therefore with the problem of seeking an interim solution to the security issue.

What is the security issue in 1990? At its base, there lies the reality of the balance of military strength in Europe. Whilst the CFE (Conventional Forces in Europe) negotiations in Vienna are aimed at massive reductions of military equipment in Central Europe, until implementation is completed in several years time, there will still be a large advantage in tanks and artillery on the Soviet side. Against the background of uncertainty about the future of the Soviet political system and of President Gorbachev, and despite the collapse of the Warsaw Pact as a military organisation, the West is reluctant to change the NATO system which has served it so well for some forty years. As NATO sees it therefore, there remains a significant military problem – the potential political instabilities of Eastern Europe and the residual military power, and particularly nuclear weapons power, of the Soviet Union.

On the Soviet side, there is at the level of ordinary citizens, still a residual concern that the United States and NATO wish to see the destruction of Soviet society as they know it, and a fear of a revival of German power and hegemony. At the level of the senior Soviet military commanders, there is a considerable sense of beleaguerment. The Soviet armed forces are under great pressure. They are suffering a post-Afghanistan syndrome, much as the US underwent the post Vietnam syndrome. They are not popular at home. They are blamed for excessive violence and brutality in crushing the pro-Georgian demonstrations in Tbilisi

Square in 1988. They are unpopular in Eastern Europe where they face calls of "Ivan go home". They face a thankless task in trying to maintain civil order between the warring Republics of Azerbaijan and Armenia. The Soviet Navy had to fire on their own merchant ships in Baku. In the Baltic Republics, they face calls for the removal of Soviet bases that are an integral part of the defence of 'the homeland'. They are conducting the removal of Soviet forces from Hungary and Czechoslovakia. They are taking part in negotiations in Vienna and Geneva to reduce nuclear, chemical and conventional weapons. They are required to conduct a speedy run down of their forces as required by Mr Gorbachev's 1988 UN commitments to reduce 500,000 men. This involves making major changes to their military deployments not only in Europe but also in Soviet Asia where there is great uncertainty about the future direction of political events in China. At home, in the first free elections to the Congress of Peoples' Deputies, several of their senior officers who stood as candidates were defeated by their juniors. From the West, they hear frequent voices calling for "caution" over any Western response to changes in the situation of the Warsaw Pact. It is the Soviet side, they hear, that must make all the concessions.

Yet they have now effectively lost the 'buffer zone' of Eastern Europe which buttressed the security of the Soviet homeland. They see the conventional balance of forces in Europe swinging firmly to the advantage of NATO. Even Mr Bush's proposal to reduce troop numbers in central Europe to a common ceiling of 195,000 requires greatly unequal reductions. And in the CFE negotiations, whilst the reductions on the Eastern side cover their forces in the most populated areas of the Soviet Union, the territory to the West of the Urals, the American forces in the continental USA are untouched by the agreement. "Now", they might say, "it appears we will be asked to remove our forces from East Germany, and 'surrender' the territory to NATO. Now too that we have surrendered the leading role of the party, what is to become of the vast political directorate of the Soviet Armed Forces? And when we want to talk to our political leaders about all this, their attention is almost entirely devoted to questions of internal politics." The interim security issue for the Soviets therefore is more of a political than a military issue. Both the Soviet military and the Russian people need to be reassured about the immediate and eventual intentions of the West: about their relations with a new style Russian State.

Two proposals are on the table. The first (which we should continue to reject) is the Soviet proposal for a neutral, unified Germany. A neutral Germany, even one guaranteed by the four powers, and with the nature and size of its armed forces limited by treaty, would be an isolated Germany. An isolated Germany would arouse genuine fears of the rise of excessive nationalism. The danger of a return to extreme nationalism throughout Europe is one we should not take lightly. The second proposal from the West is for a "unified Germany in NATO". Even if NATO troops would not go outside the territory that is now the FRG, this proposal still presents formidable problems. Would NATO territory extend eastwards to the Oder–Neisse line or would it not? If it did, then what security guarantees would NATO be giving to the 'East German' territory, particularly if Soviet armed forces were to continue to be stationed there? If it did not, what then is the meaning of "a unified Germany within NATO" in its initial form? But these are only the opening bargaining positions.

There is now widespread agreement of the need to recognise a special status for the territory of East Germany. The difficulty is in defining such a status that will meet the minimum needs of Western and Soviet security. Michael Howard in the 1990 Alastair Buchan Memorial lecture has put forward the idea of a "special military status ... comparable to that of Finland ... politically independent and free of all foreign military forces but accepting that the Soviet Union had a certain *droit de regard* which might or might not be exercised through the mechanism of the Warsaw Pact." He foresaw such a status perhaps also being eventually enjoyed by a group of countries stretching from Finland, through the Baltic States, Poland, Czechoslovakia, and Hungary to Austria and Yugoslavia, thus forming a *cordon sanitaire* which should satisfy the security interests both of the Soviet Union and of the West. It would, he argued, perhaps also conform to the wishes of the people of these countries themselves. This proposition seems doubtful, since it seems more likely that the countries of Eastern Europe will look more to the West than to the East for their security as well as their economic prosperity.

Additionally, such an arrangement, with or without the abolition of the *Volksarmee*, might well be seen by the Soviet military as not providing a sufficient security reassurance. There is a strong chance therefore that the Soviets would seek to extract a higher price for the removal of their forces (which for administrative reasons could not reasonably be completed in a short period since there is no infrastructure in the Soviet Union to receive them). That price might include the withdrawal of NATO's stationed forces from the territory of the FRG, the removal of all nuclear weapons from German territory, and perhaps that the forces of the *Bundeswehr* should leave the integrated military structure of NATO. Such measures are not likely to be acceptable to the West.

A modification of this general thesis that might be considered acceptable to both sides is that the 'special status' for the East German territory, as an interim solution, should be within the structure of the Warsaw Pact. Although the Pact is already no longer an effective military organisation, there are substantial arguments that its continuance at least for the next few years as a political element of the European security structure has advantages for both sides. For the Soviets, it is an element of continuity and thus reassurance. Here is one familiar 'landmark' remaining on their territory. For the two military alliances, each represents to the other a certain complementarity and utility, not least in the field of implementing and verifying agreements on arms control and reductions. For the West, the continuance of the Warsaw Pact produces certain modifying forces on the freedom of action of the Soviet Union. Much as the Soviets have argued that they did not wish to divide NATO across the Atlantic since they had less to fear from a Washington that remained subject to the moderating influence of West European governments than a Washington that was not, so the West should not be precipitate in removing from the Soviet Union its former allies. But in mid-1990, even the continuance of the Pact as a significant political structure seems to be in doubt.

Whatever new security structure may in the long term be evolved in Europe, it is clear both that the interim arrangements are going to be untidy, and that changes to the policies, doctrine and structure of NATO are required. Some Western leaders have already called for NATO to become a more political alliance. It has, of course, always been a political alliance in a way that the Warsaw Pact has not. In practical terms however, it is difficult to see how to give effect to such a change in the political/military balance of NATO other than by reducing its military role, a move which, arms control apart, would be resisted by a number of NATO governments – Britain, Turkey and Norway come particularly to mind. Nevertheless, if NATO is to retain public support in a situation where the public perception of the threat to the security of Western Europe has substantially reduced, then NATO itself must change. Change may be necessary not only in terms of NATO's policy and doctrine, but also in terms of its structure.

One evident direction of change is towards a greater integration of its West European forces (by for instance the formation of more multinational forces), a direction for which there is both a military and a political rationale. There is, however, an attendant danger that such increased West European integration might make the United States feel unwanted, the Russians feel threatened and the East Europeans rejected.

The extent to which NATO can be changed without undermining its essential military effectiveness and political cohesion will be a matter for delicate judgement. There is indeed an argument that NATO may begin to play a less political role. In Western Europe, it is the European Community and not NATO that stands at the core of European construction and which is the magnet for the countries of the former Eastern bloc. It is not surprising therefore that it is to the Community that the US has turned in seeking to recast its relations with a changing Europe. Recent agreements for regular meetings at Presidential and Foreign Minister level are much to be welcomed. Another strand of transatlantic dialogue is through the Conference on Security and Co-operation in Europe. The CSCE is assuming a growing importance since it is the one forum in which all the European countries (except Albania), are represented. It also, in its three 'baskets', brings together the issues of security, economics and human rights, which are becoming increasingly interwoven. Whilst NATO has, in the past, served a useful role in the CSCE process as a forum in which the Western position could be concerted before being presented to the Eastern bloc, the dismantling of the Eastern bloc has rendered even this role less useful and important. We should therefore look to a significant rebalancing of the channels of transatlantic political dialogue.

Let me turn briefly to the global issues. The fundamental question to be addressed is whether the wave of change that has swept Europe is related to the processes of change that are breaking out in other areas of the world. Southern Africa, the Middle East, Latin America and South East Asia all spring to mind as regions in which progress is now apparent towards the resolution of problems that have appeared insoluble for many years. Is peace breaking out all over the world, and if so, why? For the answer, I return to my first hypothesis. It seems to me that there has been brought about in the world an increasing recognition that common interests outweigh the narrow sectional interests. As the information revolution makes people more aware of the commonality of the problems that face all people and all Governments, there is an increasing awareness of the need for common solutions. The field of the global environment is a particular example of this. The result is that ideology is being removed from the conduct of international relations.

But changes in the effectiveness of military power is also leading to the process of their de-militarisation, a process which will provide new opportunities for the United Nations to play the role in the international security order which its founders envisaged. I should warn, however, of what I see as a threat to this spirit of optimism. It arises from considering the political philosophy of today's young reactionary who, faced with the despair that must be seen by so many in the underdeveloped countries which struggle under the burden of enormous international debt, seeks a path to a better life. Left-wing revolution has become discredited throughout almost all the world. Where then is our reactionary now to turn? One answer could be to a narrow excessive nationalism, accompanied perhaps by religious bigotry. In a world moving away from an order dominated by the two superpowers towards one in which regional powers and regional conflict may play an increasingly important part, such a movement could release very hopeful political forces. We should perhaps hesitate to express too much concern at a possible clash of Islam and Christianity, for fear of encouraging a belief that we need a new 'enemy' to replace Communism; and that we might encourage a self-fulfilling prophecy. But we need to be wary.

Finally, let me turn to particular British interests. The events of late 1989 have heightened an awareness throughout Europe both of the opportunities and the dangers of a new European construction. Change in Eastern Europe, and particularly the prospects for German unification, has brought forward the realisation that consideration of an increase in the membership of the European Community cannot be put off until after 1992, when the process of creating a single market is due to be completed. The progress in negotiations between the Community and the countries of the European Free Trade Area to complete an agreement which, by the acceptance by EFTA of the principle of the free movement of goods, people, capital and services, would form a common 'European Economic Space' has added further impetus to the concept of widening.

Thus, in the 'widening v. deepening' debate that has accompanied each phase of the Community's development, there is now increased pressure for a strengthening of the Community's institutional structures so as to deepen its internal coherence. The pressure is now such that Britain can no longer stand aside from this accelerating process of further economic and political integration. Britain has to choose whether to join the mainstream of an accelerating European development in order to play an active part in determining its outcome; or whether to stand on the touchline with much less significant influence. It is in this respect that the relationship between Britain and the two major actors in the European Community, France and Germany are of the greatest importance. By the British Government's apparent lack of enthusiasm both for European monetary union and for German unification, we have brought our relations with the Federal Republic to an unfortunate low. Efforts are being made on both sides to repair the damage and to sort out short-term differences.

But without a greater sense of a common vision of the future structure of Europe, it seems unlikely that Britain's influence in Bonn, or Brussels, will increase in the near future.

France faces a different but parallel problem. The French are concerned that the new unified Germany should remain firmly anchored within Western institutions and should not be permitted unfettered power in central Europe. Thus there is a clear French interest in retaining a 'special relationship' with Germany and also in strengthening the Anglo/French relationship as a counter-weight to German influence. The French dilemma is the extent to which these two interests are compatible. For the British, therefore, there is an important and growing interest in strengthening our relationship with France. As the two European powers that have overseas interests and some global military reach, that are nuclear powers, and are permanent members of the UN Security Council the two countries have much in common and much on which to build. Unfortunately, the past experiences of both countries of building an *entente cordiale* have not been entirely happy. We need therefore to renew our efforts to strengthen the French connection.

We must, however, not allow the events in Europe to dominate our thinking. We need to remember that there is a wider world than Europe. Race riots in Florence remind us that we have a North African problem as well as a German problem or a British problem. There are important global issues with which Europe has to deal. If Europe is to be a major global actor, then it has to be prepared to act on the world stage. Just as Europe can no longer look to the United States as the principal guardian of European security, so Europe cannot leave to others the promotion and protection of Europe's interests in other areas of the world. Britain has a major, though not unique, part to play in ensuring that the European Community looks outward as well as inward.

Sarah Humphrey

A comparative chronology of revolution, 1988–1990

This chronology was prepared using the following sources:

Keesing's Record of World Events
Economist Intelligence Unit Country Reports
Facts on File World News Digest
With the generous co-operation of the Current Affairs Research
    and Information Service at BBC Bush House.

These sources are gratefully acknowledged.

	Hungary	Poland	E. Germany	Czechoslovakia	Romania	USSR
Jan. 1988	First reports of formation of new Hungarian Democratic Forum by small group which includes reform economists, writers and scientists. Formally established in Budapest and officially recognised by government in September 1988. Around 12,000 members by January 1989.	Banned Solidarity trade union disputes government price policy of steep price rises to basic foodstuffs to amount to 110% over 3 yrs as part of economic reform programme. President Jaruzelski argues there is no alternative but chaos, as critics claim he has no coherent policy on price reform. Planned change to law to permit conscientious objection announced.	**17** 120 detained in E. Berlin at counter-demonstration to official commemoration of Rosa Luxemburg. Arrests include political, environmental, church and peace activists.	**10** Dubcek breaks 20-yr silence in interview with Italian CP paper *L'Unità*. Welcomes Gorbachev's reforms. Around 200,000 sign RC petition of 31 demands for reform of Church and religious freedoms, backed by Cardinal Frantisek Tomasek.	**25** 70th birthday of Nicolae Ceausescu. Elaborate celebrations include publication of fake congratulatory messages from the monarchs of Spain, Sweden and UK. Denials not published. Severe fuel rationing: from Nov.–Feb. electricity rationed to 1KWH per day per household in Bucharest. Food rationing and acute shortage of staple goods.	Foreign Minister Eduard Shevardnadze on visit to W. Germany calls for elimination of all tactical nuclear weapons in Europe. First international public borrowing by USSR on western capital markets since 1917. Creation of new State Committee for environmental protection.
Feb. 1988	Western reports underline gathering momentum for openness in all forms of media. Official journalists' union initiates campaign to abolish *de facto* censorship in state-controlled media.	Implementation of austerity programme with 40% rise in food costs leads to sporadic strikes and demonstrations backed by opposition and church activists. 20,000 health workers sign petition to protest collapse of health service.	E. German church leaders join W. German intermediaries in pressing for release of those detained on 17 Jan. 7 sentenced and 54 released on condition they emigrate to West Germany.	Official press attacks Cardinal Tomasek in connection with the petition for religious freedoms now signed by 300,000.	15 prominent French citizens issue open letter protesting destruction of historic and religious architecture in Bucharest.	Posthumous judicial rehabilitation of Bukharin, Rykov and 8 other prominent victims of Stalin purges by Supreme Court. Moscow implements removal of SS missiles from CZ and GDR as agreed under the US/Soviet INF treaty. Inter-ethnic violence flares in Caucasus between Christian and Shiite Muslim populations of Armenia and Azerbaijan.

In response to initiative by Charter 77 demonstrations are held outside Romanian embassies in several European capitals and in New York to protest political repression and strict austerity measures in Romania.

1988	rally to commemorate 1848 revolution. Hungarian Academy of Sciences hosts conference on alternative models of Communist economy in Gyor. Delegates from USSR, Bulgaria, CZ, Poland, Yugoslavia, China and 15 western countries. None from Romania or E. Germany.	(parliament) for first time raises the issue of Soviet crimes against Poland in WWII. including Katyn massacre.	simultaneous human rights demonstrations across E. Germany. Church Synod issues statement of solidarity with growing numbers of dissidents as Church/State relationships deteriorate.	in Prague after a mass in St Vitus' cathedral to call for religious freedom and the appointment of bishops to 10 dioceses out of 13 which remain unfilled. 25 Thousands of Catholics defy ban on demonstrations in Bratislava to protest for religious freedoms. Riot police disperse crowds and arrest 100–200.	necessity of austerity measures to accompany debt repayment programme and demands increased austerity and discipline in agriculture.	in the Armenian enclave of Nagorny-Karabach repeats Feb. vote for transfer of control to Armenia from Azerbaijan. Protests escalate after 34 die in anti-Armenian pogrom in Sumgait in late Feb. First centre to conduct public opinion polls opens in Moscow.
April 1988	Hungarian press accuses Romania of blatant violation of basic rights of its minorities, in particular a ban on the use of their native language in Romania which includes that of 2 m. ethnic Hungarians. New independent students' group (FIDESZ) formed as an alternative to official Communist Youth Union at end of March now warned by police to cease activities.	Gas, electricity and other heating costs rise 100% and coal 200%. Official claim that wage increases of 45% have met domestic price rises of 42% since Jan.	Four church newspapers raising civil rights issues temporarily banned. E. Germans receive W. German TV coverage of dissent in GDR and of reforms in USSR ignored by E. German media which retaliates with sharp criticism of W. German society.		Ceausescu announces his 'systematisation' plan to demolish 7,000 villages out of 12,000 in Romania to be replaced by 550 agro-industrial centres by the year 2000. Many of the areas involved have large ethnic Hungarian populations with persistent religious and cultural identity. Shortfall in state food targets as peasants currently produce 40–60% of essential foodstuffs on 12% of land farmed as private plots.	Gorbachev has official meeting with head of Russian Orthodox Church. First such contact since time of Stalin. New law of freedom of conscience in preparation. System of unemployment exchanges and benefits initiated as lay-offs are predicted from economic reforms to include 3 m. bureaucrats by the end of 1990.

	Hungary	Poland	E. Germany	Czechoslovakia	Romania	USSR
May 1988	Janos Kadar – leader since 1956 – jettisoned. Succeeded by Karoly Grosz. Other conservatives out and reformers in, including Imre Pozsgay, outspoken advocate of political pluralism and champion of the Hungarian minorities in Romania.	Strikes at Nowa Huta steel works and at Gdansk shipyards to demand re-legalisation of Solidarity. Students strike in support in several Polish cities. No concessions or negotiations by govt.	Increase in underground press focused on civil rights, environmental issues and anti-militarism.	Cardinal Tomasek stresses govt should make a serious response to the petition for a change in the State's approach to religion, now signed by 500,000.	Rumours that Ceausescu may be increasingly out of touch as Elena plays an enhanced role are reinforced by administrative changes as Elena takes the Chairs of State Commissions on Planning, Organisation and Production Processes.	All three Baltic republics put forward proposals for complete autonomy. Politboro agrees economic decentralisation package for Estonia. Yeltsin removed from Supreme Soviet. He calls for dismissal of Ligachev.
June 1988	27 Largest unofficial protest since 1956 as 50,000 demonstrate in Budapest against Romania's 'systematisation' policies and treatment of Hungarians in Romania. In response Hungarian consulate in Cluj on 28.	13–14 At special CP plenum Jaruzelski acknowledges tense social atmosphere and loss of reform momentum with deterioration in living standards. Airs possibility of a 'pro-reform coalition'.	20 Calls for removal of Berlin Wall and chants for Gorbachev as 5,000 young people gather in E. Berlin to listen to rock concert close to the Brandenburg Gate on other side of the Wall.	Public concern grows over environmental hazards as suppressed critical reports receive wide informal circulation (including CZ scientists warning of risks of the Danube dam project). Accused of subversive and disruptive motives in the official press.	Romania vetoes final draft of accord on Human Rights agreed by all other of 35 participants and due to be signed at Conference on Security and Co-operation in Europe (CSCE) in Vienna, on the grounds that it entails unacceptable interference in internal affairs of member states.	29–1 Reagan–Gorbachev Summit in Moscow. Supreme Court annuls 1936 verdict of treason on Zinoviev and Lev Kamenev. (School-leaving certificate history exams unexpectedly cancelled.) 1,000th anniversary of Russian Orthodox Church.
July 1988	Ctee set up to co-ordinate campaign against Danube dam hydro-electric scheme on grounds of potential severe ecological damage and doubtful economic sense. Pressure to continue work on Hungarian	11–16 Low-key 4 day official visit by Gorbachev to Poland followed by Warsaw Pact summit. Proposals for cuts in conventional forces in Europe and creation of a NATO–Warsaw Pact risk	"20 Theses" laid before the Evangelical Church Congress with very radical political demands which amount to a direct challenge to the ruling party. E. and W. German environment ministers meet in E. Berlin. Some	International appeal by Charter 77 to all states to try to stop the Romanian 'systematisation' scheme.	MFN trading status with US expires and Romania does not seek renewal on grounds that US conditions amount to unwarranted interference in Romania's domestic affairs. 7 officials jailed for illegal	Major policy speech by Gorbachev at 19th All-Union CP conference. USSR Supreme Soviet decides Nagorny–Karabach should remain part of Azerbian following formal vote.

Date					
July 1988 cont.	CZ which is near completion of its section at Gabcikovo, and from Austria which is providing finance and contractors in return for electricity, having cancelled its own similar hydro-electric scheme on environmental grounds. Announced that Budapest stock exchange to be re-activated from 1 Jan 1989.	progress on measures to control atmospheric pollution on issues of industrial effluents to the Elbe and the N. Sea.	reports from Italy by Liechtenstein firm at Sulina in the Danube delta.	under Article 70 of the Constitution of the USSR. Estonia restores prewar flag. Formation of Democratic Front in West Ukraine.	Mass rallies in Baltic republics to condemn the Hitler/Stalin pact of 1939 which provided pretext for their incorporation into the Soviet Union. Reports that the Aral Sea will dry up altogether by the year 2010 with current irrigation practice. Large areas of surrounding soil and water supplies now poisoned or salinated.
Aug. 1988	Grosz visits Romania for official talks with Ceausescu on issues of the Hungarian minorities in Romania and implication of 'systematisation' plans. No concessions by Romania and Grosz perceived to have badly mishandled the issue.	8th anniversary of founding of Solidarity. Further widespread strikes to demand re-legalisation. Authorities accuse Solidarity of taking advantage of economic hardships to manipulate unrest and underline high cost of strikes. Many leaders arrested and talks refused.	21 77 arrests at impromptu demonstration of up to 10,000 in Prague to mark 20th anniversary of 1968 invasion. Marchers chant 'Dubcek' and demand democracy. Enhanced official attacks on Dubcek's welcome of Gorbachev's reforms and emphasis on role of foreign interests in stirring up dissent.	13 27th anniversary of building of the Berlin Wall. Hard currency transfers to friends and relatives in E. Germany from W. Germany to be eased from October 1.	Party press publishes vitriolic attack on reforms in Hungary following Grosz's meeting with Ceausescu. 'Romanian Democratic Action' circulates report which blames over-rapid industrialisation for imminent environmental disaster and in particular blames Elena Ceausescu for high-risk developments in chemical and petrochemical works.
Sept. 1988	12 30,000 demonstrate in Budapest against diversion of Danube at Nagymaros in hydro-electric scheme. Presence of Austrian, Cz and W. German Greens.	Walesa states he is ready to open talks at any time with the authorities to include the RC Church without pre-conditions. Govt insists strikes must stop first but agrees in	Dubcek granted exit visa to travel to Italy to receive hon. degree at Bologna in Nov. Open press coverage of environmental and pollution issues gathers	Honecker visits Moscow to noticeably cool reception in contrast to previous visit. Repeated calls for radical change at Church Synod concerned at increased	King Michael issues call from Switzerland for full-scale rebellion against Ceausescu regime. EC and Council of Europe make formal pro-	Publication of extensive plans to reverse ecological damage to the Aral Sea area. Large-scale demonstrations in Latvia and Lithuania to protest

	Hungary	Poland	E. Germany	Czechoslovakia	Romania	USSR
Sept. 1988 cont.	MPs demand a referendum on the issue with evidence of 60% public opposition. Seen as unprecedented test of secret and centralised planning system. Hungary signs 10-yr co-operation agreement with EC.	principle to round table talks. Solidarity continues to urge round table talks on basis of official recognition of its 'sovereign' status. Poland establishes diplomatic relations with EC.	level of emigration of skilled and articulate workers. Govt renews ban on church press with particular reference to discussion of the issues of environmental pollution, emigration and alternatives to military service.	momentum with discussion of the interconnection between energy supply policies and declining standards of health. CZ establishes diplomatic relations with EC.	test to Romanian govt over planned demolition of villages. **29** Finance minister attacks policies of the IMF and World Bank as operating solely in the interests of the developed western states and banks.	about pollution of Baltic Sea. Inter-communal violence escalates in the Nagorny-Karabach area. **30** Hastily convened Party plenum agrees reorganisation of Central Committee with effective reduction in strength of conservatives and enhanced power to Gorbachev – as Chair of Presidium of Supreme Soviet – and reform members.
Oct. 1988	Law of Corporate Association passed permitting western-style capital market and foreign investment and ownership of companies. Protest in Budapest to mark anniversary of 1956 invasion: first public chants of 'Imre Nagy'. Dam protests continue in Budapest. Grosz insists on go-ahead for financial reasons despite now general consensus that project was a mistake. Parliament votes to proceed but Speaker later	Round table talks fail to be convened as scheduled in view of what are seen as provocative moves by govt, including decision to close Lenin shipyard at Gdansk on economic grounds and dispute over composition and timing of talks. Large student rallies to demand reinstatement of banned Independent Students' Association. Jaruzelski blames state of economy on labour turmoil caused by Solidarity and on 'economic	**10** 80 detained during E. Berlin demonstration against censorship of religious publications.	**28** 87 arrests at demonstration in Prague to commemorate 70th anniversary of the founding of State of Czechoslovakia in 1918. President Husak appoints PM Ladislav Adamec to head new govt in place of Lubomir Strougal. CP reshuffle strengthens position of secretary-general Milos Jakes. Frantisek Pitra replaces Ademec as PM.	**4–6** Strained Soviet-Romanian relations apparent at official visit by Ceausescu to Soviet Union. Absence of Gorbachev from welcoming party indicates cool reception reinforced by critical tone of Gorbachev's speech on 5th. Elena Ceausescu's power-base appears further confirmed. Romania finally responds to Bulgarian pressure to stop one particular source of toxic pollution	Ligachev moved from post as secretary of ideology to take charge of agriculture and loses de facto position as second in command to Gorbachev after effective demotion in Apr. Popular Front movements inaugurated in Latvia, Estonia and Lithuania and proposed at rally in Byelorussia. Finance Minister discloses budget deficit for 1988 of 36.3

1988 cont.	Renewed demands for referendum and mass rally on 30 as issue becomes test of leadership commitment to reform.

7th October: conclusion of 10-day Danube River Cruise from Russe to Budapest organised by Bulgarian 'Eco-Forum' on environmental issues for scientists and officials of all Danube Basin states and USSR (none from Romania). Experts issue collective statement that Danube River faces imminent ecological collapse.

Nov. 1988

Surprise announcement by ruling CP of proposal to move towards 'pluralism within a one-party system' seen to anticipate move to a multi-party system.
24 Miklos Nemeth appointed as PM: young, pro-reform technocrat. New law allows conscientious objectors an alternative to military service as drafts proceed on legislation to secure freedom of the press, of religion, of association, and to form independent trade unions and non-Communist political parties.

7 Prime Minister Rakowski states government committed to reform but relegalisation of the question on Walesa's terms. Walesa warns that deteriorating conditions will lead to explosion of social unrest without radical shift to social pluralism.
30 Live TV debate between Walesa and Miodowicz (head of official trade unions) clearly 'won' by Walesa.
30 Report of Polish Academy of Sciences states that ecological balance has completely collapsed in 27 areas encompassing 1/3 of Polish population. Air unsafe to breathe and water unfit for human consumption.

15 1,000 march on Romanian embassy to protest Ceausescu policies. Solemn official ceremonies to mark Reich 'Kristallnacht' of 1938 – major conciliatory gesture towards Jews who are now to receive compensation payments as in W. Germany.

11 Dubcek to Italy for 12-day visit takes opportunity to restate defence of his own policies and condemn those of his successors. CZ papers now allowed to publish articles from Soviet press strongly in favour of reform and open debate alongside normal harsh criticism of such subversive proposals and analysis. Evidence that current Czech leaders face acute problems in trying to embrace Gorbachev's 'new thinking' without admitting past mistakes.

17 Ceausescu on official visit to E. Germany receives high honours and in joint statement reasserts the right of each national CP to set its own priorities and tactics in response to concrete conditions.
28 Ceausescu reiterates his opposition to reforms in other E. bloc countries and determination to proceed with rural resettlement scheme. Strict fuel rationing to proceed throughout the winter.

16 Estonian Supreme Soviet declares Estonia sovereign. USSR Supreme Soviet declares this vote void as unconstitutional.
29–1st USSR Supreme Soviet approves constitutional amendment to create bicameral legislature with genuine powers:
Upper house of Congress of Peoples' Deputies of 2,250 members – 1,500 to be elected at local and regional levels and 750 to be chosen by CP and other organisations.
Lower house of 400–450 to be chosen by Congress and called Supreme Soviet.
New post of State President proposed.

	Hungary	Poland	E. Germany	Czechoslovakia	Romania	USSR
Nov. 1988 cont.						Transcaucasian quarrels escalate. 800,000 rally in Baku on 23rd to demand integration of Nagorny-Karabach into Azerbaijan.
Dec. 1988	Budapest MP forced to face re-election on Danube dam issue as 'Danube Circle' gains momentum. Hungary's gross hard-currency debt highest per capita in Eastern Europe: 45% of hard-currency earnings currently devoted to debt repayment. Slight reduction in gross debt to $16.6b. announced end of 1988.	10 Rakowski announces new rights for all citizens to obtain and hold passports. 10 Walesa meets Sakharov in Paris at ceremony to mark 40th anniversary of Universal Declaration of Human Rights hosted by Mitterrand.	Slight relaxation of border controls to ease East-West visiting rights. E. Germans make around 7m. visits to the West in 1988.	11 Authorities permit first officially sanctioned opposition rally since 1968 in Prague to mark 40th anniversary of Universal Declaration of Human Rights. 11 Thousands of Catholics demonstrate in Moravia to protest committal of author of January petition on religious freedoms (Augustin Navratil) to mental institution.		7 In major speech on global security at the UN General Assembly Gorbachev announces large troop reductions in E. Europe. 7 Armenian earthquake: 25,000 killed 13,000 injured 500,000 homeless 77 countries donate $100m. aid.
Gross External Debt 1988: ($billion:)	17.3	38.9	19.9	5.1	2.7	
Jan. 1989	11 Parliament passes Law of Association permitting independent associations including political parties and trade unions. Expected to lead to full multi-party political system. Over	16 Central Committee approval of resolution drafted by leadership to open round table talks with opposition on political and trade union pluralism and re-legitimisation of Soli-	15 80–100 arrested at demonstration in Leipzig to demand freedom of expression as Leipzig Church meetings of dissidents gather momentum.	15 5,000 demonstrate in defiance of official ban to mark anniversary of Jan Palach's 1968 suicide in Wenceslas Square. Violent police reaction and 91 arrests. 16–17 Demonstrations	5 Romania insists at last minute on 17 amendments to final draft of Helsinki Review conference in Vienna. Deadlock ensues. 7 Week-long celebrations of Elena	Shevardnadze confirms force reductions including some short-range nuclear weapons and immediate start to destruction of chemical weapons

1989 cont.	revived Social Democrats, Smallholders and National Peasants' parties, Green and minority groups including gypsies and one Stalinist group – Ferenc Munich Org. Press, TV and radio *glasnost* increases further. **26** Exhumation of Imre Nagy (leader of revolutionary government 1956, executed 1958) authorised for proper burial. **28** Imre Pozsgay reveals on radio the report of a Party Historical Commission that 1956 was not 'counter-revolution' but 'popular uprising'. Govt very embarrassed by unauthorised leak of this highly critical historical reappraisal: 'most damning indictment of Soviet system ever published in Eastern bloc'.	ens to resign if proposal rejected. **20** Walesa agrees to talks. Strikes in many sectors of the economy continue as inflation accelerates. Militant members of Solidarity oppose Walesa's agreement to talks.	arrests which include Vaclav Havel. No police interference on **18** but violent response on **19** with 280 arrests and beatings of participants on **20** as up to 5,000 continue to demonstrate each day. **21** 400 detained en route to Jan Palach's grave. **26** 692 sign petition to demand release of political activists. **27** Adamec accuses Cardinal Tomasek of political confrontation.	to block final draft of Vienna document but insists on **15** that it will not feel obliged to honour all the specifications on human rights and will make a selective interpretation in accordance with its own law and traditions. Other delegates condemn this as 'illegal and unacceptable'. **19** Radio Budapest says all cultural relations between Hungary and Romania are to cease after failure of bilateral talks on cultural, educational and scientific cooperation.	Karabach region put under direct rule from Moscow. Lithuanian Nationalist group hosts conference of pro-autonomy movements from several republics. Estonia and Lithuania adopt official status for their own languages causing resentment among their large Russian minorities. Large demonstrations in Moldavia to demand new status for its own language and reversion to the Latin alphabet. **21** Revised budget deficit by 1990 for USSR now projected at 11% of national income: 100b. roubles. Report in *Izvestia* cites Chernobyl clean-up and earthquake disaster with costs of solving food and housing shortages.
Feb. 1989	**11** Central Committee plenum reportedly thrown into crisis by Pozsgay's remarks amid rumours of his dismissal	**6** Round table talks start with aim of reaching agreement on programme of economic stabilisation and political	**21** Vaclav Havel tried and sentenced to 9 months in prison for incitement to anti-state activities (i.e. informing Civil rights activists organise readings of the works of Havel and demand his release.	Sweden proposes resolution to UN Commission on Human Rights to appoint special envoy to investigate allegations of	Soviet Union completes withdrawal of forces from Afghanistan. **21** Soviet Union

	Hungary	Poland	E. Germany	Czechoslovakia	Romania	USSR
Feb. 1989 cont.	but final communiqué appears to concede his position: Grosz states that potential of existing system to resolve current political and economic problems exhausted and 'cautious' transition to multi-party system necessary. 20 Subsequent plenum initiates new constitution which stipulates CP must preserve its pre-eminence on basis of merit and approves multi-party elections. 28 Announced after Politburo meeting that fortifications and alarm systems along the Hungarian border with Austria would be removed by 1991.	reform including relegalisation of Solidarity. 57 delegates set up 3 main working commissions and numerous other working groups and adjourn talks to mid-March. 10 Walesa calls for 6-week moratorium on strikes, which continue. 21 Riot police disperse a student demonstration in Krakow in support of Havel. 24–25 Confrontation between police and demonstrators in Krakow and several cities as right-wing groups opposed to round table talks coincide with students protesting at police violence and calling for re-authorisation of the Independent Students' Association.		foreign radio stations of the event in Jan.) Continued strong W. European protest at violation of Human Rights Accord just signed by CZ at Helsinki Review conference in Vienna and international protests at Havel's conviction. CZ media now reveal just enough of internal dissension and debate to make it obvious they are censoring a great deal which is of general interest and provoke resort to foreign radio stations.	serious abuse in Romania amid sustained international protest over a wide spectrum of concern.	sends first permanent ambassador to EC. Decision to halt work on new canal to avoid ecological catastrophe in Caspian Sea region. Vigorous debate in Soviet press over agricultural reform raises wider issues of history and ideology as collectivised farms policy and centralised distribution system become focus of debate on food shortages and subsidies. ⅓ of all farm produce reported to rot before it reaches consumers.
Mar. 1989	Hungary breaks ranks in E. bloc to co-sponsor Swedish resolution to UN Commission to investigate human rights abuses in Romania. 9 Government announces it will reconsider Danube dam	3 Draft report from round table working group on environment cites Poland's ecological situation as disastrous. Investment in control of pollution fell during 1988 despite the recognised heavy cost to the		21 Appeal to quash Havel's jail sentence rejected but sentence reduced. 1,000 intellectuals sign letter demanding his release. Official attempts to defuse and isolate protests in Prague by minimum and adverse	1 Abortive attempt to block UN resolution. Six former CP and senior govt officials issue open letter highly critical of Ceausescu for systematic violation of constitution, cult of self and family, ideological dogmatism	26 Direct constituency elections to new Congress of Peoples' Deputies. Many high-ranking Party members and regional Party leaders rejected. Landslide victory for Yeltsin in

	Hungary	Poland	E. Germany	Czechoslovakia	Romania	USSR
April 1989 cont.		Independent Students' Association promised authorisation. 17 President Bush promises package of aid measures to Polish economy; it is not clear these add up to real new resources beyond increased international goodwill and optimism on debt rescheduling.			19–20 Two days of speeches in National Assembly and mass rallies on daily basis to praise Ceausescu for liquidation of the debt. 20 2nd conference on ecological protection of Black Sea ends in Ankara without agreement as Romania vetoes Turkish proposal to request UN involvement in conservation programmes.	of the old guard and 24 candidate members including Gromyko. Politburo reshuffle in favour of reform. 26 Praesidium issues decrees liberalising leasehold of land and price-control mechanisms.
May 1989	Hungary begins to demolish fence and alarm system of fortified border with Austria. 13 Hungary announces 2-month suspension of work on Danube dam project to study feasibility of complete withdrawal. Pozsgay describes the scheme as a 'monument to Stalinism'. CZ warns it would demand compensation as do Austrian banks but Hungary calculates to proceed would cost more than to stop despite losses and	5 Launch of Solidarity daily: *Gazeta Wyborcza.* 11 Parliament drafts law pardoning all political crimes re. strikes and protests committed since Gdansk accords of 1980 and abolishes jail terms for printing and distributing underground literature or possessing radio transmitters. 17 Parliament creates liberalised legal framework for Church/State relations. 30 Walesa thanks RC Church for its support at	Pro-democracy demonstrations start in Beijing Demonstrations in E. Berlin and Leipzig to protest at invalidity of electoral process in nation-wide communal elections.	17 Havel released. CZ confirms it will proceed with Danube dam project at Gabcikovo and accuses Hungary of violation of international law in halting project confirming it will seek compensation. Denounces CZ scientists who oppose dam and accuses Hungarian govt of touting for electoral popularity. 20 Havel interviewed by Radio Budapest and broadcast received in CZ.	Ceausescu visits CZ. Subsequent joint communiqué reiterates criticism of Hungarian reforms. International concern that debt repayment will release funds to accelerate the systematisation programme and demolition of centre of Bucharest. Evidence that new blocks for rural resettlement are of very low quality as construction resources overstretched.	15–18 Gorbachev on state visit to China – first Sino-Soviet summit for 30 yrs. New Congress of Peoples' Deputies convenes on 25. Gorbachev elected to post of State President as sole nominee. 2 weeks' live TV coverage of debates as radicals test limits. 26 Supreme Soviet of 542 elected by Congress. Roy Medvedev only radical member and 3,000 rally in

May 1989 cont.

Moscow in support of Yeltsin's election. Deputy stands down in his favour on **29**.
22 In letter to UN Assembly Shevardnadze calls for global treaty on protecting environment and for UN environment fund to be derived from savings on arms control. Gorbachev reveals exact defence budget at 13% of national income.

penalties. 150,000 sign petition to demand referendum on the issue.
30 Grosz states on TV that Imre Nagy could not yet be rehabilitated. Seen as an isolated stance by Grosz.

gathering of 300,000 in annual pilgrimage for miners.
Official protest that Radio Free Europe is violating Polish sovereignty in supporting Solidarity in the election campaigns.

25 After talks with Hungarian ministers Adamec agrees to reassess environmental impact of dam project.

June 1989

12-15 Gorbachev visits W. Germany to very enthusiastic reception. Signs agreements with Köhl on human rights, economic and environmental co-operation and envisages 50% cut in strategic nuclear weapons. Congress votes to establish Commission of Enquiry into Soviet annexation of the Baltic republics in 1940.

17 Romania registers 'vigorous protest' to Hungary over the 'fascist hostile manifestations' in Budapest on occasion of reburial of Imre Nagy, interpreted as a direct threat to Romania.
26 Announcement in Brussels that 1,000 European communities had 'adopted' 1,000 Romanian villages to protest demolition. Reports that Romania had reinforced its border with Hungary by wire

> Invasion of Tiananmen Square by troops on 3 June

29 Announced by opposition that more than 11,500 people have signed a petition 'A Few Sentences' calling for political reforms. Many new signatories who are not recognised opposition including Party members and well-known personalities in public life. Demands include freedom of assembly, respect of religious belief and release of all political prisoners, and to

Growing official criticism and concern at events in Hungary and the historical reassessment there. In report to Central Cttee reiteration that E. Germany is economically dynamic and guarantees freedoms not assured in capitalist economies of work, housing and amenities to all citizens with stress on the apparent 'chaos' of the reforming E. European economies. *Neues Deutschland* carries

1 Hungary applies to become full member of Council of Europe.
13 Trilateral talks start between govt, opposition and other interests.
16 Imre Nagy re-buried with other leaders in State funeral in Heroes Sq. All Warsaw Pact leaders except Romania send delegations and encourage media reports of the event.
23-24 Central Cttee elects new 4-man Praesidium: President

4 First round of elections. Solidarity victory in 99 out of 100 seats it is permitted to contest in Senate and in all seats it contests in Sejm (parliament) (62% turnout). Gov't's unopposed list rejected including the PM and several Politburo members. After the second round (25% turnout) commitment to totally free elections confirmed within 4 yrs.

	Hungary	Poland	E. Germany	Czechoslovakia	Romania	USSR
June 1989 cont.	Reszo Myers plus Pozsgay, Nemeth and much-weakened Grosz with reduced portfolio. Agreed that Pozsgay would be Party candidate for President in 1990 elections.	28 Solidarity clashes with govt over new price increases and is accused of avoiding responsibility for essential austerity measures.	solely the official Chinese version of events in Tiananmen Square. Viewers in E. Berlin see contrary reports on W. German TV as E. German govt gives vocal support to Chinese leadership.	manipulation of the media and to the persecution of independent movements.	fence to deter refugees followed within weeks by its being dismantled.	Serious inter-ethnic violence erupts in Soviet Central Asian Republic of Uzbekistan. Clashes between majority Uzbeks and minority Mezkhetians (Turkic group deported by Stalin from Georgia in 1944).
July 1989	6 Janos Kadar dies aged 77. 7 Nagy formally rehabilitated by Supreme Court. Release to the press of many documents about 1956 and early Kadar years which arouse much public interest. 11 Bush first US President to visit Hungary. Proposed aid will finance cultural and educational exchanges, environmental research centre for E. and Central Europe in Budapest and boost private sector. Relaxation of export and emigration restrictions.	4 New bi-cameral parliament convenes with Solidarity as formal opposition in decisive majority. 9–10 President Bush visits Warsaw. Addresses Polish Parliament. 11 Bush and Walesa address crowd of 20,000 in Gdansk. Jaruzelski and Walesa both stress that loans or aid now critical to stabilisation as strikes and shortages continue. World Bank states loans contingent on credit arrangement with IMF and debt rescheduling by Paris Club.	Honecker taken ill. Protests to Hungary about relaxed border with Austria as many E. German holidaymakers in Hungary overstay with view to leaving via Austria. E. and W. Germany reach agreement on first scheduled flights between the territories to commence in Aug. Strained relations with W. Germany over high levels of air and water pollution in E. Germany in particular from lignite extraction and industrial and agricultural effluent. Clear evidence of health	Sharp attacks in official media on organisation and content of June petition and police harassment of leading signatories accused of association with foreign subversives and neo-fascists. Czech authorities report incontrovertible evidence indicates no danger to wild-life, agriculture or water supplies from Danube dam project and cast doubt on integrity of Hungarian case for suspension or reappraisal. Czech section at Gabcikovo cannot run on full power	7–8 Warsaw Pact summit in Bucharest: relations with Hungary reach new low in heated debate between Romanian and Hungarian delegates. Hungary now perceives military threat from Romania and can make no headway with Ceausescu about halting systematisation programme. 10 Sharp criticism in Romanian press of President Bush's discriminatory policies towards East European countries on eve of his visits to Hungary and	4–6 Gorbachev official visit to France and speech to Council of Europe. Over 20 economic, scientific and cultural agreements signed. Gorbachev restates theme of 'common European home' raised in Bonn in June stressing inadmissibility of interference by one state in another's internal affairs and ruling out use or threat of force to settle disputes. Characterises scientific and technological

July 1989 cont.	16 Hungarian Foreign Minister repeats note of alarm concerning Romania's military capability and intentions in interview with Italian press. 31 Reports of 100 E. German refugees in W. German embassy in Budapest.	Full diplomatic relations restored between Poland and the Vatican. 19 Jaruzelski elected President by very narrow margin of National Assembly. 24 EC approves emergency food aid package for Poland. 25 Walesa rejects Jaruzelski suggestion of 'grand coalition' of all parties on basis Solidarity should form a govt. 29 As President, Jaruzelski resigns Party leadership.	...hazards and raising water tables. Agreements on limiting environmental damage signed with CZ, Poland and W. Germany in early July.	Hungarian section cancelled: Hungary argues compensation cannot include benefits foregone, only costs incurred.	11 In speech to Arab Inter-Parliamentary Union Ceausescu castigates West for manipulation of 3rd world debt to plunder and impoverish debtor nations and to finance subversion. EC suspends negotiations for trade and co-operation agreement with Romania in progress since April 1987.	...ridiculous', as ... Cold War was over. 10 Miners' strikes commence in W. Siberia and spread to E. Ukraine. 112,000 on strike in Siberia by 17. 25 Strikes stop in response to promises of reform and agreement to key demands to cover whole Soviet mining industry. 300 radical deputies form unofficial parliamentary opposition known as 'Inter-Regional Group'. 29 Latvia declares itself 'sovereign'. Escalation of inter-ethnic violence in Armenia. Cotton monoculture in Cent. Asia becomes hot political/ecological issue.
Aug. 1989	Increasing numbers of E. Germans start to leave via Austrian border as Hungary relaxes controls. By early September some 6,500 out of 200,000 E. Germans on	1 Abolition of state food price controls and meat rationing. Food price increases of up to 500%. Wildcat strikes as workers press for wage rises.	Hundreds of East Germans begin to gather in Budapest hoping to leave via the W. German embassy – closed on 14 due to overcrowding. Groups of E. Germans	8 Cardinal Tomasek offers to mediate at round table discussions modelled on the Polish example. 10 Discussion in official press (Rude Pravo) by	1 Hungarian TV broadcasts interview with King Michael – accuses Romania of being equivalent to absolute monarchy in which people are treated like	8 Estonian Supreme Soviet passes law which imposes residence requirements for voting and holding office in Estonia.

	Hungary	Poland	E. Germany	Czechoslovakia	Romania	USSR
Aug. 1989 cont.	holiday have taken refuge in 3 camps and many more are staying on as visas expire. **14** W. German embassy in Budapest closed due to overcrowding. **22** Polituburo issues statement condemning Molotov/Ribbentrop Pact but recognising current borders cannot be changed.	**1** Brussels meeting of 24 Western countries to discuss support for Polish reforms including emergency food aid. **7** Walesa proposes Solidarity-led coalition. Accepted by Jaruzelski on 17. On 24 leading Solidarity member Tadeusz Mazoweiki sworn in as PM obtaining votes of almost all CP deputies. Evidence of chaotic wage/price spiral with collapse of food market as international relief effort and food aid programme starts.	now begin to cross the Austro-Hungarian border. **19** 600 cross after 'picnic' on the border, with Austrians permitted to join in by Hungarian border guards. **23** For first time E. Germany openly acknowledges existence of secret protocol to the 1939 Molotov–Ribbentrop pact which allowed Moscow and Berlin to divide Poland and the Baltic states between them.	legal and constitutional experts of first draft of new constitution indicates marked shift towards Gorbachev's position. Govt warns it will not tolerate street demonstrations and opposition reluctant to force street violence but in defiance of warnings on 21 3,000 rally in Wenceslas Square to commemorate 1968 invasion. 400 arrests.	cattle and sold for hard currency if they wish to emigrate. Romania recalls its ambassador to Hungary in protest. **8** Hungarian TV broadcasts part of interview by Canadian TV with Laszlo Tokes, Hungarian priest in Timisoara, who is then briefly detained by police. In interview with Yugoslav magazine Ceausescu underlines debt repayment as essential to avoid pressure or interference of foreign states or agencies such as IMF in domestic economy.	Declared unlawful by Supreme Soviet and amended after strikes by ethnic Russians. **14** Soviet press reports Nagorny-Karabach close to anarchy. **21** More than 1m. people in Baltic republics link to mark 50th anniversary of Nazi/Soviet pact forcing their annexation by Soviet Union. Official Soviet confirmation of secret protocols in pact.
Sept. 1989	**10** Hungarian govt announces suspension of 1969 agreement with E. Germany under which citizens without valid travel documents were sent back. As a result more than 24,000 E. Germans leave via Austro-Hungarian border by the end of Sept. **23** Confirmation that 265 E. Germans had swum Danube from CZ to Hungary since 11,	**12** Solidarity-led govt under PM Tadeusz Mazoweiki sworn in. Communists get Interior and Defence Ministries as agreed but external Finance and Foreign Affairs which go to Solidarity with Labour and Education. **22** Legalisation of Independent Students' Assoc. Polish United Workers' Party (Communists) proposes to transform itself into party of broad Left	Weekly demonstrations in Leipzig outside Nikolae Kirche throughout Sept. Since Austro-Hungarian border thrown open on 10 12,000 E. Germans leave in 72 hrs. Formal protest to Hungary and demands to stop the exodus on 12. **10** Formation of nation-wide opposition group, New Forum, with 100 signatories to appeal for open dialogue on need	**19** Reports that more than 500 E. Germans have moved in to W. German embassy in Prague. **26** More than 1,100 E. Germans camped in W. German embassy. By mid-Sept. the June petition 'A Few Sentences' has 27,000 signatures.		**8** Formation of Ukrainian Popular Front. **9–10** Yeltsin tours US. **20** CPSU 'retires' many conservatives in favour of reformers. **19–20** CPSU holds plenary meeting on nationalities policy. Gorbachev points out that 21% of Soviet Union citizens live outside their national republics, and stresses

Sept. 1989 cont.	19 Delegates to trilateral round table sign agreement outlining moves to multi-party democracy. Free Democrats oppose timing of Nov. presidential elections and by mid-October 200,000 petition to force debate in parliament on this issue.		and former party activists. 21 Permission refused for authorisation of New Forum which will launch appeal. Denies it is an 'anti-State' movement and will proceed regardless of ban. Honecker seriously ill after operation in Aug.			cut road and rail links to Armenia. Appeals for help to Supreme Soviet which has to send in army to run the rail link through Azerbaijan. 7 20,000 demonstrate in Moscow to accelerate reform process. 9 New labour law includes right to strike. 22 Russian Popular Front set up at Yaroslavl. 24 Supreme Soviet abolishes reserved seats for CP and social organisations in Congress of Peoples' Deputies. 26 Gorbachev visits Finland. Reiterates wish for nuclear-free Baltic Sea. Armenian/Azerbaijani violence intensifies as rail blockades continue. 17 Re-admission of Soviet Psychiatric Society to World Psychiatric
Oct. 1989	12 At tense party congress Hungarian Socialist Workers' Party (Communists) votes to rename itself Hungarian Socialist Party and to condemn Stalinist past with commitment to build social market economy and promote democracy. New image forced by imminence of elections. 17–20 Parliament adopts new transitional constitution legalising multi-party system and redefining Hungary as representative democracy. Mixed system of proportional and direct representation which favours smaller parties. Votes to withdraw Party cells from workplace and to disband Workers' Militia. 23 On anniversary of	12 Govt publishes plan to abolish command economy and establish full market economy with programme of selective privatisation. Retail prices soar and soup kitchens introduced for poorest as govt forced to focus on control of hyperinflation expected to reach 1000% by the end of year. Farmers withold sale of produce to state food-processing industries in favour of private markets or hoarding in response to price chaos and meat supplies fall by over 30%. 30 Solidarity proclaims release of last political prisoner in Poland.	1 4,000 E. Germans camped in W. German embassies in Prague and Warsaw leave for West by train through E. Germany. 3 Visa and passport-free travel to CZ suspended. 4–5 Another 10,000 leave by train by same route. Riots in Dresden as thousands more seek to board trains in transit. Leipzig and Dresden demos get bigger with up to 700 arrests on 7. 6–7 Gorbachev visit for 40th anniversary of GDR. Presence encourages demonstrations. 7 Violent arrests as 6,000 march in E. Berlin. 8 30,000 march in Dresden. 9 50,000 march in Leipzig. Honecker reportedly authorises use	11 Adamec and Hungarian PM Nemeth fail to reach agreement on Danube dam issue at meeting in Prague. 11 Milos Jakes highly critical of developments in Hungary and Poland at CPCz plenum. 28 Up to 10,000 rally in Wenceslas Sq. to commemorate founding of the Republic of Czechoslovakia in 1918. Riot police move in and detain over 300.	Hungarian Interior Minister tells UN High Commission on Refugees that 21,000 had crossed the border from Romania to Hungary since mid-'87. 2,600 in September of '89 of whom one third were ethnic Romanians. 17 Laszlo Tokes reported to have been ousted as head of his Reformed Church congregation in Timisoara.	7 20,000 demonstrate in Moscow to accelerate reform process. 9 New labour law includes right to strike. 22 Russian Popular Front set up at Yaroslavl. 24 Supreme Soviet abolishes reserved seats for CP and social organisations in Congress of Peoples' Deputies. 26 Gorbachev visits Finland. Reiterates wish for nuclear-free Baltic Sea.

	Hungary	Poland	Czechoslovakia	E. Germany	Romania	USSR
Oct. 1989 cont.	declared a Republic (rather than a People's Republic) before a crowd of 70–80,000.			reportedly overruled by Krenz and/or Soviets. 16 100,000 march in Leipzig. 18 Honecker 'resigns' – replaced by Krenz. 23 150,000 march in Leipzig. 30 300,000 march in Leipzig. 31 Krenz to Moscow for talks with Gorbachev.		
Nov. 1989	3 Hungary gives formal notification to CZ of decision taken in Oct. to abandon work on the Danube dam. Protocol calls for renegotiation of 1977 treaty (between Kadar and Husak) agreeing the Project. Officially this is an ecological and not a political decision. Analysis indicates that irreparable damage could be caused to the river and drinking water supplies if completed. CZ claims total damages for cancellation of £1.1bn. Austrian state banks claim £240 million. Apparent to both there is no obvious source of cash to meet these claims.	Solidarity-led govt makes it clear its economic programme will not survive without substantial Western aid. Measures to control inflation expected to lead to unemployment. Crisis in food supplies due to disastrous policy of 'marketisation' of food economy in August.	17 30–50,000 in student-led demonstration in Prague. Police ambush and beatings with serious injuries and alleged death of student Martin Smid. 19 100,000 rally in protest with no police interference. Actors congregate in Prague and demand immediate national theatre strike. Authorities deny death and attribute rumours of it to Charter 77: arrest of Petr Uyl. Havel and others leave to avoid arrest. 19 400 activists form Civic Forum. Havel demands unconditional resignation of Jakes and	1 Travel restrictions to CZ lifted. W. German embassy in Prague soon overflowing. 2 Krenz to Warsaw for talks. 3 Announced that E. Germans would no longer have to renounce their citizenship before being allowed to leave, and could simply present identity papers at the Czech border. 50,000 leave in the next 5 days by this route. 4 Rally of 500,000 in E. Berlin. 7 Entire Cabinet resigns. 8 Entire Politburo resigns. New Cabinet appointed under Hans Modrow. Legalisation of	20–24 14th Congress of Romanian CP. Ceausescu elected unanimously to further 5-year term.	Throughout Oct./Nov. unofficial groups in Transcaucasian and Baltic republics discourage conscription to Soviet armed forces. Further miners' strikes in N. European Russia. 12 Estonian Supreme Soviet votes to effectively annul 1940 vote to join Soviet Union. 17–19 Meeting of Georgian Supreme Soviet declares Georgian sovereignty. 28 Moscow ends direct rule over Nagorny-Karabach and Azerbaijan resumes control.

...ctions and ... multi-party legislative elections to give opposition candidates more time and then for Parliament to choose the president.

early afternoon that 'All border crossings to W. Germany and W. Berlin can be used and are now open.' Crowds gather on both sides and then on top of the Wall. People begin to attack it with picks and chisels.

10–11 2m. E. Germans visit W. Berlin. By 23 11m. visas had been issued. Vast Leipzig demonstrations continue on 13 and 20.

18 50,000 at first authorised rally of New Forum in Leipzig. Calls for free elections and end to guaranteed leading role for CP.

24 Green Party established. Opposes abrupt translation of E. German society to western values without radical ecological reappraisal.

25 Free Democratic Party formed.

and release of all prisoners of conscience.

20 200,000 in Wenceslas Square. Live TV broadcasts of demonstrations start. Protests spread to other cities including Bratislava and strikes close universities and theatres. Civic Forum moves to the Magic Lantern theatre.

21 PM Adamec opens discussions with Civic Forum and rules out further police violence against demonstrators.

22 Dubcek at rally in Bratislava. Public Against Violence formed in Slovakia.

23 TV employees vote for only 'objective' reporting.

23 People's Militia refuses to restore order in Prague.

24 Milos Jakes and entire Politburo resigns including Stepan who is shouted down by workers. Dubcek at rally of 500,000 in Wenceslas Square.

	Hungary	Poland	E. Germany	Czechoslovakia	Romania	USSR
Nov. 1989 cont.				26 Adamec, Havel and Dubcek address crowds of over 500,000 in Prague and over 1m. across the country. Announce release of all political prisoners. 27 2-hour general strike called by Civic Forum observed by 3m. workers throughout the country. Rally of 200,000 in Wenceslas Sq. Civic Forum announces suspension of demonstrations. 28 Adamec announces effective capitulation to opposition demands agreeing to drop the concept of the leading role of the Party from the Constitution. 30 CP concedes free elections inevitable.		
Dec. 1989	21 Hungary's National Assembly votes to dissolve itself from 16 March 1990 so that national elections can be held.	Economic reform and austerity package agreed to ensure IMF standby credit. Walesa tours western states appealing for aid to beleaguered Polish economy. 29 People's Republic becomes simply Republic	2 Huge demonstrations call for action in response to evidence of corruption in previous regime when press articles are confirmed by evidence of parliamentary committee. Stasi (secret police) offices ransacked. 4–6 Entire CP leader-	3 New govt announced with mainly CP members: massively rejected. 4 Vast demonstrations in Prague and elsewhere in protest. 4 Heads of the 5 Warsaw Pact countries involved condemn the 1968 invasion.	15 Deportation order served on Laszlo Tokes (ethnic Hungarian pastor openly critical of the regime) in Timisoara. 16 Several hundreds blockade his home to obstruct the order. 17 Street protests continue and are fired on by	1 Armenia reasserts claim to Nagorny–Karabach. 2–3 US/USSR Malta Summit on the *Maxim Gorky*. Unscheduled joint press conference of Bush and Gorbachev. 4 40,000 besiege

1989 cont.

tional 'leading role' of CP cancelled. Royal eagle restored to national flag and 'Lenin' dropped from titles of Gdansk shipyards and Nova Huta steelworks.

Krenz. 12 members expelled. Gregor Gysi (lawyer and defence council for members of New Forum) elected leader.

6 Round table talks agree to general elections in May 1990.

22 Köhl and Modrow meet to formally open Brandenburg Gate.

and Stepan expelled from CPCz.

9 Gustav Husak resigns.

10 New govt formed with non-Communist majority.

17 Ceremonial cutting of wire on Czech-Austrian border as all crossing restrictions lifted.

20 Adamec elected to new post of party chairman of CPCz. CPCz and Opposition parties agree that Federal Assembly should elect President to serve in interim capacity until free elctions for new Federal Assembly in 1990.

28 Dubcek elected Chairman of Federal Assembly.

29 Havel elected President by unanimous vote.

troops. 71 killed, (early reports exaggerate numbers killed).

18–20 Demonstrations reported from other parts of the country as protests grow in Timisoara.

20 Troops withdraw from streets after workers occupy and threaten to blow up petrochemical plant in Timisoara. 50,000 demonstrate and CP offices ransacked. Timisoara committee formed to demand free elections and an end to repression meets PM Dascalescu.

20 Ceausescu returns from trip to Iran and declares state of emergency in Timisoara.

21 Ceausescu calls staged rally in Bucharest – his authority collapses and troops fail to intervene. Securiate police fire on demonstrators in clashes in Bucharest and elsewhere.

22 Ceausescu declares national state of emergency and tries to address crowds who break into CP Central Committee building as he and Elena flee by helicopter from roof.

Soviet to protest defeat of radical proposals.

6 Pressure in Congress to debate Article 6 defining guaranteed leading role of CP. Sakharov demands strike to force the issue. Conservatives attack Gorbachev who makes rhetorical offer to resign.

14 Death of Sakharov.

18 Soviet Union signs 10 yr trade and economic cooperation agreement with EC.

19 CP of Lithuania declares its independence of CP of Soviet Union which decides on 25 to send Gorbachev to negotiate.

23 Yakovlev Historical Commission confirms illegitimacy of Hitler/Stalin pact of 1939. Protocols deemed to be "legally invalid and null and void from the moment of their signing".

Hungary	Poland	E. Germany	Czechoslovakia	Romania	USSR
Dec. 1989 cont.				22 Army joins people and battles with Securitate after shooting of Defence Minister for non-compliance with orders to shoot crowds. Crowds capture TV and radio stations and National Salvation Front organises itself with HQ in TV station. Heavy fighting with Securitate. 22 Ceausescus detained and held in armoured car until tried and shot on 25. Council of the Front set up to include well-known dissidents and religious leaders. 27 Final small-scale Securitate assault on TV station. Many Securitate shot on capture. 27 New NSF govt headed by Iliescu as President announces programme of multiparty system with free elections in April and comprehensive political and economic reforms. Abolition of death penalty. Prominent dissident Doina Cornea voices widespread suspicion of composition and real	

from streets of Bucharest.

3–4 First visit by South African Foreign Minister to Warsaw Pact country with surprise arrival of Pik Botha. Reports of interest in joint economic ventures and of SA attempts to recruit skilled E. European workers. Sharp criticism of visit by UN and European anti-apartheid movements.
5 'Danubegate' scandal: press conference announcement by opposition parties that Security police has continued undercover surveillance of opposition politicians – resignation of head of Interior Ministry and dissolution of State Security Service confirmed on 21.
14–15 Japanese PM Toshiki Kaifu visits Warsaw and Budapest on whirlwind tour of Europe. Announces loans of $500 million to both Poland and Hungary.

Sharp rise in fuel and transport costs and 36% drop in real incomes in Jan. plus currency devaluation.
Solidarity-led govt has to argue IMF case for austerity measures in face of continued strikes and sharp rise in number of unemployed.
12 Daihatsu reported to be planning joint car-making venture with Poland.
18 Walesa demands complete withdrawal of Soviet troops by end 1991.
27 Polish United Workers' Party (Communists) meets to dissolve itself. Protests to demand forfeit of all its assets. New party emerges committed to parliamentary democracy and rule of law under the name Social Democracy of the Polish Republic.
29 Aleksander Kwasneiwski elected

Around 2,000 E. Germans continue to leave for W. Germany each day.
The Communist Socialist Unity Party to be renamed Party of Democratic Socialism damaged by attempt to set up successor to Stasi security police. Proposal aborted but suspicion remains. Measures are announced to ease foreign investment, permit civilian alternative to conscription and start transition to market economy. Cuts in consumer and business subsidies.
12 German Social Union founded in Leipzig to unite Christian, Liberal and Conservative Opposition groups.
15 Demonstrators storm and sack Stasi HQ in E. Berlin.
16 Modrow to W. Berlin for talks on linking the two halves of Berlin.

1 Havel's New Year address describes the current Czech economy as inefficient, wasteful and environmentally destructive and describes the State as 'humiliating and exploiting workers'. ...'Out of a gifted and sovereign people the [Communist] regime made us little screws in a monstrously big, rattling and stinking machine.' Recalls pre-40s strength of Czech economy and culture. Denounces vengeance on Communists.
1 Havel announces amnesty of benefit to ⅔ of total prison population.
2 Havel visits E. and W. Germany: talks with leaders and opposition. Civic Forum's new programme centres on cultural freedom and freedom of information and travel, opening of links to western Europe and economic reform

1 Securitate formally abolished by decree of NSF Council.
1 Iliescu announces partial redistribution of State agricultural and land assets to farm workers and migrants, retaining city workers and co-operatives in a free market.
3 Ceausescu's ban on foreign borrowing lifted. Emphasis on urgent need for new technology imports.
8 Passports to be freely issued for foreign travel. (No accompanying hard cash available.)
Growing popular criticism of National Salvation Front. Charges it is too closely identified with Ceausescu regime and distrust of its decision to contest free elections in April. Delay of elections sought by opposition.
12 10,000 demonstrate outside NSF HQ in Bucharest. Crowd told by

4–6 Gorbachev meets leadership of Lithuanian CP and Sajudis in Moscow.
8 Advance party of 40 CPSU officials to Lithuania.
11–13 Gorbachev to Lithuania to sound out opinion and explain priorities. Announces draft law in preparation for 'mechanism to allow a republic to leave Soviet Union' and envisages restructuring of SU as a federation of sovereign states. But stresses interdependence of all republics in the success of *Perestroika* and his personal stake in this: Lithuanian leadership not impressed. Sajudis rally of 300,000 in Vilnius.
11 Latvian Supreme Soviet abolishes Article 6 which guarantees leading

	Hungary	Poland	E. Germany	Czechoslovakia	Romania	USSR
Jan. 1990 cont.	18 Govt decision to severely restrict exports to COMECON countries to reduce rouble surplus under pressure from IMF. Leads to massive lay-offs in state-owned bus company in February. Joint venture with Suzuki for first car plant in Hungary and biggest Japanese investment to date in E. Europe agreed on 9. Rupert Murdoch acquires 50% interest in two Budapest tabloids for total of $4m. Robert Maxwell's Mirror Group expected to buy 40% stake in government daily: *Magyar Hirlap.* General Electric takes 50% stake in Tungsram (lightbulbs). General Motors agrees joint venture to produce engines. Imre Pozsgay loses face over disputed dismissal of highly respected head of TV news and current affairs, Endre Aczel. Free Democrats gain electoral advantage in this by linkage of Democratic Forum (HDF) with	Party Chairman. Breakaway party insisting on complete break with Communist past forms Social Democratic Union under Tadeusz Fiszbach. Renounces all former CP assets.	20 Krenz and 13 other Politburo members expelled and 39 executive members resign from Socialist Unity Party. 22 Modrow calls for immediate formation of grand coalition. Talks agreed on 28. Honecker to be charged with treason. Leaves hospital on 29 too ill for arrest.	with room for private enterprise. Independent judiciary, free elections, socially just State, widely accessible education and environmental protection. 15–16 Talks on withdrawal of Soviet troops start and adjourned without agreement. 15 Formal application by CZ to join IMF and World Bank. Proposed access to expert advice rather than loans. 17 CZ applies to join OECD. 25 Havel addresses Polish Parliament. Suggests informal liberal alliance of Poland, Hungary and CZ to co-operate on economic and disarmament issues. 26 Havel addresses Hungarian National Assembly. Complete withdrawal of Soviet troops agreed in principle by 23.	Iliescu that Romanian CP has been outlawed but this decision reversed on 13. Plans for referendum on this and abolition of the death penalty cancelled on 17. Clear internal power struggle in NSF. 18 Seizure of all assets and property of CP including 60 industrial enterprises, 50,000 hectares of land and 21 palaces used by Ceausescu. 18 Resignation of discredited patriarch of Russian Orthodox Church. 23 Elections rescheduled to 20 May. 24 Cordon of troops surround NSF HQ in face of further demonstrations. 26 Systematisation plan formally cancelled. Grandiose construction and prestige projects halted. Food exports stopped but serious food shortages necessitate emergency EC food aid. USSR promises increased fuel supplies to aid critical shortages.	role of CP in Latvia. 31 Dec.–5 Organised attacks on the Azerbaijani border defences with Iran. Protests in Baku in support of Azerbaijani separatism and union of Soviet and Iranian Azeris. 8–10 Renewed disputes over Nagorny-Karabach and rival claims to run it leading to 13–15 anti-Armenian pogrom in Baku. 60 killed. Serious armed conflict in Nagorny-Karabach. 16 Large troop reinforcements sent to control the situation. 19 Troop assault on Baku. 22 750,000 protest in Baku. Hundreds of party cards burnt. Azerbaijani Supreme Soviet issues secession ultimatum and general strike starts. 24 Arrest of 43 leading members of Azerbaijani Popular Front. 30,000 Armenians

1990 cont.	over 12,000 reform Communists form 'Democratic Platform of CPSU' calling for full multi-party system. 31 McDonald's opens in Pushkin Square in Moscow serving 30,000 on first day.				4 150,000 march in Moscow. Unprecedented media coverage and advance publicity. Demands include end of Communist monopoly of power, removal of conservative leadership and end of privileges for party functionaries (*nomenklatura*). 5–7 CPSU Central Committee meets to draft new platform. Gorbachev announces CP's intention to renounce guaranteed monopoly of power and its accommodation to democratic process plus leadership changes to counteract 'authori-
Feb. 1990	2 Detailed negotiations start in Budapest on withdrawal of 65,000 Soviet troops but timing as USSR resists pressure for 1991 deadline. Announced Fuji Bank of Japan to be first Japanese bank to open for business in E. Europe in Hungary in summer 1990. 9 Full diplomatic relations restored with Vatican.	5 Poland finalises first IMF credit agreement back-dated to 1 Jan. 1990. 6 1st World Bank loans to Poland confirmed. 9 Mazoweiki appeals to western creditor governments for loan rescheduling or cancellation. Current external debt around $40 billion, more than ½ GNP. 16 Paris Club meeting agrees re-scheduling but no overall debt reduction. (Some eventual write-off considered inevitable but reluctance to set visible precedent to other debtor states.) 9 Green Party candidate defeats Solidarity candidate to become mayor of	1 New travel law permits cross-border freedom to come and go at will. On return from visit to W. Germany Modrow announces proposals for unification in response to increased popular pressure and exodus to West. 85,000 leave in first 6 weeks of 1990. E. German critics of union focus on defence posture and implications of currency union. 5 Christian Democrat parties form 'Alliance for Germany' to contest elections with full support of Köhl and W. German equivalent. 5 Hundreds of right-wing skin-heads shouting Nazi slogans disrupt Leipzig demonstration.	1 Total abolition of State security police announced. New security system composed. 6 Petr Pithart (spokesman for Civic Forum) replaces Pitra as PM. 17 CPCz expels 22 former members including Gustav Husak (General Sec. 1969–87). 17–21 Havel visits Iceland, Canada and USA. 20 Havel talks with Bush: trade agreements. 21 Havel addresses joint session of US Congress. Calls for new pan-European defence structure. Advises US to aid Soviet Union in path to democracy.	1 Round table talks of 29 opposition parties agree to power-sharing arrangement with NSF in Council for National Unity: 180 seats – 3 for each party and 90 reserved to assorted interest groups whom critics anticipate will all be NSF Council members. 2 4 senior Ceausescu officials sentenced at start of series of show trials. Economic reforms anticipate cautious move to market economy and extend farm-workers' rights to land, assets and sales. Major devaluation of currency. 9 After 1st session CNU expands to 253 seats. By now 37 other parties –

	Hungary	Poland	E. Germany	Czechoslovakia	Romania	USSR
Feb. 1990 cont.		Krakow. Economic austerity measures cause fast contraction of demand with falling output and wages and rising unemployment. **13** Poland presses for inclusion in second phase of "2 + 4" talks which open in Ottawa. **28** Köhl proposes W. and E. German govs issue joint commitment guaranteeing Oder-Neisse border after 18 March.	**6** Köhl proposes German monetary union and advocates immediate negotiations. **7** Three left-wing citizens' movements including New Forum form 'Electoral Alliance 90' to contest elections. Favours gradual unification leading to demilitarised Germany. New Forum split between those who want to run political campaign and those who want to remain outside the political process. **12** Liberal grouping of 'League of Free Democrats' set up in W. Berlin. **13–14** Modrow visits Bonn with high-level delegation representing all coalition parties. Stress on principle that 'unification' must not translate into 'annexation' of East by West. **13** "2 + 4" (Allied States & Germanies) meet in Ottawa to discuss security implications of	**26–27** Havel to Moscow for talks with Gorbachev. Agree to complete withdrawal of Soviet troops by July 1991. Lays wreath at grave of Sakharov and meets opposition including Yeltsin.	any more to get observer status only. The extent of the AIDS problem and other health hazards emerges as suppressed statistics and tests are published and international medical aid sought. Accurate economic statistics have also been sparse, false or unreliable for many years. Trials of Securitate personnel appear delayed by fear of revelations of widespread complicity and corruption. **12** Air Force officers from Timisoara begin 3-day occupation of NSF HQ in protest at continuity of Ceausescu and Securitate elements in the military. **14** Demonstration in support includes officers, cadets and conscripts. Iliescu pledges investigation of Defence and Interior Ministers. **16** Defence Minister replaced.	tarianism, bureaucratism and ideological dogmatism'. Proposes new post of President of USSR. Furious response from conservatives who characterise Gorbachev's policies as spineless capitulation to pragmatism fast leading to destabilisation and anarchy. But despite vehement opposition from floor entire Politburo including Ligachev back draft reforms – Yeltsin sole vote against. (Western analysts see new platform as full of contradictions in trying to accommodate to both radicals and conservatives.) Nationalist and inter-ethnic rioting erupts in Soviet Cent. Asia. **11** Tadjikistan rioters inflame rumours of influx of Armenian refugees and besiege

...Soviet Union prefers neutral and demilitarised Germany to western option for inclusion in NATO.

21 Mazoweiki calls for treaty guaranteeing Oder-Neisse border. Special EC summit on these security issues convened for April.

Contrary to E. Germany's initial intention, W. Germany plays large and increasing role in E. Germany's election campaign (for 18 March). Political groups emerge corresponding to W. German parties. Selective funding disadvantages certain groups with no corresponding W. German equivalents such as New Forum.

5 Vote to ban activities of W. German neo-Nazis.

5,000 in Victory Sq. denounces NSF and invades its HQ.

19 5-8,000 miners arrive in Bucharest to rally in support of Iliescu and NSF.

shanbe. Other minorities including Russians attacked, 22 killed.

Inter-ethnic unrest spills over into Uzbekistan from Samarkand to Tashkent by 21.

Attacks on minorities.

13 Rail freight starts to move again between Baku and Armenia.

Inter-ethnic tension escalates in Moldavia. Soviet Moldavia presses for reunification with Romania. Large Russian minority in Estonia counteracts Estonian calls for independence by demands for re-structured Soviet Federation. Latvia restores pre-war flag.

24 Lithuanian Supreme Soviet passes into control of Sajudis in multi-party elections.

25 Massive demonstrations in support of radical democratic reforms in several cities. 50,000 rally in Moscow.

	Hungary	Poland	E. Germany	Czechoslovakia	Romania	USSR
Feb. 1990 cont.	1 Parliament amends constitution to allow direct presidential election after general election. Contradicts Nov. referendum decision for parliamentary vote for president. Seen to increase Pozgay's chances. 14 IMF approves standby credit arrangement for Hungary. 22 Hungarian Foreign Minister accuses Romania of deliberately allowing Magyars (ethnic Hungarians) to be 'slaughtered' in Tirgu Mores in violent conflict on 20. On 21. Romania had accused Hungary of stirring up Magyar nationalism with ultimate					27 Supreme Soviet approves draft bill to create new presidency after heated debate. Elections to local Soviet and Republican legislatures confirm loss of support to Communists and increased separatist/nationalist gains.
Mar. 1990		2 W. German statement by Köhl on Oder–Neisse border draws sharp criticism from EC and outrage from Poland as it appears to fudge earlier commitment to guarantee established borders by insisting on link with Poland renouncing claims to WW II reparations. 6 After emergency cabinet meeting Köhl backs down on demand for linkage of border with reparations issue. W. German Cabinet backs plan that the 2 German Parliaments would adopt identical resolutions renouncing territorial claims on Poland. Passed by	12 Final session of round table discusses draft constitution to be reviewed by newly elected Volkskammer and put to referendum on 17 June. 12 Köhl suggests elections for a United German Parliament in 1991. 13 Köhl pledges E. Germans will receive one-to-one exchange rate for D. marks for all currency held in savings in planned monetary union. Seen as political tactic to support electoral allies. Recognised that high overall conversion rate could make E. German labour expensive and increase unemployment whereas low rate would increase	1 Govt approves bill to remove certain limits on private enterprise including number of employees, level of profits and foreign ownership. 15 W. German President von Weizscker on 1-day official visit to Prague at invitation of Havel to mark reconciliation of CZ with W. Germany. 17 Warsaw Pact meeting in Prague discusses German unification and position re. membership of NATO, opposed by USSR but favoured by Poland, Czechoslovakia and Hungary over the option of a neutral Germany. New European	1. Suicide of judge who condemned Ceausescu to death on 25 Dec. following threats and breakdown. 2 Trials of police and Securitate officials begin in Timisoara. 17 Electoral law of 99 Articles sets out detailed rules for procedure, eligibility and financing of general election to be held on 20 May. Conflict erupts between groups of Romanian nationalists and ethnic Hungarians (Magyars) in Transylvania following restoration of rights to 2m. Hungarians to bilingual education and media denied by Ceausescu. Romanian	11 Lithuania declares unilateral independence. Vote of Lithuanian Supreme Soviet timed to preempt possible new powers of new Presidency of USSR. Elects Landsbergis as President. 12 Heated debate in Congress of Peoples' Deputies on proposal to create the post of President of USSR. 13 Proposal approved after amendments passed to control power to veto and of emergency powers. Boycott of vote by deputies opposed to strengthened central executive.

1990 cont.

Transylvania (once part of Hungary). Hungary retorts that Bucharest condones rise of racist groups including anti-Semitic, anti-gypsy and anti-Hungarian. Anti-gypsy element also exists in Hungary.

Events in Romania reinforce Nationalist vote in first round of elections to the National Assembly held on 25.

Results of first round give 24.71% to populist centre-right Hungarian Democratic Forum (HDF).

21.38% to liberal Alliance of Free Democrats (SzDSz), Independent Smallholders' Party third with 11.76%.

Hungarian Socialist Party (reformed Communists) 10.89%, League of Young Democrats 8.94%,

HWP (hardline Communists) less than 4% with no representation. In contrast to the HDF the SzDSZ favoured more radical and rapid restructuring of the economy and integration into western Europe with disengagement from the

---

during heated debate Köhl again urges Poles to renounce claims to reparations.

– already source of considerable friction.

14 'Two + Four' talks on security issues open in Bonn. Agreement to include Poland on all related issues.

18 Elections for 400-seat Volkskammer (turnout 93.4%).

48.12% of votes to Alliance for Germany led by Christian Democrats (CDU). (22% in E. Berlin, 60% in south). Substantial backing from W. German equivalent with emphasis on rapid unification of two Germanies.

21.88% to Social Democrats. (SPD). 16.4% to Party of Democratic Socialism led by Modrow (PDS) (polled 30% in E. Berlin – low vote in industrial south)

'Alliance 90' consisting of E. German groups who took initiative in the collapse of the previous regime receive 2.91%.

'Alliance 90' and Green Party agree to form a joint fraction in the Volkskammer (20 seats – 4.88%).

Parties in the Alliance for Germany resist W. Ger-

---

mooted.

19-23 Havel state visits to France and UK. Makes clear preference for common security system subsuming NATO and Warsaw Pact.

27 Revised state budget aims to reverse forecast deficit for 1990 by cutting spending on subsidies to state enterprises including agricultural cooperatives, cutting defence and security budget by 10% and cancelling subsidies to the CPCz.

29 Federal Association votes to re-name the State dropping the word 'Socialist' and settling for 'Czechoslovak Federalist Republic' and 'Czecho-Slovak hyphenated in Slovakia.

30 Thousands demonstrate in Bratislava in protest at compromise on hyphenation.

---

territorial claims at root of demand for cultural autonomy and force confrontation in Tirgu Mores after celebration of Hungarian National Day on 15 despite joint efforts to stop hostilities and calls for resignation of Iliescu for complicity on 18. Nationalists storm HQ of Hungarian Democratic Union of Romania and on 20 an armed crowd of 2,000 attacks peaceful demonstration of 9,000 Hungarians. 3 dead and many seriously injured.

20 70,000 Hungarians demonstrate in Bucharest.

Govt denounces attacks and sets up Commission of Enquiry.

13 Agreement signed with US for $80 million aid to agriculture.

No. killed in Dec. uprising now known to have been greatly exaggerated and early official reports of 60,000 deaths reduced to 7,000 in Jan. and now put at 700 overall with 70–100 killed in Timisoara.

In conjunction with evidence that the NSF was

---

repeal Article 6 and abolish guaranteed leading role of the CP in the constitution. Law on establishing new political parties being drafted.

15 Election of Gorbachev as President – sole candidate.

15 Congress votes to condemn Lithuanian UDI as illegitimate and invalid.

17 Lithuania forms non-Communist coalition govt.

18 Soviet forces begin large scale manoeuvres in Lithuania after it ignores deadline to rescind UDI and on 19. Gorbachev goes on TV to announce other measures to enforce Congress resolution.

20 Paramilitary security force forms in Lithuania and is ordered by Soviet ground forces to disarm as increased numbers of Lithuanian soldiers desert Soviet army.

25 Soviet troops take over HQ of Lithuanian CP.

	Hungary	Poland	E. Germany	Czechoslovakia	Romania	USSR
Mar. 1990 cont.	Warsaw Pact. Expected from pre-election polls to come first. Second round of polling due on 8 April. **30** First payment of 5-yr loan agreed with EC of ECU 87,000,000 ($1,000m.)		man pressure to join as one fraction. **20** W. Germany announces closure of emergency reception centres for East German immigrants from 1 July. **23** Köhl tells EC commission that German unification reinforces process of European integration but should not be too precipitous.		in existence at least 6 months before late Dec. speculation occurs that the source of the revolution was not in a spontaneous uprising in Timisoara.	**25** Estonian CP votes in principle to become independent of CP of SU (with 6-month transition) Vote boycotted by ethnic Russian delegates. **28** Lithuania indicates willingness to discuss referendum on independence as Soviet Parliament drafts law on secession. **28** First session of new USSR Presidential Council composed of wide diversity of interests and political commitments. **30** Estonian Supreme Soviet declares start of transitional phase to independence.

Index